EPHESIANS AND COLOSSIANS
In the Greek New Testament

WORD STUDIES IN
THE GREEK NEW TESTAMENT
For the English Reader

by Kenneth S. Wuest

Also by Kenneth S. Wuest

THE NEW TESTAMENT
IN EXPANDED TRANSLATION

EPHESIANS
AND COLOSSIANS
in the
Greek New Testament

FOR THE ENGLISH READER

by

KENNETH S. WUEST, LL.D.

WM. B. EERDMANS PUBLISHING COMPANY
Grand Rapids   Michigan

Set up and printed, February 1953
Eighth printing, August 1974

ISBN 0-8028-1233-3

Dedicated

To Rev. and Mrs. Harold E. Garner, in glad recognition of their splendid work for the advancement of Christian Education in The Moody Bible Institute and in the Church at large. Their enthusiasm for their task and their gracious Christian spirit are a blessing to all of us.

CONTENTS

INTRODUCTION

This book is written for the student of the New Testament who does not have access to the Greek text, but who would like to work beneath the English translation in the untranslatable richness and added accuracy which the original autographs afford. This book, with its twelve predecessors, is an attempt to put the Greek text on a level where the student of the English Bible can successfully work.

This is done by the use of Greek word studies, interpretive material, and an expanded translation. The word studies bring out a far richer, more fully developed and clearer meaning of the Greek word than any single English word could do. In the interpretive material, the author gives the student the benefit of the rich studies of the great Greek masters, plus his own comments at times. In the expanded translation, a translation using more English words than the standard versions do, the author gives the English reader what the Greek reader of the first century read. In the process of translating, the standard versions leave much rich material behind in the Greek text, since these are held down to a minimum of words. This material, the Bible student should know if he expects to do the best kind of work.

This book is not armchair reading. Its place is next to the student's open Bible on his study desk. With its aid, the student can work slowly through the Ephesian and Colossian letters, and obtain a far clearer and richer understanding of their contents than he could from a study of any number of translations. After he has worked through these epistles, he can use this book as a reference work.

The sources consulted in the writing of this book are as follows: *The Expositor's Greek Testament*, S. D. F. Salmond writing on Ephesians, A. S. Peake writing on Colossians; *Word Studies in the New Testament*, by Marvin R. Vincent; *Alford's*

Greek Testament, by Henry Alford; *Paul's Epistles to the Colossians and to Philemon,* by J. B. Lightfoot; *Biblico-Theological Lexicon of New Testament Greek,* by Hermann Cremer; *Vocabulary of the Greek Testament,* by J. H. Moulton and George Milligan; *Greek-English Lexicon of the New Testament,* by J. H. Thayer; *Greek-English Lexicon* (classical), by Liddell and Scott; *Synonyms of the New Testament,* by R. C. Trench. The Greek text used is that of Nestle. The translation quoted is the Authorized Version, since most Christians still use that translation. The expanded translation offered must not be used as a substitute for but as a companion translation to the standard version the student is using.   K. S. W

PREFACE

Ephesians and Colossians are two of the so-called Prison Epistles, written by Paul during his first Roman imprisonment, the date, about A.D. 64. They were sent by the same messenger (Tychicus) who also carried the letter to Philemon. They are companion letters, not only because written at the same time, but primarily because Ephesians speaks of the Body of Christ of which He is the Head, and Colossians presents Him as the Head of the Body.

Colossians was written to combat the Colossian heresy, a discussion of which the reader will find in the introduction to that book. In Colossians we find the Person of the Lord Jesus more clearly presented than in any other of Paul's letters. The very necessity of defining His Person in view of the heresies about Him, made this imperative.

As to the Ephesian letter, *Expositors* has this to say: "In the judgment of many who are well entitled to deliver an opinion, it is the grandest of all the Pauline letters. There is a peculiar and sustained loftiness in its teaching which has deeply impressed the greatest minds and has earned for it the title of the 'Epistle of the Ascension.' It tarries largely among 'the heavenlies.' . . . . It is characterized by a dignity and a serenity which is entirely in harmony with the elevation of its thoughts. It has little to do with the questions of ceremonialism or with the personal vindications which fill so large a space in others of the great epistles of St. Paul. The polemical element is conspicuous by its absence. There is scarcely even an echo of the great controversies which ring so loudly in the Epistles to the Romans and Galatians."

While the Colossian letter was addressed to the local church at that place, the Ephesian epistle appears to have been a circular letter sent from church to church. The reader will find a discussion of this latter subject in the exegetical material of Ephesians 1:1.   K.S.W.

THE
EXEGESIS
OF
EPHESIANS

CHAPTER ONE

(1:1, 2) The name "Paul" is from the Latin, meaning "small." Hebrew parents often gave their sons a Gentile name in addition to a Jewish one. From the meaning of this name and from I Corinthians 10:10, "His bodily presence is weak," it is thought that Paul was of diminutive stature. His Hebrew name was Saul, which word meant "to ask or pray." He designates himself an apostle; the Greek word is *apostolos*, from the verb *apostellō*, "to send one off on a commission to do something as one's representative." The word was used in an official capacity to refer to an ambassador or envoy. Paul considered himself an official envoy or ambassador of Christ Jesus. The Greek text has these names in the above order. "Christ" is the transliteration of *christos* which means "anointed," and this Greek word is the translation of the Hebrew word which we take over into English in the word "Messiah," and which itself means "The Anointed One." However, in the Church Epistles, the word does not refer to our Lord in His official capacity of the Messiah of the Jewish nation, but as The Anointed of God, the Person chosen from the Godhead to be the anointed Prophet, Priest, and King to accomplish the purposes of God in the plan of salvation. The name "Jesus" is the transliteration of the Hebrew word which comes over into English in the name "Jehoshua." It is *Iēsous* in the Greek language. The Hebrew word means "Jehovah saves." In it we find the deity, humanity, and vicarious atonement of the Lord Jesus. God incarnate died for sinners to satisfy the just demands of His law which sinners violated.

Paul designates himself an ambassador of Christ Jesus. The grammatical form is genitive of description. The great apostle looked upon himself as honored in being chosen as the representative of Christ Jesus. The allusion to his apostleship was for the purpose of giving this letter an official character. He became an apostle, he says, through the will of God. These words emphasize the fact that his apostleship was by divine appointment.

Paul addresses his letter "to the saints." The word is *hagios*. It is one of the great doctrinal words in this epistle. The word demands a careful and full treatment. Paul took it right out of the terminology of the pagan Greek religions. He had to. There were no other terms which he could use so long as he was confined to the Greek language. There it meant "devoted to the gods." For instance, a Greek worshipper would bring an offering to the god as a gift. He devoted it to that god. Or, the Greeks would build a magnificent temple and devote it to a certain god. The building was thereby set apart from any secular use, and separated to a religious one. It was consecrated to the worship of that particular Greek god. The building was therefore holy, holy, not in our sense of the term, pure, for the Greek temples were filled with immoral practices that were part of their religious worship (the temple at Corinth housing 3000 "sacred" harlots), but holy in the sense of being non-secular, and therefore religious in nature, set apart for the worship of the Greek divinities. The term was also used of persons who were devoted to the service of a god, separated to the service of the god, thus, *hagios,* consecrated, non-secular in character, but on the other hand, distinctively religious in nature and occupation. This is the genius of the Greek word translated "saint." The verbal forms *hagizō* and *hagiazō* mean "to hallow, make sacred," especially by burning a sacrifice. The foregoing estimate of *hagios* is taken from *Greek-English Lexicon* by Liddell and Scott.

We turn now to the *Biblico-Theological Lexicon* of Hermann Cremer which specializes in the great doctrinal and theological words of the Greek New Testament. Cremer says that *hagios* "is the rarest of five synonyms which the Greeks had to express the idea of holiness, so far at least as they knew such an idea. In biblical Greek on the other hand, of the Old as well as the New Testament, it is the only word by which the *biblical* conception of holiness is expressed, that conception which pervades the Bible throughout, which molds the whole divine revelation, and in which, we may say with perfect truth, are centered the fundamental and leading principles and aims of that revelation. What constitutes the essence of holiness in the biblical sense is not primarily contained in any of the above named synonyms (*hieros, hosios, semnos, hagios*); the conception is of purely biblical growth, and whatever the Greeks surmised and thought concerning the holiness of Divinity in any sense remotely similar to that in which Holy Scripture speaks of it, they had not one distinct word for it, least of all did they express it in any of the terms in question. . . . As Greek of itself did not possess the right word for it, the only term presenting itself as in any degree appropriate — *hagios* — had to be filled and coined afresh with a new meaning; and thus *hagios* is one of the words wherein the radical influence, the transforming and newly fashioning power of revealed religion is most clearly seen. Of all the ideas which, within the world subjected to the influence of Christianity or in the modern languages, are bound up in the word *holy*, none are to be found in the ancient tongues, Greek or Latin, in the terms above named, save those of 'the sublime,' 'the consecrated,' 'the venerable.' The main element — the moral — is utterly wanting. Hence it is not merely a topic of linguistic interest; it is a significant moral phenomenon which here presents itself to our inquiry."

The word, *hagios* when applied to God signifies "His opposition to sin manifesting itself in atonement and redemption or in judgment. Or as holiness, so far as it is embodied in law, must be the highest moral perfection, we may say. . . . holiness is the perfect purity of God, which in and for itself excludes all fellowship with the world, and can only establish a relationship of free electing love, whereby it asserts itself in the sanctification of God's people, their cleansing and redemption" (Cremer).

The words, "saint, sanctify, sanctification, hallow, holy, holiness" in the New Testament are all translations of this same Greek root *hagi*. The verb means "to set apart for God," and refers to the act of the Holy Spirit setting apart for God the sinner who has been elected to salvation, taking him out of the first Adam and placing him in the Last Adam. This is positional sanctification, an act performed once for all the moment the sinner places his faith in the Lord Jesus as his Saviour. This is followed by progressive sanctification, a process that goes on all through the earthly life of the Christian and continues throughout eternity, in which that person is being gradually conformed to the image of the Lord Jesus. That person is called a *hagios,* a set apart for God person, a consecrated person. He is, as such, looked upon as a non-secular person, a distinctively religious person, in that he has been set apart for God, His worship and service. This he 'is positionally. It is easy to see that this set apart position of separateness demands a separation of life in his experience, separation from the age system of evil, separation in his own sphere of life from everything that would interfere in the least from the worship and service which is due to the God to whom he is set apart. This is a saint in the Bible sense of the term.

Paul is writing to the saints which are in Ephesus. The words "in Ephesus" are within brackets in the Nestle and the Westcott and Hort texts. Tradition has it that this letter was sent to the local church in that city. But certain considerations have led recent expositors to believe that it was not sent to that church alone, but that it was an encyclical letter, sent to all the churches in Asia Minor. The oldest and best manuscripts, Aleph and B, do not contain the words "in Ephesus." Origen did not have them in his copy. Marcion called it the Epistle to the Laodiceans. Paul in Colossians 4:16 alludes to the letter from Laodicea. Marcion was familiar with the copy in Laodicea. Basil in the fourth century, mentions some manuscripts with no name in the address. Paul was intimately acquainted with the members of the Ephesian church, but he makes no personal reference to any of them in the letter, nor does he send any word of greeting to any of them, as is his habit in other letters. From the above, it has been concluded that this letter was a general epistle to be circulated among the churches of the Roman province of Asia, and it is supposed that the name of the church was inserted in the space provided in each instance.

These saints are described as "the faithful in Christ Jesus." The Greek word is *pistos,* another important word which must be considered. It is the word used when the New Testament writers speak of a sinner exercising faith in the Lord Jesus. Moulton and Milligan in their *Vocabulary of the Greek Testament,* give some illustrations of its use in the secular documents of that time, which throw a flood of light upon the way the average person used the word in ordinary conversation. The Bible writers used the terminology of the average person of that time in the writing of the New Testament manuscripts.

In the sentence "whom no one would trust, even if they were willing to work," we see its meaning of confidence in the person's character and motives. The sentence, "I have trusted no one to take it to her," speaks of a person's lack of confidence in the ability of another to perform a certain task. From the standpoint of the one trusted, we have, "I am no longer trusted, unless I behave fairly." Paul uses the word in I Thessalonians 2:4; Galatians 2:7; I Corinthians 9:17; and I Timothy 1:11, "I was put in trust with the gospel, the gospel . . . was committed unto me, the gospel . . . which was committed to my trust." This is the verb usage.

When we come to the noun, we have the meaning of "faith and confidence, fidelity and faithfulness." The adjective gives us "faithful and trustworthy." Paul uses the word in his directions to the Philippian jailer, "Believe on the Lord Jesus Christ, and thou shalt be saved, and thy house" (Acts 16:31). He exhorts him to consider the Lord Jesus worthy of trust as to His character and motives. He exhorts him to place his confidence in His ability to do just what He says He will do. He exhorts him to entrust the salvation of his soul into the hands of the Lord Jesus. He exhorts him to commit the work of saving his soul to the care of the Lord. That means a definite taking of one's self out of one's own keeping and entrusting one's self into the keeping of the Lord Jesus. That is what is meant by believing in the Lord Jesus Christ.

The words, "the faithful," refer in this context not to the fact that the saints at Ephesus were faithful in the sense of being true to the Lord Jesus in their lives, but to the fact that they were those who had put their trust in Him. They were believers as contrasted to unbelievers. The word "and" (*kai*) should here be translated "even." Paul is writing to the saints. He identifies these saints as believing ones in Christ Jesus. There were two kinds of saints (*hagios*) in Ephesus, those who were devotees of the pagan religions, and those who were devotees of Christianity. The Greek word was taken by Paul from the Greek mystery religions and transplanted into Christianity. It therefore needed careful definition. It was the saints who were believers in Christ Jesus to whom Paul was writing, not the "saints" in the pagan religions.

We come now to one of the most important words in this epistle, and indeed in the New Testament — "grace." It deserves a detailed treatment.

Archbishop Trench in his *Synonyms of the New Testament* says of this word, "It is hardly too much to say that the Greek mind has in no word uttered itself and all that was at its heart more distinctly than in this." This was his comment regarding the word "grace" as it was used in the language of pagan Greece. In the case of the use of the same word in the Greek New Testament, we can repeat this Greek scholar's words, substituting the word "God" for the word "Greek." *It is hardly too much to say that the mind of God has in no word uttered itself and all that was in His heart more distinctly than in this.*

We will look first at the way the word was used in pagan Greece with its philosophy, its athletics, its poetry and drama, its wonderful architecture and statuary, its blue skies and rugged mountains, its love of the beautiful. The word itself is a beautiful word, *charis*. It is pronounced as follows: *ch* as in Scotch lo*ch,* or as in our word *ch*asm, *a* as in father, *i* as in police, and the *s* as in cerise. The voice is stressed on the first syllable. The

Christian poet wrote "Grace! 'tis a charming sound, Harmonious to the ear; Heav'n with the echo shall resound, And all the earth shall hear. Saved by grace alone! This is all my plea: Jesus died for all mankind, And Jesus died for me." But of the latter, the Greeks of the pre-Christian era knew nothing.

Charis referred first of all to "that property in a thing which causes it to give joy to the hearers or beholders of it. . . . After awhile it came to signify not necessarily the grace or beauty of a thing, as a quality appertaining to it; but the gracious or beautiful thing, act, thought, speech, or person it might be, itself — the grace embodying and uttering itself, where there was room or call for this, in gracious outcomings toward such as might be its objects . . . There is a further sense which the word obtained, namely, the thankfulness which the favor calls out in return. . . . In the ethical terminology of the Greek schools *charis* implied ever a favor freely done, without claim or expectation of return. . . . Thus Aristotle, defining *charis,* lays the whole stress on this very point, that it is conferred freely, with no expectation of return, and finding its only motive in the bounty and free-heartedness of the giver" (Trench). *Charis* was also used to describe an act that was beyond the ordinary course of what might be expected, and was therefore commendable.

This word, the inspired writers take over into the New Testament. In a few instances, it has its distinctively classical meaning, but in the other places where it is used, it takes an infinite step forward to a deeper, richer, more wonderful content of meaning. Luke uses it in its purely classical meaning when he says (4:22), "And all bare Him witness, and wondered at the gracious words which proceeded out of His mouth." Here the word has its classical meaning of that property in our Lord's words which caused them to give joy to the hearers. How wonderful it must have been to hear the Lord Jesus speak in human speech and human tones. Not only was the content of His words gracious and beautiful, but the tones of His voice must have reflected all the depth of His personality, the intensity of His convictions (John 2:17), the fervor of His desire to serve

(Matt. 20:28), the pathos and tenderness of His sorrow (Matt. 23:37-39). It was the infinite God speaking with human lips and in human tones.

Both Luke (17:9), and Paul in Romans 6:17 and II Corinthians 8:16 use *charis* in its classical meaning of "thankfulness." Peter uses the word in its meaning of "that which is beyond the ordinary course of what might be expected and is therefore commendable," in his first epistle (2:19, 20), where the words "thankworthy" and "acceptable" are the translations of *charis* which appears in the Greek text. Surely, for a slave to manifest a spirit of patient submission toward a master who mistreats him, is an action beyond the ordinary course of what might be expected and is therefore commendable. The usual reaction on the part of a slave who is mistreated is to rebel against his master.

But how this purely classical meaning of the word describes what took place at Calvary. All the human race could expect in view of its sin, was the righteous wrath of a holy God, that and eternal banishment from His glorious presence. But instead, that holy God stepped down from His judgment seat and took upon Himself at Calvary's Cross, the guilt and penalty of human sin, thus satisfying His justice and making possible the bestowal of His mercy. And this He did, not for those who were His friends, but His bitter enemies, unlovely creatures saturated with sin. *Charis* in classical Greek referred to a favor conferred freely, with no expectation of return, and finding its only motive in the bounty and free-heartedness of the giver. This favor was always done to a friend, never to an enemy. Right here *charis* leaps forward an infinite distance, for the Lord Jesus died for His enemies (Rom. 5:8-10), a thing unheard of in the human race. Surely this was beyond the ordinary course of what might be expected and is therefore commendable. This is what John is speaking of in his first epistle (3:1) when he says, "Behold, what manner of love the Father has bestowed on us, that we should be called the children of God." The words "what manner of" are from a Greek word which means "what foreign kind of." That is, the love shown by God at the Cross is foreign to the human race. Man simply does not act that way (Rom. 5:7, 8, 10). That is why God's action at the Cross in dying for lost humanity is an action beyond the ordinary course of what might be expected and is therefore commendable. Here is one of the strongest proofs of the divine source of the Bible. The substitutionary atonement never came from the philosophies of man but from the heart of God.

Thus, the word *charis* comes to its highest and most exalted content of meaning in the New Testament. It refers to God's offer of salvation with all that that implies, which salvation was procured at Calvary's Cross with all the personal sacrifice which that included, offered to one who is His bitter enemy, and who is not only undeserving of that salvation but deserves condign punishment for his sins, offered without any expectation of return, but given out of the bounty and free heartedness of the giver. This means that there is no room for good works on the part of the sinner as a means whereby he could earn his salvation, or after salvation, whereby he might retain that salvation. Paul sets grace over against works as things directly in opposition to one another so far as the means of salvation is concerned (Rom. 4:4, 5, 11:6). But Paul is very careful to make plain that good works naturally issue from and are required by grace (Titus 2:11-12).

Furthermore, he shows that this grace is unlimited in its resources. In Romans 5:20 he says, "Where sin abounded, grace did much more abound." The word "abound" is from a different Greek word than that which is translated "abounded." It is a compound word made up of a verb which means "to exist in superabundance," and a prefixed preposition which means "above." The translation could read, "grace existed in superabundance and then more grace added to this superabundance."

Thus, salvation is a gift, to be received by the open hand of faith, not something to be earned. Dear reader, if you have been depending in the least upon any personal merit, will you not now cast aside all this, and accept the free grace of God by faith in Jesus Christ as your personal Saviour, the One who died on the

Cross for you, pouring out His precious blood as the God-appointed sacrifice for sins? "For God so loved the world that He gave His Son, the only begotten One, that whoever believes in Him might not perish but might be having eternal life" (John 3:16).

"Peace" is another word rich in meaning. The Greek noun is *eirēnē*, the verb, *eirō*. The latter means "to join." That is, when things are disjointed, there is lack of harmony and well being. When they are joined together, there is both. Hamlet cried, "The times are out of joint. O, cursed spite that I was ever born to set them right." Peace is defined by Cremer as follows: "a state of untroubled, undisturbed wellbeing." It is used in contrast to strife, and to denote the absence or end of strife. Our Lord "made peace through the blood of His cross" (Col. 1:20) in that He by His death, satisfied the just demands of the law which we broke, thus making it possible for a righteous and holy God to bestow mercy upon a believing sinner and do so without violating His justice. Our Lord thus bound together again the believing sinner and God, thus making peace. There is therefore a state of untroubled, undisturbed wellbeing for the sinner who places his faith in the Saviour. The law of God has nothing against him, and he can look up into the Father's face unafraid and unashamed. This is justifying peace. But Paul, in writing to the Ephesian saints, was writing to those who were enjoying this kind of peace already. Therefore, the peace he is speaking about is sanctifying peace, that state of untroubled, undisturbed tranquility and wellbeing produced in the heart of the yielded saint by the Holy Spirit (Gal. 5:22). We have this peace to the extent that we are yielded to the Spirit and are intelligently conscious of and dependent upon His ministry for us.

Paul says that this grace and peace come from God the Father and from the Lord Jesus Christ. In associating these names together as the apostle does, the conclusion is inescapable that the Lord Jesus must be Very God of Very God Himself, possessing Expositors comments: "The *grace* and *peace* desired for the co-eternally with God the Father, the same essence, that of deity.

readers by the writer are blessings which come only from God the Father and from Christ. The 'Lord Jesus Christ' is named with 'God our Father' as the giver of the grace and peace — a collocation impossible except on the supposition that the writer held Christ to be of the same rank with God or in a unique relation to Him. There is a distinction indicated here between God and Jesus Christ. But it is not in what they are able to give, for the gifts of grace and peace come from both. Nor is any distinction suggested here in respect of *nature*. But there is a distinction in respect of *relation* to believers. To the receivers of grace and peace God is in the relation of *Father;* to the same subjects Christ is in relation of *Lord.* God is *Father,* having made them His children by adoption. Christ is *Lord,* being constituted Head of the Church, and having won the right to their loving obedience and honor."

Translation. *Paul, an ambassador of Christ Jesus through the will of God, to the saints, the ones who are (in Ephesus), even believing ones in Christ Jesus. Grace to you and peace from God our Father and the Lord Jesus Christ.*

(1:3, 4) The contents of verses 3-14 make one long sentence, possibly the longest sentence of connected discourse in existence. Here we have some of the most important doctrinal words and profoundest and richest truths regarding what God has done for the saints, in all the Pauline writings.

We will look first at the distinctive Greek word translated "blessed" here. There are two words translated "blessed," *makarios,* which means "happy" in the sense of "prosperous," used in Matthew 5:3-11, for instance, "Spiritually prosperous are the poor in spirit"; and *eulogētos,* used here, which is made up of *legō,* "to speak," and *eu,* "good," thus, "to speak well of" (our word "eulogize"). The first speaks of character, the second of repute. *Eulogētos* is used exclusively of God in the N.T. The verb of being is usually left out and is supplied by the reader or translator. It is, "Let the God and Father of our Lord Jesus Christ be well spoken of, be eulogized." When David says,

"Bless the Lord, O my soul," he is praising God, speaking well of God.

The phrase, "The God and Father of our Lord Jesus Christ," needs some attention. God the Father is the God of our Lord Jesus Christ as He (the Lord Jesus) is seen in His humanity. He cried on the Cross, "My God, My God, why hast thou forsaken Me?" The Persons of the Godhead also recognize each other as co-equal deity and address each other as God. The Father addresses the Son, "Thy throne, O, God, is for ever and ever" (Heb. 1:8). But in our Ephesian passage Paul is thinking of the humanity of our blessed Lord as it relates Him to God the Father. Our Lord recognized God as His Father in a twofold relation. In John 6:18, the Jewish leaders accused Him of making Himself equal with God because He said that God was His (*idios*) own, private, peculiar, individual Father, His Father in a different way from that in which He is the Father of believers. Here our Lord speaks of Himself as Son of God the Father from whom He proceeds by eternal generation in a birth that never took place because it always was. Thus, God is the Father of the Lord Jesus as He (the Lord Jesus) is seen in His deity. Again, He says to Mary (John 20:17), "I ascend unto my Father, and your Father, and to my God and your God." In the expression "my God," we see the humanity of our Lord, and also the fact that in His humanity He bore a different, unique relation to God as His Father from that of the believer. It would seem that since He is speaking of His human relationship to God in this phrase, He is also doing so in the phrase "My Father and your Father." Our Lord regarded God as His Father also in His humanity.

"Hath blessed" is aorist tense in the Greek text, referring merely to the fact of an action. The translation should read "The One who blessed." The same Greek word for "blessed" is used, but in a different form. When we bless God, we praise Him, speak well of Him. When He blesses us, it is not that He speaks us good but He does us good. Our blessing is in word. His is in deed. He confers benefits upon us. Expositors says, "In word and thought we bless God because in deed and positive effect He blesses us." The "us" refers to Paul and the Ephesian saints, and extends to all saints down the ages.

And now to come to grips with the phrase, "with all spiritual blessings." Alford and Vincent concur in the teaching that the word "spiritual" describes the blessings, not as spiritual as contrasted to physical, but to blessings produced and given us by the Holy Spirit. Alford says, "*Pneumatikos* (spiritual) in the N.T., always implies the working of the Holy Spirit, never bearing merely our modern inaccurate sense of spiritual as opposed to bodily." Vincent says, "Another leading word. *Spirit* and *spiritual* occur thirteen times. Paul emphasizes in this epistle the work of the divine Spirit upon the human spirit. Not spiritual as distinguished from bodily, but *proceeding from the Holy Spirit.*" Expositors says, "It is best . . . to take *pneumatikos* (spiritual) to define the blessings in question as *spiritual* in the sense that they are the blessings of grace, blessings of a divine order, belonging to the sphere of immediate relations between God and man. It is true that these come from God through the Spirit. But the point in view is what they are, not how they reach us. There is little to suggest either that a contrast is drawn between the blessings of the gospel and the more temporal blessings of the O. T. economy . . . . There is still less to suggest that the statement is to be limited to the extraordinary gifts of the Spirit, healing, tongues, etc. This latter supposition is refuted by the all inclusive 'all.' The expression is a large one, covering all the good that comes to us by grace — whether the assurance of immortality, the promise of the resurrection, the inheritance of the kingdom of heaven, the privilege of adoption, etc." Moule, in his *Ephesian Studies,* offers this translation and paraphrase, "all spiritual benediction; spiritual as shed from Him who is Spirit." Summing up the above authorities we would say that the expression, "spiritual blessings" refers to blessings that are by their very character such as come from the Holy Spirit. We have here therefore, a balance, on the one hand, the kind of blessings, Spirit-produced, and on the other hand, the source of these blessings, the Holy Spirit.

We come now to a consideration of the phrase, "in heavenly *places*" (A.V.). The word "places" is in italics, showing that the word as such is not in the Greek text, and is supplied by the translators in an attempt to make plain to the English reader, the thought in the Greek text. The original has *en tois epouraniois;* a preposition (in), the definite article, and an adjective meaning "in or above heaven, existing in heaven, the heavenly regions, i.e., the abode of God and angels." Thayer applies the last meaning to Ephesians 1:3, 20, 2:6, 3:10, where the same expression is used. In 6:12, the expression applies to the lower heavens or the heaven of the clouds (Thayer). Vincent says, "another key-word; one of the dominant thoughts of the epistle being the work of the ascended Christ. *Places* is supplied, the Greek meaning, *in the heavenlies.* Some prefer to supply *things,* as more definitely characterizing *spiritual blessing.* But in the four passages where the phrase occurs, 1:20, 2:6, 3:10, 6:12, the sense is local, and *epouranios heavenly,* is local throughout Paul's epistles. The meaning is that spiritual blessings are found in heaven and brought thence to us." Expositors concurs with Vincent in viewing the expression as referring to heaven as a locality, and says, "It is not merely that the blessings with which God blessed us are blessings having their origin in heaven . . . , but that they are blessings which have their seat where God Himself is and where Christ reigns." It is that we saints while still in the body on earth, are enjoying some of the blessings which we will enjoy in heaven.

Paul has already given us a two-fold description of these blessings. They are of such a character that they are Spirit-produced ones. They are blessings which have their natural abode in and come from heaven. He adds another. They are blessings that are "in Christ." Expositors comments, "Not merely *through* Christ. The phrase expresses the supreme idea that pervades the Epistle. Here it qualifies the whole statement of the *blessing* in its bestowal, its nature, and its seat. The divine blessing has its ground and reason in Christ, so that apart from Him it could have no relation to us. It is ours by reason of our being in Him as our Representative and Head, 'by virtue of our incorporation in, our union with, Christ' (Lightfoot). 'In Him lay the cause that God blessed us with every spiritual blessing, since His act of redemption is the meritorious cause of this divine bestowal of blessing' (Meyer)."

We come now to the words, "according as He hath chosen us." The words "according as" are *kathōs* "even as, in conformity with the fact." Vincent says: "Explaining *blessed* us, in v. 3. His blessing is in conformity with the fact that He chose." Expositors comments: "Here *kathōs* designates the ground of the 'blessing' and so is also the note of its grandeur. The 'blessing' proceeded on the divine election, and took effect in accordance with that. It has its foundation, therefore, in eternity, and is neither an incidental thing nor an afterthought of God." "He hath chosen" is *exelexato,* the first aorist middle of *eklegō* "to pick out, choose," in the middle voice where the subject of the verb acts in his own interest, "to pick or choose out for one's self." This is another of those important doctrinal words in Ephesians. We turn to *Biblico-Theological Lexicon of the Greek New Testament,* by Hermann Cremer, which specializes in the important doctrinal and theological words of the Christian system. Cremer, in discussing the meaning and usage of this verb, makes the following points; *first,* the word is used of God choosing out Israel from amongst all nations to be the channel through which He will bring salvation to all those in these other nations who will receive it. This choosing out of Israel from among the nations does not imply that those nations not chosen are rejected or refused salvation. Indeed, the salvation of Israel was for the purpose of making salvation possible to the other nations. The same usage applies in the case of individual sinners selected out from amongst mankind. These are selected for the purpose of being channels through which the knowledge of salvation might be brought to the rest of mankind, so that those who put their trust in the Lord Jesus as Saviour might be saved. This precludes the idea that those not selected are rejected or refused salvation; *second,* the middle voice of the verb gives it the meaning of taking or setting apart something for one's self, to seek or choose out something for one's self; however, Cremer says "it is unwarranted to give special prominence either to the element of *selection from among others,* or to that of *preference* above *others.* The main import is *appointment for a certain object or goal; third,* the word is used of the act of choosing some person or thing for a definite object or calling. The middle voice in Greek represents the subject of the verb acting in his own interest or for himself. Thus, this selection of the saints in this age of grace is the act of God choosing out from among mankind, certain for Himself. These become His own, to be used for a certain purpose.

The word "elect" (A.V.) of I Peter 1:2, is the translation of the noun form of this verb *eklegō.* Here these are said to be "selected out ones, this selection being dominated by the foreordination of God the Father in the sphere of the setting apart work of the Spirit resulting in obedience and the sprinkling of the blood of Jesus Christ." We have here three steps God takes in the salvation of a sinner. God the Father selects him out from among mankind. This selection is made in the sphere of the setting apart work of the Spirit, in which the Holy Spirit brings that sinner to the act of faith in the Lord Jesus, which faith is answered by the act of God the Son cleansing him in His precious blood. God the Father selects, God the Spirit brings to the act of faith, and God the Son cleanses the believing sinner in His precious blood. This is the same election or selection spoken of in Ephesians. In our I Peter passage, the *method* God uses in saving the individual is in view. In our Ephesian text, the *result* of this salvation is in view. Commenting on the words "according as He hath chosen us," Expositors says: "What is meant, therefore, is that the blessing which God bestowed on these Ephesians was not a thing of time merely, but the issue of an election prior to their call or conversion, a blessing that came to them in accordance with a definite choice of them out of a mass of others by God for Himself."

This selection of certain out of mankind to be channels through which God could reach the rest of mankind with the message of the gospel, was "in Him," the pronoun referring back to the name "Christ." The grammatical classification is locative of sphere, the translation, chosen out "in the sphere of Christ." That is, those chosen out were chosen with the provision and limitation that this choice would be followed by the inclusion of the person thus chosen, within the sphere of the saving work of the Lord Jesus, which in turn would result in their position in Him as the Last Adam who would confer upon them righteousness and life as the first Adam by his fall brought sin and death upon the entire human race.

This choice, Paul tells us was made "before the foundation of the world." The word "foundation" is *katabolē*, from *ballō*, "to throw," and *kata*, "down," the word meaning "a throwing or laying down." It describes the act of the transcendant God throwing down a universe into space, speaking a material universe into existence which had no existence before. The writer to the Hebrew says, "Through faith we understand that the ages were framed by the Word of God, so that things which are seen were not made of things which do appear" (Heb. 11:3). This leaves no room for the theory of evolution which holds that the things that are seen today were made of pre-existing material. The word "world" is *kosmos*, "an apt and harmonious arrangement or constitution, order." The Greeks had a word, *chaos*, which comes into our language in its exact spelling, "chaos." The Greek word was used by the pagan Greek philosophers of what they considered to be the first state of the universe. The word meant "unformed matter." It spoke of darkness, a vast gulf or chasm, a pit, the nether abyss. But the Bible writers speak of the original state of the universe as one of a harmonious arrangement of things. They use the word *kosmos* not *chaos*. God, speaking of the laying of the cornerstone of the universe, speaks of the sons of God, the angels, shouting for joy at its creation (Job 38:6, 7). The holy angels did not shout for joy over a chaos. How long ago did God create the universe? Astronomers recently have discovered stars that are over 500,000,000 light years from the earth. That means that the universe is over 500,000,000 years old. But God chose us out before that. Commenting on the phrase, Expositors says: "It expresses most definitely the fact that the *election* in question is not the setting apart of certain persons at a definite period, an act in time, a *historical* selection, as some . . . strive to prove, but an eternal choice, a determination of the Divine Mind before all time. The idea of the Divine election in the N. T., is not a philosophical idea expressing the ultimate explanation of the system of things or giving the *rationale* of the story of the human race as such, but a religious idea, a note of grace, expressing the fact that salvation is originally and wholly of God. In Pauline teaching, the subjects of this Divine election are neither the Church as such (Ritschl), nor mankind as such (Beck), but Christian men and women, designated as *hēmeis* (us), *humeis* (you). It is, as is here clearly intimated, an eternal determination of the Divine Will, and it has its ground in the freedom of God, not in anything forseen in its subjects. Of a prevision of faith as the basis or motive of the election, there is no indication here. On the contrary, the character or distinguishing inward quality of the subjects of the election is presented in the next clause as the *object* of the election, the end it had in view."

And yet, there is more to be said. The above is what is called an anthropomorphic statement of the matter, that is, a manner of stating a fact in a way so as to accommodate it to human intelligence and a human viewpoint. We were chosen in eternity before the universe was created. But, wonder of wonders, this choice was never made. God cannot be said, in the last analysis, to decide upon any course of action. That choice is as eternal as God is. The name of every Christian is as eternal as God is, for God has had that individual in His heart for salvation as long as He has been in existence. What a salvation, based upon an eternal choice, which extends through time, into, and throughout the eternity after time ceases. And then some dear children of God are afraid that after God has saved them, they can be lost.

We were chosen out from amongst mankind before the foundation laying of the universe, "that we should be holy and without
blame before Him." We must be careful to note that the words
"that we should be" do not refer to an obligation put upon a
Christian to be holy and without blame in his Christian experience.   That responsibility is spoken of in Chapters 4-6.   The
context here is doctrinal in character, not hortatory.   Paul bases
exhortation on doctrine.   The latter must always precede the
former, for only in doctrine can one see the sweet reasonableness
of the exhortation and find the way to avail one's self of the power
to obey that exhortation.

The words "holy" and "without blame," do not refer to the
Christian's standing as a justified person, but to his character as
a child of God.   Paul perhaps had in mind the words in Deuter-
onomy 7:6 and 14:2, "For thou art a holy people unto the Lord:
the Lord thy God hath chosen thee to be a special people unto
Himself, above all people that are upon the face of the earth."
The word "holy" is again *hagios,* the same word we studied in
our consideration of the word "saints" of 1:1.   The root means
"separated to God."   The verb means, "to separate from things
secular and dedicate to God."   Thus, we are in our character as
Christians, a separated people, separated from evil and dedicated
to the worship and service of God.   That is what we are in the
position in which God in salvation has placed us, in Christ.   The
position has to do, not with justification, which is a legal position
in which the guilt and penalty of sin is taken away and a positive
righteousness, even Christ Jesus, bestowed, but with sanctification, positional here, namely, the saint's position in the Last
Adam, which is a matter of character, and is followed by progressive sanctification spoken of in chapters 4-6, namely, growth
in the Christian experience. The Greek word translated "without blame" is *amōmos,* "without blemish," free from faultiness,
as a sacrificial animal without spot or blemish (Lev. 22:21), or
as the Lamb of God (I Peter 1:19).

The words, "before Him," are *katenōpion autou.* The first
word we break up as follows; *kat,* "down," *en,* "in," and *ōp,* "to

see," namely, "to see down in." The word speaks of a penetrating gaze that sees right down into a thing. It refers here to the penetrating gaze of the Holy Spirit as He sees right down into our innermost being, through all of the superficialities, hypocrisies, and shams of human existence. This refers to a present, searching gaze of God into the inner character of the saint, not to a future judgment at the Judgment Seat of Christ. And it is not a searching gaze conducted in a critical attitude which looks for faults, but a satisfied, delighted contemplation of the reflection of the holiness and spotlessness of the Lord Jesus in the character of the saint, for Alford says; "implying an especial nearness and dearness to Him — and bearing a foretaste of the time when the elect shall be before (*enōpion*) the throne of God (Rev. 7:15)."

The words, "in love," are, in the A.V., construed with what has gone before, but Nestle in his Greek text punctuates so as to relate them to what follows, thus, "in love having predestinated."

(1:5) Expositors and Alford take it with the preceding "that we should be holy and without blame in love." Bible expositors are in hopeless disagreement as to whether the words "in love" qualify that which precedes or that which follows. We cannot report the discussion of the matter by Expositors and Alford, since it is too lengthy. Vincent takes the words "in love" to go with "predestinated." The author can only give his opinion as to what he thinks is the correct interpretation here after weighing the arguments on both sides, each of which has cogent reasons for its position. In either case, we have the truth. It is true that "the electing act and the object it had in view, namely, holiness and blamelessness on our part, were both due to God's love and had their explanation in it" (Expositors). It is also true that the motivating factor in God's act of predestinating us, was divine love. Perhaps we will have to wait until we see the great Apostle in heaven before we can settle the matter with certainty. While the present author would not be at all dogmatic in his interpretation, and not even sure that he is right, he leans to the opinion that the words "in love" are to be construed with "predestinated." The verb "chosen" (selected out) is too remote from the words "in love," and the word "predestinated," so near, that it would seem to decide the case for, "in love having predestinated." As one reads the Greek, the grand sweep of the sense of the passage tends to the same thing, for instance; "even as He selected us out for Himself in Him before the laying down of the foundations of the universe, to be holy and without spot in His penetrating, searching gaze, in love having predestinated us, etc."

We now come to grips with the word translated "having predestinated." The word is *proorizō*, made up of *pro*, a preposition, and the simple verb *horizō*. The noun *horos* means "a boundary, a limit." The verb itself means "to mark out the boundary or limits" of any place or thing. When used of persons, it means "to put limitations upon that person," thus, "to determine his destiny." The preposition *pro*, prefixed to the verb means "before." The compound verb means "to mark out the boundary or limits of a place, thing or person previously," thus "to predestine." Cremer defines it, "to determine or decree beforehand." He says, "The matter to be considered when the word is used is not *who* are the objects of this predestination, but *what* are they predestined to. This second object of the verb, as it has been called, forms an essential part of the conception expressed by it; what is called the first object, *i.e.*, the persons, is an accidental one, a contingency belonging to history, whereas *proorizō* itself precedes history."

Expositors suggests the word "foreordain" as a better translation than the word "predestine." This authority says; "While in Romans and Ephesians the A.V., adopts 'predestinated,' in I Corinthians 2:7 it has 'foreordained.' It is best to adopt 'foreordain' all through, as *proorizō* means *to determine before* . . . . In the N.T., it is always used of God as determining from eternity, sometimes with the further definition 'before the age' (I Cor. 2:7) — decreeing to do something (Acts 4:28); foreordaining things or persons (I Cor. 2:7, Rom. 8:29); or as here,

appointing one beforehand to something. The *pro* (before) in
the compound verb expresses the fact that the decree is prior
to the realization of its object. The aorist participle may be taken
as *temporal,* in which case the foreordination would be something
prior (not in *time,* indeed, but in *logical* order) to the *election,*
and the election would be defined as proceeding on the foreordination. But it may also be taken as *modal,* not prior to the
election, but coincident with it, and expressing the mode of its
action or the form which it took — 'in that He foreordained us'
. . . . This is the more probable view, because no real distinction
appears to be made between the *eklegō* (to select out from) and
the *prooorizō* (to mark out or set limits upon previously) beyond
what may be suggested by the *ek* (out of) in the one and the *pro*
(before) in the other; the idea in *eklegō* being understood to be
that of the *mass from* which the selection is made, and that of
prooorizō, the priority of the decree." Alford says: "In God,
indeed, all is one; but for our anthropomorphic way of speaking
and treating, which is necessary to us, there follows on His first
decree to adopt and to sanctify, the nearer decision, how and by
what this shall be brought about, because it *could* only be thus
brought about."

We consider now the words "unto the adoption of children."
The preposition is *eis,* which is sometimes translated "with a
view to," signifying purpose or result. This marking out beforehand, this setting limits upon, this predestinating had in view the
act of God adopting these selected out ones as children. The
Greek word is *huiothesia,* from *tithēmi,* "to place," and *huios,* "an
adult son." Thus, the word refers to the act of God placing these
selected-out ones as adult sons. Paul speaks of this in Romans
8:15 in the words "Spirit of adoption." The apostle here uses
as an illustration the Roman practice of legally adopting a child,
and thus not only bequeathing to him the material possessions of
the one adopting, but also giving him his civil status. Thus God
takes a believing sinner, regenerates him, and by means of this
child and places him in a legal position as an adult son (*huios*).
makes him His child (*teknon,* a born one). Then He takes this

We thus become joint-heirs with Christ, having been raised to a civil status as adult sons, in which we become heirs of God, inheriting jointly with Christ all that He possesses as an heir of God the Father by virtue of His Sonship and work on the Cross. This is one object of God's predestination. The other is that the believer is to be conformed to the image of God's Son (Rom. 8:29). Thus, God selected certain from among mankind to be included within the saving work of Christ, and those selected, He predestined to be placed as adult sons and to be conformed to the image of His own Son. Hence, predestination follows election, not in point of time, for the acts were simultaneous, but in point of divine economy or logical order.

This act of God the Father placing believing sinners as adult sons was "by Jesus Christ." The preposition is *dia,* the preposition of intermediate agency. Jesus Christ was the intermediate agent of God the Father to bring to fruition His purpose of placing believers as adult sons. He did that through His work on the Cross where He satisfied the just requirements of God's law which we broke, making it possible for Him to bestow mercy upon a believing sinner on the basis of justice satisfied.

This placing of believing sinners as adult sons was "to Himself." The words, "to Himself," refer, of course, to the subject of "predestinated," namely, God the Father. He previously marked us out with a view to placing us as adult sons for Himself, for His own satisfaction, that He might lavish His love on us as His sons, that He might give us the high privilege of sonship to and fellowship with Him, that He might be glorified in saving us and being the recipient of our worship and service.

All this was "according to the good pleasure of His will." Of the word *eudokian* ("good pleasure"), Vincent says; "Not strictly in the sense of *kindly* or *friendly feeling,* as Luke 2:14, Phil. 1:15, but *because it pleased Him,* see Luke 10:21; Matt. 11:26. The other sense, however, is included and implied, and is expressed by *in love."* Expositors gives the meaning of *eudokia* as follows: "good will, delight, satisfaction, purpose, counsel." The word "will" is *thelēma,* "a desire which proceeds from one's heart or emotions." The same authority says: "In the present passage it is only in relation to the grace of His dealings with sinful men that reference is made to the will of God. The clause in question presents that grace in the particular aspect of its sovereign, unmerited action. It adds the last note to the statement of the wonders of the Divine election by expressing the fact that that election and God's foreordination of us unto adoption are not due to any desert in us or anything outside God Himself, but are acts of His own pure goodness, originating wholly in the freedom of His own thoughts and loving counsel."

(1:6) This act of God in previously marking out certain to be placed as adult sons through Jesus Christ for Himself according to the good pleasure of His will was "to the praise of the glory of His grace." Vincent comments: "The ultimate aim of *foreordained* . . Glory is an attribute of grace: that in which grace grandly and resplendently displays itself. *Praise* is called forth from the children of God by this divine glory which thus appears in grace. The *grace* is not merely *favor, gift,* but it reveals also the divine character. In praising God for what He does, we learn to praise Him for what He is. *Glory* is another of the ruling words of the epistle, falling into the same category with *riches* and *fulness.* The apostle is thrilled with the sense of the plentitude and splendor of the mystery of redemption." Alford says: "The end, God's end, in our predestination to adoption is, that the glory, glorious nature, brightness and majesty, and kindliness and beauty, — of His grace might be the object of men and angel's praise: both as it is in Him, ineffable and infinite, — and exemplified in *us,* its objects."

This grace is described as that "wherein He hath made us accepted in the Beloved." The better manuscripts have "which" referring to "grace," not "wherein." The translation reads "Which (grace) He freely bestowed upon us in the Beloved." The words "freely bestowed" are the translation of *charitoō,* "to pursue with grace, to compass with favor, to honor with blessings." This verb has the same stem as the noun *charis* (grace). One could render the clause, "which (grace) He graced us with in the Beloved." The word "Beloved," referring to the Lord Jesus, is the translation of a Greek verb "to love," (*agapaō*), which here is a participle in the perfect tense. This Greek word for "love" is the same one found in John 3:16, Romans 5:5, 8, Gal. 5:22, I John 4:8. It speaks of the love that God is, and with which He loves the lost, the love which is the product of the Holy Spirit in the heart of the yielded believer. The perfect tense speaks of an action completed in past time having present, and in a context like this one, permanent results. It speaks of the fact that God the Father has always loved God the Son with an absolute love which is a permanent attitude on His part.

The words "in the Beloved" are locative of sphere. That is, God the Father freely bestowed on us the grace which saved us, and did so in the sphere of the Lord Jesus, His Person and His work on the Cross. His grace could not operate in our salvation apart from the atoning death of our Lord, for God is not only a loving God, but a righteous and just God who cannot pass by sin, but must require that it be paid for. Only thus can He manifest His grace. The word "Beloved" is a perfect participle, the perfect tense being used by Paul to show the degree of the love with which the Father loves the Son. Vincent says: "Beloved *par excellence.*" He refers us to Col. 1:13 and the expression, "the Son of His love."

(1:7) "The Beloved" is described as the One "in whom we have redemption." The verb is present in tense, and durative in action, thus, "in whom we are having redemption." The redemption is an abiding fact from the past, through the present, and into the future. The fact of redemption is always a present reality with the believing reader of this passage whether he reads it today or ten years from now. The definite article appears before "redemption." It has a two-fold significance, pointing to the particular redemption spoken of in the Bible with which both the writer and reader are acquainted, and speaking of ownership. It is "in whom we are having our redemption." The word "redemption" is *apolutrōsis* which Thayer defines as follows; the verb, "to redeem one by paying the price, to let one go free on receiving the price"; the noun, "a releasing effected by payment of ransom, deliverance, liberation procured by the payment of a ransom." The story of redemption can be told in three Greek words; *agorazō,* "to buy in the slave market" (I Cor. 6:20, 7:23, 30, II Pet. 2:1, Rev. 5:9) ; the Lord Jesus bought us in the slave market of sin, the ransom price, His blood; we are his bond-slaves; *exagorazō,* "to buy out of the slave market, to buy off, to buy for one's self" (Gal. 3:13, 4:5) ; the redeemed are the possession of the Lord Jesus forever, and will never be put up for sale in any slave market again; *lutroō* "to liberate by payment of ransom" (Tit. 2:14, I Pet. 1:18) ; the redeemed are set free from the guilt and power of sin now, to be finally set free from the presence of sin at the Rapture. The particular aspect of redemption spoken of here is redemption from the guilt and condemnation of sin, for the qualifying phrase, "the forgiveness of sins" is added.

This redemption is said to be "through His blood." The preposition is *dia,* the preposition of intermediate agency. The out-poured blood of the Son of God at the Cross is the *lutron,* "the price for redeeming, the ransom," used of the act of buying slaves, of paying the ransom for a life or of captives. The blood of Christ paid for the sins of the human slaves of sin in the sense that it satisfied the just demands of God's holy law which decreed that "the wages of sin is death"; and outpoured blood means death.

This redemption is defined as "the forgiveness of sins." The word "forgiveness" is *aphesis* from *aphiēmi,* "to send from one's self, to send away, to bid go away or depart." The noun *aphesis,* used in relation to "sins," means "a release, the letting them go as if they had not been committed, thus, forgiveness, a remission of their penalty" (Thayer). Trench says that the image underlying the verb is that of releasing a prisoner (Isaiah 61:1), or letting go, as of a debt (Deut. 15:3). One is reminded of the one goat who was offered as a sin-offering on the Day of Atonement, and of the other goat upon which was placed the sins of the people (symbolically) and which was let go in the wilderness, never to be seen again by Israel, the latter goat typifying that aspect of redemption in which the sins of the human race were put away, never to be charged against the individual again. All of which means that sinners are lost today, not because they sin, but because they have not availed themselves of the salvation which is in Christ Jesus. God's forgiveness of sin refers therefore to His act of putting sin away on a judicial basis, to His remitting the guilt and penalty. It is for the sinner to avail himself of salvation by appropriating the Lord Jesus as his Saviour by faith in what He has done for him on the Cross. The particular word for "sins" here is *paraptōma*, from *parapiptō*, "to fall beside a person or thing, to slip aside"; the noun form *paraptōma* means, "a fall beside or near something; a lapse or deviation from truth and uprightness, a sin, a misdeed, a trespass."

This forgiveness is "according to the riches of His grace." The words "according to" are the translation of *kata*, a preposition which in its local meaning has the idea of "down." The word "down" speaks of domination. The word "domination" speaks of control. The degree of this forgiveness was controlled, dominated by the riches, (*ploutos*) wealth, abundance, plenitude of God's grace. This forgiveness is therefore a complete, an unqualified, an unchanging one, since it is controlled by the plenitude of God's grace, and that plenitude is infinite in proportion. Expositors comments: "The freeness of this divine favor in the form of grace, the *unmerited* nature of the divine goodness, is what Paul most frequently magnifies with praise and wonder. Here it is the mighty measure of the largesse, the grace in its quality of *riches*, that is introduced. This magnificent conception of the *wealth* of the grace that is bestowed on us by God and that which is in Christ for us, is a peculiarly Pauline idea."

(1:8) Greek grammar refers the word "wherein" back to "grace," "in which grace He hath abounded toward us." The word "abounded" is *perisseuō*, "to exceed a fixed number or measure, to be over and above a certain number or measure, to exist or be at hand in abundance" (Thayer). Moulton and Milligan give as the papyri usage, the meaning of the verb, "to remain over," and the meaning of the adjective, "over and above, superfluous," and quote extracts as follows: "more than enough has been written; if you find any purchasers of the surplus donkeys"; of the noun they say; "superfluity." Thus, the verb means "to exist in superfluity, to super-abound." The translation reads "which (grace) He super-abounded to (*eis*) us." That is, God's grace was manifested to us in superabundance. It is an oversize grace. It is more than enough to save and keep saved for time and eternity, every sinner who comes to God in Christ Jesus. Paul uses this same verb in Rom. 5:20 but prefixes the preposition *huper,* which preposition means "above," and the translation reads; "Where sin existed in abundance (*pleonazō*), grace existed in super-abundance, and then some on top of that." The A.V., translates *eis,* "toward." But the preposition reaches farther than *pros* which means "to, toward." *Eis* means "in, into," and reaches not only toward the believing sinner, but into his very being. The grace comes not only towards him, but grips him in its irresistible working and brings him into salvation.

This grace God superabounded to us "in all wisdom and prudence." It is locative of sphere. This superabundance of grace was ensphered within the guiding limitations of all wisdom and prudence. The word "all," occurring as it does here with a singular substantive without the article, is to be translated "every." The word wisdom is *sophia.* "This was a great word with the Greeks. With them the word included the ideas of cleverness and skill in handicraft and art, skill in matter of common life, sound judgment, intelligence, practical wisdom, learning, speculative wisdom, natural philosophy and mathematics" (Liddell and Scott). Trench says that *sophia* is recognized in the N.T. and in Christian writers as expressing the highest and noblest in wisdom. He says; "We may affirm with confidence that *sophia* is never in Scripture ascribed to other than God or good men, except in an ironical sense. . . . For, indeed, if *sophia* includes the striving after the best ends as well as the using of the best means, is mental excellence in its highest and fullest sense, . . . there can be no wisdom disjointed from goodness."

Thayer says that when *sophia* is used of God, it refers to supreme intelligence such as belongs to God. The word "prudence" is *phronēsis,* "understanding." Trench says of the word; "It skillfully adapts its means to the attainment of the ends which it desires; but whether the ends themselves which are proposed are good, of this it affirms nothing." Moulton and Milligan say: " 'prudence' as leading to right action, as compared with the more theoretical *sophia."* To compare the two words, we would say that *sophia* refers to wisdom as such, and *phronēsis,* to the right and effective use of that wisdom in order to attain desired ends.

This wisdom and prudence is bestowed upon the recipients of God's grace. Expositors says; *"Sophia* is the collective moral intelligence, 'insight into the true nature of things' (Lightfoot) and in the Pauline Epistles it is this intelligence in especial as knowledge of the divine plan of salvation long hidden and now revealed; while *phronēsis* is the practical use of wisdom, the product of wisdom, 'the right use and application of the *phrēn* (the mind)' (Trench), the faculty of discerning the proper disposition or action. The riches, the abounding riches, of the grace expended on us stood revealed in the bestowal of these gifts of spiritual discernment with reference to the deep things of the divine counsel and the divine revelation."

(1:9) The words, "having made known to us the mystery of His will," are explanatory of the previous verse. It is, "Wherein He hath abounded, having made known." The participle is modal, indicating the manner in which the action of the main verb is performed. "He hath abounded, in that He made known." The word "mystery" is *mustērion,* in classical Greek, "a hidden thing, a secret, a mystery," in N.T., "the secret purposes and counsels which God intends to carry into effect in His kingdom." It is something which is not understood until revealed, and when revealed, not difficult of being understood by the Spirit-enlightened believer. Vincent says: "Another key-word of this epistle. God's grace as manifested in redemption is a mystery in virtue of its riches and depth — as the expression of God's very nature. The mystery of the redemption in Christ, belonging to the eternal plan of God, could be known to men only through revelation — *making known. Of His will;* pertaining to His will." Expositors translates "the mystery touching or pertaining to His will." The word "will" is the translation, not of *boulē,* a desire based upon the reason, but *thelēma,* a desire based upon the emotions. God's will or desire here, comes from His heart of love.

This will or desire is "according to His good pleasure." The words "according to" are *kata,* the preposition meaning "down" and suggesting domination. This desire on God's part is dominated by His good pleasure (*eudokia*). This Greek word is made up of *dokeō,* "to seem, to be accounted." It is often used in the question, "What does it seem to you?" The word *eu* means "well, to be well off, to prosper." Thus *eudokia* means "that which seems good or well" to one. God's good pleasure, therefore, is not an arbitrary whim of a sovereign, but represents that which in the wisdom and love of God would contribute most to the well-being and blessing of the saints. The word means "will, choice, delight, pleasure, satisfaction." In the case of God, all these are dictated by what is good or well. Thus, the delight, pleasure, and satisfaction which God has in blessing the saints is found in the fact that what He does for them is dictated by what is good for them.

This good pleasure is that "which He hath purposed in Himself." "Purposed" is *protithēmi,* "to set before one's self," thus, "to determine." This good pleasure God purposed "in Himself." As Expositors so aptly puts it, "The purpose is God's own free determination, originating in His own gracious mind."

(1:10) The purpose God had in mind is given us in the words, "that in the dispensation of the fulness of times, etc." The preposition is *eis,* "with a view to," indicating what direction the purpose took. The word "dispensation" requires some study. It is not preceded by the definite article. The word is *oikonomia,* which is made up of *oikos,* "house," and *nomos,* "law." The compound word means, "the management of a household, or of household affairs, the management, oversight, administration of other's property, the office of a manager, overseer, stewardship."

Thus, it speaks here of an administration by God of a certain period of human history designated as "the fulness of times." Our word "dispensation," used in Bible teaching nomenclature, refers to a certain period of time marked by a certain method in which God administers the affairs of mankind, such as the dispensation of grace, etc. It does not have that meaning here. Instead of referring to a dispensation itself, it speaks of the method by which God administers the particular time referred to in the words "the fulness of times."

We now address ourselves to the question as to what this fulness of the times has reference. The Greek word translated "times" here is *kairos*. In Gal. 4:4 we have the words, "when the fulness of time was come." The Greek word for "time" here is *chronos,* which refers to "time, contemplated simply as such, the succession of moments" (Trench). In our Ephesian passage, the word is *kairos* which Trench defines as "the joints or articulations in these times (*chronos*), the critical, epoch-making periods foreordained of God . . . when all that has been slowly, and often without observation ripening through long ages is mature and comes to the birth in grand decisive events, which constitute at once the close of one period and the commencement of another." The word could be translated "seasons." The word "fulness" is *plērōma,* "fulness, completeness." The *kairos* ("times") refer to the various periods of human history as they have to do with Israel and the Church in which God deals with these in a particular manner, each season, age, or dispensation being marked by a separate and distinct manner of dealing, such as the Age of Law and Age of Grace. By the fulness of these seasons is meant the time when the succession of the ages has come to a close in the plan of God. We are now living in the age of Grace. The season or dispensation which will complete the succession of seasons is the Messianic Kingdom.

God will, after this last age comes to a close, "gather together in one all things in Christ both which are in heaven, and which are on earth, in Him." The words "gather together," are the translation of *anakephalaioō,* "to bring back to and gather round the main point." Vincent says, "It does not indicate Christ (the Head) as the central point of regathering, though He is in fact. That is expressed by *in Christ*. The compounded preposition *ana* signifies *again,* pointing back to a previous condition where no separation existed. *All things.* All created beings and things; not limited to intelligent beings. Compare Rom. 8:21, I Cor. 15:28. . . . God contemplates a regathering, a *restoration* to that former condition when all things were in perfect unity, and normally combined to serve God's ends. This unity was broken by sin. Man's fall involved the unintelligent creation (Rom. 8:20). The mystery of God's will includes the restoration of this unity in and through Christ; one kingdom on earth and in heaven — a new heaven and a new earth in which shall dwell righteousness, and 'the creation shall be delivered from the bondage of corruption into the liberty of the glory of the children of God.' "

The purpose of God, tnerefore, is with a view to the administration that has to do with the completion of the seasons. At the close of the Messianic Kingdom, the Great White Throne judgment will take place at which all lost human beings, fallen angels, and demons will be judged. The material universe cursed by sin will be brought back to its pristine state, the saved of the human race will live on the new earth, and the endless eternal ages will begin. This is what is meant by an administration of the completion of the seasons. God will accomplish all this restoration work in and through the Lord Jesus and His atoning death on the Cross. He is the Head, the center around which God revolves everything He does in relation to sin and salvation.

(1:11) The word "also" (*kai*) gives the connection. Expositors comments: "Not only was it the purpose of God to make known the secret of His grace to us Christians, but this purpose was also fulfilled in us in point of fact and we were made His own — not only chosen for His portion but actually made that." The best Greek texts have, not, "we have obtained an inheritance," but "we were made an inheritance," or, "we were designated as a heritage." Thus, the saints are God's heritage, His possession through the work of Christ on the Cross.

This "being made an inheritance" is explained by the words "being predestinated (to such a destiny) according to the purpose of Him who worketh all things after the counsel of His own will." The word "predestinated" is *proorizō* "to mark out the boundaries or limits beforehand." The translation reads "in whom we were made an inheritance, having been previously marked out (for this) according to the purpose of His will." Expositors comments: "The *panta* (all) has the absolute sense, and is not to be restricted to 'the all things' that belong to divine grace and redemption. The foreordination of men to a special relation to God is connected with the foreordination of things universally. The God of the chosen is the God of the universe; the purpose which is the ground of our being made God's heritage embraces the whole plan of the world; and our position as the heritage and possession of God has behind it both the sovereignty and the efficiency of the Will that energizes or is operative in all things."

The word "counsel" is *boulē* which has in it the ideas of intelligence and deliberation. The word "will" is "a desire that springs from one's emotions." Here the emotional nature is governed by reason and deliberation. Expositors says: "Here, therefore, the will of God which acts in His foreordaining purpose or decree, in being declared to have its *boulē* or 'counsel,' is set forth as acting, not *arbitrarily*, but intelligently and by deliberation, not without reason, but for reasons, hidden it may be from us, yet proper to the Highest Mind and Most Perfect Moral Nature. 'They err,' says Hooker, 'who think that of God's will there is no reason except His will.' It is also implied in this statement that the divine foreordination, whether of things universally or of men's lots in particular, is neither a thing of necessity on the one hand nor of caprice on the other, but a thing of freedom and of thought; and further, that the reasons for that foreordination do not lie in the objects themselves, but are intrinsic to the divine Mind and the free determination of the divine Will."

(1:12) The saints were made God's heritage "that we should be to the praise of His glory." "That" is *eis*, a preposition often showing result. Translate, "to the end that we are to the praise of His glory." The words "should be" too often carry the idea of obligation to the English reader, and thus suggest here the obligation of the Christian to live a life that will be to the praise of God's glory. But Paul is speaking here of the saint's position, not his Christian experience, which latter he takes up in chapters 4-6. Expositors comments: "This clause states the ultimate end which God had in view in foreordaining us to be made His inheritance. It was not for our own privilege (as the Jews with their limited and exclusive ideas had misinterpreted the object of God in His election of them), but that through us His glory might be set forth. Compare the prophetic declaration, 'this people which I formed for myself, that they might show forth my praise' (Isa. 43:21)."

The "we" are described as those "who first trusted in Christ." The word "trusted" is not *pisteuō*, the Greek word which means "to believe, to trust," but *proelpizō*, "to hope before, to repose hope in a person or thing before the event confirms it." Vincent says: *"We* refers to Jewish Christians, and the verb describes their Messianic hope *before* (*pro*) the advent of Christ. Hence Rev., correctly, *we who had* (have) *before hoped. In Christ* should be 'in *the Christ*,' as the subject of Messianic expectation and not as *Jesus,* for whom *Christ* passed into a proper name. It is equivalent to *in the Messiah.*" The English word "Christ" is the transliteration (spelling) of the Greek word which means "the anointed," and this is the translation of the Hebrew word "Messiah."

(1:13) The word "trusted" is in italics and is therefore not in the Greek text. It is not needed. We have in the Greek what is called an interrupted construction. The translation reads, "in whom also as for you (Gentiles), having heard the word of the truth, the good news of your salvation, in whom having believed, you were sealed with the Spirit of the promise, the Holy (Spirit)." The word "sealed" is *sphragizō,* "to set a seal upon, mark with a seal." The papyri afford the following examples of its use: "If the *fruit* is *sealed,* then everything is in order: the sealing is the last thing that must be done prior to delivering;" "let him seal a sample," obviously to prevent the corn from being tampered with during its transit; "I gave the letter sealed (to the messenger);" "send the ass to be branded" (Moulton and Milligan, *Vocabulary of the Greek Testament*). The Scofield Bible footnote is helpful: "The Holy Spirit is Himself the seal. In the symbolism of Scripture a seal signifies (1) A finished transaction (Jer. 32:9, 10; John 17:4, 19:30), (2) Ownership (Jer. 32:11, 12; II Tim. 2:19), (3) Security (Esth. 8:8; Dan. 6:17; Eph. 4:30)." Thus, God places the Holy Spirit in us permanently ("The Spirit who has been caused to take up His permanent residence in us, has a passionate desire to the point of envy" Jas. 4:5), indicating that the great transaction in which God the Son paid for sin, thus satisfying the just demand of God's holy law, is finished; that we saints belong to Him as His heritage, and that we are eternally secure. The Holy Spirit is described as the Spirit of the promise, namely, the Spirit who was announced by promise; see Acts 2:16, Joel 2:28; Zech. 12:10; Isa. 32:15, 44:3; John 7:39; Acts 1:48; Gal. 3:14 (Vincent).

(1:14) The Holy Spirit is described as "the earnest of our inheritance." The word "earnest" is *arrabōn*. Vincent defines it as "caution-money deposited by a purchaser in pledge of full payment." The papyri give us the following examples: "a woman who was selling a cow received 1000 drachmae as earnest money; regarding Lampon the mouse-catcher, I paid him for you as earnest money 8 drachmae in order that he may catch the mice while they are with young" (M. and M.). They say: "The above vernacular usage amply confirms the N.T., sense of an 'earnest' or a part given in advance of what will be bestowed fully afterwards." The bestowal of the Holy Spirit is God's part payment in the salvation He gives the believing sinner, that part payment guaranteeing the full delivery of all parts of the salvation given.   Salvation is in three parts; *justification,* the removal of the guilt and penalty of sin and the bestowal of a positive righteousness, Jesus Christ, is given at the moment the sinner puts his faith in the Lord Jesus as Saviour; *sanctification,* a progressive work of the Spirit in the life of the believer, is a present possession in which He eliminates sin from the experience of the believer and produces His own fruit; *glorification,* the act of God transforming the present bodies of believers into perfect, sinless, deathless bodies.   The believer has the first two now.   The Holy Spirit, indwelling the believer, is God's earnest money, guaranteeing to him the future glorification of his body.

The Holy Spirit is this guarantee until "the redemption of the purchased possession."   The words "purchased possession" are *peripoiēsis,* which "expresses the general idea of *preserving, acquiring, gaining for one's self,* without specific reference to a *price*" (Expositors).   It refers to the saints as God's heritage which He preserves for Himself.   The final redemption of this possession is glorification, when the physical body will be the recipient of the work of salvation.   The soul and spirit are now the recipients of God's saving grace.   The body will experience that work at the Rapture when the first resurrection takes place. This will result to the praise of God's glory.

Translation (1:3-14).   *May the God and Father of our Lord Jesus Christ be eulogized, the One who conferred benefactions upon us in the sphere of every spiritual blessing in the heavenly places in Christ, (4) even as He selected us out for Himself in Him before the foundations of the universe were laid, to be holy ones and without blemish before His searching, penetrating gaze; (5) in love having previously marked us out with the result that He placed us as adult sons through the intermediate agency of Jesus Christ for Himself according to that which seemed good in His heart's desire, (6) resulting in praise of the glory of His grace which He freely bestowed upon us in the Beloved, (7) in whom we are having our redemption through*

*His blood, the putting away of our trespasses according to the
wealth of His grace* (8) *which He caused to superabound to us
in the sphere of every wisdom and understanding,* (9) *having
made known to us the mystery of His will according to that
which seemed good to Him, which good thing He purposed in
Himself,* (10) *with respect to an administration of the completion of the seasons, to bring back again to their original state the
all things in the Christ, the things in the heavens and the things
on the earth, in Him,* (11) *in whom also we were made an inheritance, having been previously marked out according to the
purpose of the One who operates the all things according to the
counsel of His will,* (12) *resulting in our being to the praise of
His glory who had previously placed our hope in the Christ,*
(13) *in whom also, as for you, having heard the word of the
truth, the good news of your salvation, in whom also having
believed, you were sealed with the Spirit of the promise, the
Holy* (*Spirit*), (14) *who is the earnest of our inheritance guaranteeing the full payment of all to the redemption of the possession which is being preserved, with a view to the praise of His
glory.*

(1:15, 16) "Wherefore" is *dia touto,* "on this account," on
account of all that is true of the saints which is stated in verses
3-14, and in particular, because of what is said of them in verse
13, Paul thanks God for the Ephesian saints and prays for
them. "Your faith" is *tēn kath' humas pistin,* literally, "the
down among you faith." The preposition, *kata,* "down," when
used with the accusative case as it is here, means "down along."
It has a distributive sense. Paul referred to the faith existent
among the Ephesian saints, not the initial act of appropriating
faith when they were saved, but the day by day faith exercised
in the Lord Jesus for daily living. This faith resulted in love
exhibited toward all the saints. The word "love" here is *agapē,*
referring to that love produced in the heart of the yielded believer by the Holy Spirit (Gal. 5:23).

Translation. *On account of this, I also, having heard of the
faith in the Lord Jesus which is among you, and of your love*

to all the saints, do not cease giving thanks for you as I constantly make mention of you in my prayers.

(1:17) The expression, "the God of our Lord Jesus Christ," refers to our Lord in His humanity as worshipping and being obedient to God the Father. "The Father of glory" is "the Father of the glory," the definite article appearing in the Greek text. He is the Father of the glory in the sense that He is the Father to whom glory belongs.

Paul prays that God might give the spirit of wisdom and revelation to the Ephesians. Are we to understand the word "spirit" which here is without the article, to refer to the human spirit or the Holy Spirit? The Ephesian saints had both. How could God give them something they already had? Vincent and Expositors say that it is the Holy Spirit to which reference is made. Alford says: "Certainly it would not be right to take *pneuma* (spirit) here as solely the Holy Spirit, nor as solely the spirit of man: rather as a complex idea, of the spirit of man indwelt by the Spirit of God that as such, it is His special gift of wisdom (not, which *gives wisdom,* but which possesses it as its character — to which appertains wisdom) and of revelation (i.e., that revelation which belongs to all Christians)." The word *pneuma* has among its various uses the meaning, "a disposition or influence which fills and governs the soul of anyone." What Paul is praying for is that God might so work in the lives of the Ephesian saints that they will have the spiritual wisdom and a revelation from Him that is the result of the Holy Spirit's work of energizing their human spirit. That spiritual disposition should characterize these saints.

This spiritual wisdom and revelation is "in the knowledge of Him." The word "knowledge" is *epignōsis,* "knowledge that is true, accurate, thorough, full knowledge." Expositors says: "It was by a knowledge of God Himself, or, as it may be better put, *within* the sphere of that knowledge that the gift of enlightenment and the reception of further disclosures of the divine counsel were to make themselves good. The only gifts desired for these converts were gifts of a spiritual order, meaning a better acquaintance with God Himself."

Translation. *That the God and Father of our Lord Jesus Christ, the Father of the glory, might give to you a spirit of wisdom and revelation in the sphere of a full knowledge of Him.*

(1:18) The words, "the eyes of your understanding being enlightened," are explanatory of the act of God giving the saints a spirit of wisdom and revelation in the sphere of a full knowledge of Him. The Greek is, "the eyes of your heart," the heart referring not only to the emotional nature, but also to the reason and to the faculty of intelligence. The words, "being enlightened," are a perfect participle in the Greek text, referring to a past complete act having present results. The translation reads, "the eyes of your heart having been enlightened with the present result that they are in a state of illumination." That is, Paul is praying that a permanent work of the Holy Spirit be done in the human spirits of these saints, that their inner spiritual capacities for understanding the truth may be the recipients of a lasting benefit, and this with a view to their knowing three things.

The *first* is that they may know "what is the hope of their calling." The word "what" is *tis,* not "how great," nor "of what kind," but "what" — what the hope really is. "The 'His calling' is the call of which *God* is the author, and that is an effectual call. . . . The hope is not the *object* hoped for, . . . but the attitude of mind, the subjective hope, the assured Christian expectation" (Expositors).

The *second* is that they may know "what is the wealth of the glory of His inheritance in the saints." The words "in the saints" are locative of sphere. God's inheritance is within the sphere of the saints. That is, the phrase "in the sphere of the saints" is definitive of the word "inheritance." This takes us back to verse 11 where Paul says we saints were made God's inheritance. In verse 18, Paul prays that we might know how precious the saints are in God's eyes as His inheritance. He is glorified in His saints, and this glory is valuable. It is part of the wealth that God possesses, dearer to Him than all the splendors of creation.

Translation. *The eyes of your heart being in an enlightened state with a view to your knowing what is the hope of His calling, what is the wealth of the glory of His inheritance in the saints.*

(1:19, 20)   The *third* thing Paul prays for is that the saints might know "what is the exceeding greatness of His power to us-ward who believe." Expositors comments: "In these three clauses Paul leads the readers on from the hope itself which becomes theirs in virtue of their being called of God, to the splendor of the inheritance to which the hope points, and from this again to that in God Himself which makes the fulfillment of the hope and the possession of the inheritance certain, namely, the limitless efficiency which is His prerogative." This power of God working in our behalf with reference to our salvation is not thought of here as operating only in the future, but also at present. The word "exceeding" is *huperballon*, literally, "a throwing beyond," thus metaphorically, "superiority, excellence." It speaks of power here that is beyond measure, more than enough, of surpassing power.

This power is described as "according to the working of His mighty power which He wrought in Christ when He raised Him from the dead." The word "working" is *energeia* from which we get our word "energy." It speaks of energy put forth, in operation. This surpassing power which God in salvation uses in ministering to our spiritual needs, is in accordance with, commensurate with the divine energy "of His mighty power." The Greek has it, "of the manifested power of His strength." Paul uses four words here, all having the general meaning of "power;" the first use of "power" is *dunamis,* "natural ability, general and inherent;" "working" is *energeia,* "power in exercise, operative power;" "mighty" is *kratos,* "manifested strength;" the second use of "power" is *ischuos,* "strength, power as an endowment." To put these together we have, "And what is the superabounding greatness of His inherent power to us who are believing ones as measured by the operative energy of the manifested strength of His might."

This might "He wrought in Christ when He raised Him from the dead." The word "wrought" is *energeō,* "to be operative, be at work, put forth power." The idea here is that this might or power was operative in Christ when God raised Him from the dead. It operated to raise Him from the dead. We can translate, "which might was operative in Christ." The words, "from the dead" are literally, "out from among the dead." "Set" is *kathizō,* "to make to sit down."

Translation. *And what is the superabounding greatness of His inherent power to us who are believing ones as measured by the operative energy of the manifested strength of His might, which (might) was operative in the Christ when He raised Him out from among the dead and seated Him at His right hand in the heavenly places.*

(1:21) "Principality" is the translation of *archē,* literally, "a first one, a leader," and is used usually to refer to the holy angels or to demons. Here it refers to the former since the exaltation of Christ is in view, not His victory over the hosts of Satan. "Power" is the translation of *exousia,* "delegated authority." It has reference to the holy angels also. The word "might" is *dunamis,* "power," and "dominion" is *kuriotēs,* "lordship." Alford says that "in this enumeration not only earthly, nor only heavenly authorities are meant to be included, but both together. That the evil spirits are included, is therefore manifest." The words "far above" are the translation of *huperanō,* literally, "over above."

Of the words, "and every name that is named," Vincent says: *"And* has a collective and summary force — *and in a word. Every name,* etc. Whatever a name can be given to. 'Let any name be uttered, whatever it is, Christ is above it; it is more exalted than that which the name uttered affirms' (Meyer). Compare Phil. 2:9. 'We know that the emperor precedes all, though we cannot enumerate all the ministers of his court: so we know that Christ is placed above all, although we cannot name all' (Bengel)."

The word "world" is, not *kosmos,* "the created universe," but *aiōn,* "age"; it speaks of duration; it speaks of this present state of things, and in the words, "but also in that which is to come," of the future state of things.

Translation. *Over above every government and authority and power and lordship and every name that is constantly being named not only in this age but also in the one about to come.*

(1:22, 23) "Put under" is *hupotassō,* a military term, "to put in subjection under one." Expositors says: "The act referred to, therefore, by the aorist of *hupotassō,* may be the definite gift of absolute dominion consequent on the exaltation. The raising of Christ to God's right hand was followed by the placing of all things under His feet and making Him sovereign over all."

The Greek has it, "and gave Him as Head over all things to the Church." Christ is therefore God's gift to the Church. He as Head over all things and as Head of the Church is a love gift of God the Father to the Church. The word "church" is *ekklēsia,* "a body of called out individuals." It refers to the invisible Church, composed of only saved individuals, not to the visible, organized Church on earth.

The Church is described as that "which is His body." The word "which" is *hētis,* "which is of such a nature as," and has a qualitative nature to it. Of the word "body," *sōma,* Expositors says: "The word *sōma,* which passes readily from its literal meaning into the figurative sense of a *society,* a number of men constituting a social or ethical union (compare Eph. 4:4), is frequently applied in the N.T., epistles to the Church, . . . as the mystical body of Christ, the fellowship of believers regarded as an organic spiritual unity in a living relation to Christ, subject to Him, animated by Him, and having His power operating in it. The relation between Christ and the Church, therefore, is not an external relation, or one simply of Superior and inferior, Sovereign and subject, but one of life and incorporation. The

Church is not merely an institution ruled by Him as President, a Kingdom in which He is the Supreme Authority, or a vast company of men in moral sympathy with Him, but a Society which is in vital connection with Him, having the source of its life in Him, sustained and directed by His power, the instrument also by which He works."

Commenting on the words, "the fulness of Him that filleth all in all," Expositors has this preliminary note: "The preceding sentence carries the idea of the *Church* far beyond the limited conception of a concrete institution or outward, visible organization, and lifts us to the grander conception of a great spiritual fellowship, which is *one* under all varieties of external form and constitution in virtue of the presence of Christ's Spirit in it, and *catholic* as embracing all believers and existing wherever any such are found. It is the conception of the Church which pervades this epistle (compare 3:10, 21; 5:23, 24, 25, 27, 29, 32). It appears again in similar terms in the sister epistle (Col. 1:18, 24), and elsewhere in the varied phraseology of the 'royal priesthood' (I Pet. 2:9) and the 'Church of the First born' (Heb. 12:23). It is this supreme idea of the Church as a spiritual order, the essence of which is a living relation to Christ, that receives further expression in the profound sentence with which the paragraph closes."

The word "fulness" is *plērōma*. Thayer gives the following: "that which is or has been filled; used of a ship inasmuch as it is filled (i.e., manned) with sailors, rowers, and soldiers; in the N.T., the body of believers, as that which is filled with the presence, power, agency, riches of God and of Christ." Alford says, "the meaning being, that the Church, being the Body of Christ, is dwelt in and filled with God: it is His *plērōma* (fulness) in an especial manner — His fulness abides in it and is exemplified by it." Expositors comments: "The idea is that the Church is not only Christ's body but that which is *filled by Him*. In Col. 1:19, 2:9, the whole *plērōma* or every plenitude of the Godhead, the very fulness of the Godhead, the totality of the divine powers and qualities, is said to be recognized as Framer and Governor

of the world, and there is neither need nor place for any intermediate beings as agents in those works of creating, upholding
and administering.   Here the conception is that this plenitude
of the divine powers and qualities which is in Christ is imparted
by Him to His Church, so that the latter is pervaded by His
presence, animated by His life, filled with His gifts and energies and graces.   He is the sole Head of the universe, which is
supplied by Him with all that is needed for its being and order.
He is also the sole Head of the Church, which receives from Him
what He Himself possesses, and is endowed by Him with all
that it requires for the realization of its vocation."   "The all
things" is "the whole system of things, made by Christ, and having in Him the ground of its being, its continuance, its order
(Heb. 1:3, Col. 1:16, 17, I Cor. 8:6), 'with all things,' . . . the
universe itself and all the things that make its fulness" (Expositors).

Translation.   *And all things He put in subjection under His
feet, and Him He gave as Head over all things to the Church,
which is of such a nature as to be His body, the fulness of the
One who constantly is filling the all things with all things.*

CHAPTER TWO

(2:1) The words "And you," "take up the closing thought of the preceding chapter, the magnitude of God's power toward believers as exhibited in Christ's resurrection. He now shows that the same power is applied to his readers. Hence the connection is, 'When He raised Him from the dead, etc., and *you* did He quicken, even as He quickened Christ.' The structure of the passage is broken. Paul having prominently in mind the thought *God quickened you as He did Christ,* begins with *you also.* Then the connection is interrupted by vv. 2, 3, which describe their previous condition. Then v. 1 is taken up in v. 4, by *but God,* God introducing a new sentence" (Vincent). The words "hath He quickened" are in italics and therefore not in the Greek text of v. 1. They are found in v. 5. The connection is as follows: in v. 5, those who are addressed in v. 1 are said to have been quickened by God. We therefore include them in v. 1 to fill up the gap left by Paul. "Quickened" of v. 5 is *zōopoieō,* "to cause to live, to make alive, to give life." The translation reads, "And you He made alive." The reference is to the act of God imparting divine life in regeneration to the believing sinner. "Were" is a present participle. The literal translation so far reads, "And you He made alive, being dead." Vincent translates "when you were dead," thus giving, as he says, the sense of the continued state in the past expressed by the participle "being." The word "dead" is *nekros,* "spiritually dead, that is, destitute of a life that recognizes and is devoted to God, because given up to trespasses and sins, inactive as respects doing right." It should be kept clearly in mind that death is not extinction of being or inactivity. Spiritual death is the state of separation from God and His life. Death itself is a separation, whether physical, the separation of the person from his body, or spiritual, the separation of the person from God.

The state of death spoken of here is "in trespasses and sins." It is the dative of reference, "dead with reference to trespasses and sins." That is, this state of death had to do with trespasses and sins. It was not physical death, although that is caused in the last analysis by sin. This state of death was linked with trespasses and sins in that it had to do with the moral and ethical part of the individual, his reason, will, and emotions. He was living in a state of separation from God and His life in that the latter did not energize and control the reason, will, and emotions of the person. These were very active, but were energized by the totally depraved nature. The word "trespasses" is the translation of *paraptōma* from *parapiptō,* "to fall beside a person or thing, to slip aside, hence, to deviate from the right path, to turn aside, to wander." Thus, in the word *paraptōma,* sin is looked upon as a lapse or deviation from truth or uprightness, a trespass, a misdeed. "Sins" is the rendering of *hamartia* from *hamartanō,* "to miss the mark." It was used in the Greek classics of a spearman missing the target at which he aimed the spear. It was used in the ethical terminology of the Greeks to mean "to fail of one's purpose, to go wrong." In the N.T., it speaks of sin as the act of a person failing to obey the Word of God, failing to measure up in his life to the will of God. Its use is excellently illustrated in Romans 3:28, "All have sinned (missed the mark), and at present come short of the glory of God." The mark or target is the glory of God. Man was created to glorify God. His attempt, where the attempt is made, to live a life pleasing to God, falls short of the target, like a spear thrown by an athlete, falls short of the target at which it is thrown.

Translation. *And you being dead with reference to your trespasses and sins, He made alive.*

(2:2) The word "wherein" goes back to "trespasses and sins." The idea is, "in which trespasses and sins ye walked." The word "walked" is *peripateō,* from *pateō,* "to walk," and *peri,* "around" or "about," thus, "to walk about." It then came to mean, "to make one's way, to make progress, to make due use of one's opportunities," finally, "to live, to regulate one's life, to conduct one's self, order one's behavior." We have here the locative of sphere. The unsaved order their behavior, regulate their lives within the sphere of trespasses and sins. All their thoughts, words, and deeds are ensphered by sin. Not one of their acts ever gets outside this circle of sin. That is what is meant by total depravity. The word "walked" is in the aorist tense, the classification, constative, a construction which looks at a thing or an action as a complete unit, looks at it in a panoramic view. The whole life of the unsaved person is nothing but sin.

The unsaved person orders his behavior within the sphere of trespasses and sins "according to the course of this world." "According to" is *kata,* a preposition which in its local and root meaning has the idea of "down," which latter word speaks of domination and control. His act of ordering his behavior in the sphere of trespasses and sins is dominated or controlled by "the course of this world." "Course" is *aiōn,* which Trench defines as "All that floating mass of thoughts, opinions, maxims, speculations, hopes, impulses, aims, aspirations, at any time current in the world, which it may be impossible to seize and accurately define, but which constitutes a most real and effective power, being the moral, or immoral atmosphere which at every moment of our lives we inhale, again inevitably to exhale, — all this is included in the *aiōn,* which is, as Bengel has expressed it, 'the subtle informing spirit of the *kosmos,* or world of men who are living alienated and apart from God'" (Trench). The Germans have a word for it, *zeitgeist,* "the spirit of the age." "World" is is the head, his demons are his emissaries, and all the unsaved *kosmos,* which here refers to the system of evil of which Satan are his slaves, together with the purposes, pursuits, pleasures, and places where God is not wanted. To distinguish the words, one could say that *kosmos* gives the over-all picture of mankind alienated from God during all history, and *aiōn* represents any distinct age or period of human history as marked out from another by particular characteristics.

But not only does the sinner order his behavior as dominated by the spirit of the age in which he lives, which spirit is just part of that *kosmos* human-history-long alienation of the human race from God. He is dominated or controlled by the "prince of the power of the air." The word "prince" suggests the son of a king. We use the word in the expression "he is a prince of a fellow." The Greek word is *archōn* which refers to the first in an order of persons or things. It speaks here of Satan who is the first one in power and authority in his kingdom. "Power" is *exousia,* "authority," and refers to the demons. The word "air" here is *aer,* "the lower, denser atmosphere" as against the *aithēr,* "the rarer atmosphere above the mountain tops." The kingdom of Satan is in this lower atmosphere where we human beings are, in order that that sinister being, filled with a bitter hatred of God and the human race, might with his demons, prey upon humanity. Satan is the leader of the authority (demons) of the lower atmosphere. The unsaved order their behavior according to his dictates and those of his demons. It is significant that Paul ascribes the origin of the false religions to the demons (I Tim. 4:1).

In the A.V. translation, one would naturally think that "spirit" is in apposition with "prince" and in the same construction as that word is to the words "according to," interpreting as follows: the prince is the spirit who works in the children of disobedience. That is, Satan is that spirit. Now, it is true that Satan is an angel, and in that sense could be called a spirit. It is true that he works in the unsaved. But according to the rules of Greek Grammar, it is impossible to so relate the words. "Prince" is in the accusative case, "spirit" in the genitive. They could not therefore be in apposition. The connection is as follows: the prince of the power of the air is also the prince of the spirit that now works in the children of disobedience. The question now is as to what this spirit is? It is the principle or power that comes into men from Satan, the spirit that is operative in the unsaved. The word "spirit" is used here as in the expression, "the spirit of Antichrist." The word refers to one's way of thinking and acting. We say, "the spirit of that man is beautiful." It is an evil tendency, a way of living, a characteristic of the unsaved, the spirit of the unsaved. Satan is the one who dominates and controls this spirit in man. This spirit or disposition is said to work in the children of disobedience. "Worketh" is *energeō*, "to be operative, to be at work." "Children" is *huios*, "sons" and is a Hebrew idiom in which one calls a person having a peculiar quality, or subject to a peculiar evil, a son of that quality. The unsaved are called sons of disobedience in the sense that they have the character of being disobedient. The word "disobedient" is the translation of *apeithēs*, "impersuasable, uncompliant." Stephen called Israel stiffnecked in heart. This gives the picture of a person who is impersuasable and uncompliant. The definite article before "impersuasable" seems to point to a particular act of that character, possibly the original sin of Adam.

Translation. *In the sphere of which (trespasses and sins) at one time you ordered your behavior as dominated by the age-spirit of this world system, as dominated by the leader of the authority of the lower atmosphere, (the leader also) of the spirit that is now operating in the sons of the impersuasableness.*

(2:3) The words, "among whom," refer back to "the children of disobedience." It is not "in the midst of whom," but "numbered among whom." The saints at one time were numbered among the sons of the impersuasableness. It is, "among whom, as for us, we all had our conversation." The latter word today refers to converse between individuals, in short, to talk. The Greek word is *anastrephō*, "to conduct or behave one's self, to order one's behavior." Thus, the saints at one time ordered their behavior, conducted themselves among the sons of the impersuasableness, in the lusts of their flesh. "Lusts" is *epithumia*, "a passionate longing, a craving," good or bad, depending upon the context. Here it is an evil craving since it comes from the flesh. The word "flesh" is *sarx*, which here refers to the totally depraved nature as dominating the unsaved individual.

In ordering our behavior in the sphere of the totally depraved nature, we "were fulfilling the desires of the flesh and of the mind." The word "flesh" is again *sarx,* referring to the totally depraved nature. "Mind" is *dianoia,* "the mind as the faculty of understanding, feeling, desiring"; when used in the plural as it is here, it refers to the thoughts, here to evil thoughts. "Fulfilling" is *poieō,* "to do, perform, accomplish." The participle is present in tense, thus, durative in action. It speaks of the habitual performing of acts that satisfy the desires of the evil nature and of the evil thoughts, thus a fulfilling of those desires. We went the limit in sin. The evil nature had full sway. "Desires" is *thelēma,* "desires that come from the emotions." Thus, the life of the unsaved is swayed by the emotions rather than the reason.

We "were by nature the children of wrath." "Were" is in the Greek text, imperfect in tense, which tense speaks of continuous action or state of being. Our totally depraved condition before salvation was a continuous one, from birth on without a cessation of that condition. "Children" is *teknon,* from *tiktō,* "to give birth to." Thus, *teknon* emphasizes the birth relationship. We were born children having a totally depraved nature. Vincent says: "Children (*teknon*) emphasizes the connection by birth; . . . *By nature* accords with *children,* implying what is innate. *Wrath* is God's holy hatred of sin; His essential antagonism to everything evil, (Rom. 1:18)." Expositors comments: "This holy displeasure of God with sin is not inconsistent with His love, but is the reaction of that love against the denial of its sovereign rights of responsive love. The term *phusis* (nature), though it may occasionally be applied to what is habitual or to character as developed, means properly what is *innate, implanted* in one by nature, and this with different shades of meaning (compare Rom. 2:14; Gal. 2:15, 4:8 etc.). The clause means, therefore, that in their pre-Christian life those meant by the *hemeis pantes* (we all) were in the condition of subjection to the divine wrath; and that they were so not by deed merely, nor by circumstance, nor by passing into it, but by nature. Their universal sin has already been affirmed. This universal sin is now described as sin by nature. Beyond this, Paul does not go in this present passage. But the one is the explanation of the other. Universal sin implies a law of sinning, a sin that is of the nature; and this, again, is the explanation of the fact that all are under the divine wrath, for the divine wrath operates only where sin is. Here is the essential meaning of the doctrine of *original sin.*"

Translation. *Among whom also we all ordered our behavior in the sphere of the cravings of our flesh, continually practicing the desires of our flesh and of our thoughts, and were continually children of wrath by nature, as also the rest.*

(2:4-6) Expositors comments: "A return is now made to the statement which was interrupted at verse 2. The resumption might have been made by *oun* (therefore). The adversative *de* (but), however, is the more appropriate, as the other side of our case is now set forth — the divine grace which meets the sinful, condemned condition, and which stands over the dark background of our death by sin and our subjection by nature to the divine wrath. God who is wroth with sin, is a God of grace. His disposition towards those who are dead by trespasses and sins is one of mercy, and this is no stinted mercy, but a mercy that is *rich,* exhaustless." The word "rich" is the translation of *plousios,* "wealthy, abounding in material resources, abounding, abundantly supplied."

God who is rich in mercy is so "for His great love wherewith He loved us." The word "for" is *dia,* "because of, on account of," thus, "in order to satisfy" His great love. The distinctive word for "love" here is *agapē* which speaks of a love called out of one's heart by the preciousness of the one loved, a love that impels one to sacrifice one's self for the benefit of the object loved. It is the love shown at Calvary (John 3:16).

There are two parallel phrases here, "God being wealthy in the sphere of mercy," and "we being dead with respect to our trespasses." The entire translation is, "But God being wealthy in the sphere of mercy, on account of His great love with which He loved us, and we being dead with respect to our trespasses, hath quickened us together with Christ." The word "quickened" is *zōopoieō,* "to cause to live, to make alive, to give life."

This takes us to Romans 6:3, 4, "Or, do you not know that as many as were placed into Christ Jesus (by the Holy Spirit), into His death were placed. We were entombed therefore with Him through this aforementioned placing into His death, in order that just as there was raised up Christ out from amongst the dead ones through the glory of the Father, thus also as for us, in the newness of a life (imparted) we may order our behavior." This newness of life is a new life imparted through our identification with Christ in His resurrection. Our identification with Christ in His death broke the power of indwelling sin. Our identification with Him in His resurrection resulted in the impartation of divine life. This is what Paul has reference to when he says, "We were made alive together with Him."

Now comes the interjection, "by grace ye are saved." We have here in the Greek what is called a periphrastic construction. This is used when the writer cannot get all of the details of action from one verbal form. So he uses two, a finite verb and a participle. The participle here is in the perfect tense, which tense speaks of an action that took place in past time and was completed in past time, having results existent in present time. The translation reads, "By grace have you been completely saved, with the present result that you are in a saved state of being." The perfect tense speaks of the *existence* of finished results in present time. But Paul is not satisfied with showing the *existence* of finished results in present time. He wants to show the *persistence* of results *through* present time. So he uses the verb "to be" in the present tense which gives durative force to the finished results. Thus, the full translation is, "By grace you have been saved in past time completely, with the result that you are in a state of salvation which persists through present time." The unending state of the believer in salvation could not have been put in stronger or clearer language. The finished results of the past act of salvation are always present with the reader. His present state of salvation is dependent upon one thing and one thing only, his past appropriation of the Lord Jesus as Saviour. His initial act of faith brought him salvation in its three aspects, *justification,* the removal of the guilt and penalty of sin and the impartation of a positive righteousness, Jesus Christ Himself, an act which occurs at the moment of believing, and a position that remains static for time and eternity; *sanctification, positional,* the act of the Holy Spirit taking the believing sinner out of the first Adam with his (Adam's) sin and death, and placing him in the Last Adam (Jesus Christ) with His righteousness and life, an act that occurs at the moment of believing; *progressive,* the process by which the Holy Spirit eliminates sin from the experience of the believer and produces His fruit, gradually conforming him into the image of the Lord Jesus, a process that goes on all through the life of a Christian and continues all through eternity, and which never is completed, for a finite creature can never equal an infinite one in any quality; and *glorification,* the act of the Holy Spirit, transforming the mortal bodies of believers into glorified, perfect bodies at the Rapture of the Church. The believer has had his *justification,* he is having his *sanctification,* and he is yet to have his *glorification.* The earnest of the Spirit guarantees to him his glorification.

"Hath raised us up together" is *sunegeirō.* Expositors translates, "Raised us with Him," and comments: "That is, to life now, in a present spiritual sense. The *sunegeirō* expresses the definite idea of *resurrection,* and primarily that of physical resurrection. The introduction of this term and the following makes it not improbable that both ideas, that of the present moral resurrection and that of the future bodily resurrection, were in Paul's mind, and that he did not sharply distinguish between them, but thought of them as one great gift of life."

"Made us sit together" is the translation of *sunkathizō,* which Expositors translates, *Seated* us (or, enthroned us) *with Him* in the *heavenlies,* and comments: "Made us sharers with Him in dignity and dominion, so that even now, and in foretaste of our

future exaltation, our life and thought are raised to the heavenlies where He reigns."

As to the phrase "in Christ Jesus," the same authority says:
"Not the 'seated us with Him' only, but the whole statement is
qualified by this. This quickening, this resurrection, this seating
of us with Him take effect in so far as we are *in* Him as our
Representative, having our life and our completeness in our
Head."

Translation. *But God, being wealthy in the sphere of mercy,
because of His great love with which He loved us, and we being
dead with respect to our trespasses, made us alive together with
the Christ, by grace have you been saved completely in past time,
with the present result that you are in a state of salvation which
persists through present time, and raised us with Him and seated
us with Him in the heavenly places in Christ Jesus.*

(2:7) Now comes the purpose for which God saved us,
namely, "that in the ages to come He might show the exceeding
riches of His grace in His kindness toward us through Christ
Jesus." Expositors says: "The satisfaction of His love was
God's motive in quickening and raising them. The manifestation
of His glory in its surpassing wealth is His final purpose in the
same." The expression, "the ages to come" are in the Greek, *en
tois aiōsin tois eperchomenois,* literally, "in the ages that are
coming one upon another," that is, in the eternal ages that roll
in, one after another in the future eternity after the universe is
returned to its pristine glory. Expositors comments: "God's
purpose, therefore, is that in the eternal future, the future which
opens with Christ's Parousia (His personal presence in His
second coming), and in all the continuing length of that future,
the grace of His ways with those once dead in sins should be
declared and understood in all the grandeur of its exceeding
riches." "Kindness" is *chrēstotēs,* "benignity, kindness." "Toward" is *epi,* "upon," with the accusative case as here, "to."
"Show" is *endeiknumi,* in the middle voice, which voice indicates
that the subject of the verb acts in his own interest. God will exhibit His kindness to the saints for His own glory, in order that

He may be glorified. And the spectators will be the angels. We saints will be the objects of this kindness. We will be on display before the angelic world, basking in the sunshine of God's smile, enjoying the riches of His blessings, all, in order that He might be glorified by the angelic hosts.

Translation. *In order that He might exhibit for His own interest (glory) in the ages that will pile themselves upon one another in continuous succession, the surpassing wealth of His grace in kindness to us in Christ Jesus.*

(2:8-10)   The definite article appears before the word "grace" here, pointing the reader back to the same statement in verse 5, and informing him that the writer is to elaborate upon this previously mentioned statement.   The reader of this exposition is urged to go back to the exegesis of verse 5 and refresh his memory as to the total meaning of Paul's statement, "by grace are ye saved."

The words, "through faith" speak of the instrument or means whereby the sinner avails himself of this salvation which God offers him in pure grace.   Expositors says: "Paul never says 'through the faith,' as if the faith were the ground or procuring cause of the salvation."   Alford says: "It (the salvation) has been effected by grace and apprehended by faith."   The word "that" is *touto*, "this," a demonstrative pronoun in the neuter gender.   The Greek word "faith" is feminine in gender and therefore *touto* could not refer to "faith."   It refers to the general idea of salvation in the immediate context.   The translation reads, "and this not out from you as a source, of God (it is) the gift."   That is, salvation is a gift of God.   It does not find its source in man.   Furthermore, this salvation is not "out of a source of works."   This explains salvation by grace.   It is not produced by man nor earned by him.   It is a gift from God with no strings tied to it.   Paul presents the same truth in Romans 4:4, 5 when speaking of the righteousness which God imputed to Abraham, where he says: "Now, to the one who works, his wages are not looked upon as a favor but as that which is justly or legally due.   But to the one who does not work but believes on the One who justifies the impious, his faith is computed for righteousness."

One reason why salvation is a free gift of God and not earned by works, is given us in the words; "lest any man should boast." Grace glorifies God. Works would glorify man. Commenting on the words, "For we are His workmanship," Vincent says: "A reason why no man should glory. If *we* are God's workmanship, our *salvation* cannot be of ourselves." Expositors comments: "We ourselves are a *work,* the handiwork of God, made anew by Him, and our salvation, therefore, is due to Him, not to ourselves." The word "workmanship" is *poiēma,* from *poieō,* "to do, to make." Thus, *poiēma* means "something that is made."

The words, "created in Christ Jesus unto good works," Expositors says are "a further definition of 'His workmanship.' We are God's spiritual handiwork in the sense that we were *created* by Him, made a new spiritual *creature* by Him when His grace made us Christians. This new creation was *in Christ,* so that except by union between Him and us it could not have taken place (Eph. 2:15, 4:24, II Cor. 5:17; Gal. 6:15; Col. 3:10). Also it was with a *view* to good works . . . . We ourselves then having been created anew by God, and good works being the *object* to which that new creation looked, not the cause that led to it, all must be of grace — not of deeds, and there can be no room for boasting."

"We were created in Christ Jesus for good works," and these good works are described as those good works "which God hath before ordained that we should walk in them." The word "ordained" is *proetoimazō,* "to prepare before, to make ready beforehand." Vincent says: "God prearranged a sphere of moral action for us to walk in. Not only are works the necessary outcome of faith, but the character and direction of the works are made ready by God." Expositors says: "Before He created us in Christ by our conversion, He had destined these good works and made them ready for us in His purpose and decree. There is the unseen source from which they spring, and there is their final explanation."

These good works were prepared beforehand "that we should walk in them." The word "walk" is *peripateō,* "to regulate one's life, to conduct one's self, to order one's behavior." "In them" is *en toutois,* "in these," namely, the good works, locative of sphere. We are to order our behavior within the sphere of these good works. Expositors comments: "God's purpose in the place which He gave to good works in His decree was that they should actually and habitually be done by us. His final object was to make good works the very element of our life, the domain in which our action should move. That this should be the nature of our walk is implied in our being His handiwork, made anew by Him in Christ; that the good works which are the divine aim of our life shall be realized, is implied in their being designed and made ready for us in God's decree; and that they are of God's originating, and not of our action and merit, is implied in the fact that we had ourselves to be made a new creation in Christ with a view to them."

Translation. *For by the grace have you been saved in time past completely, through faith, with the result that your salvation persists through present time; and this (salvation) is not from you as a source. Of God it is the gift; not from a source of works, in order that no one might boast; for we are His handiwork, created in Christ Jesus with a view to good works which God prepared beforehand in order that within their sphere we may order our behavior.*

(2:11, 12) Expositors comments: "As *dio* (wherefore) indicates, what follows is a personal, ethical application of what has been said; and the application is drawn, not from the immediate preceding sentence, but from the contents of the prior paragraph as a whole. The great things done for them by God's grace should incline them to think of the past from which they have been delivered. The remembrance of that past will make them more thankful for their present privilege, and more careful to walk in the good works which God has in view for them." The word "Gentiles" is preceded by the definite article in the Greek text, marking Gentiles out as a distinct class. The word "flesh" in this verse does not refer to the unregenerate man, but to the actual physical body, as Expositors says: "The term *sarx* (flesh) also is to be taken literally, not as referring to the former unregenerate life, but (as the subsequent sentences show) in the sense of the *flesh* to which *circumcision* is applicable. They are reminded that they belonged to the class of the Gentiles, their bodies proclaiming their heathen character." As to the clause "that which is called Uncircumcision," Expositors says: "A further definition of what they were as *ethnē* (Gentiles), suggestive of the low regard in which they were held as members of that class. The name *Uncircumcision!* — a name of contempt, was flung at them." The same authority has this to say also: "This sentence also is introduced with reference to the poverty of the previous condition of these Godless, Christless Gentiles. The point seems to be that the inferiority in which they were held, and which was expressed by the contemptuous name *Uncircumcision,* meant all the more as it was fastened on them by those to whom, while proudly calling themselves the Circumcision, the distinction was nothing more than an outward manual act performed on their bodies. The rite, when its spiritual significance and use are in view, is spoken of with honor by Paul (Rom. 4:11). As a mere performance, a barrier between Jew and Gentile, a yoke imposed by the former on the latter, a thing made essential to salvation, he spoke of it in terms of scorn and repudiation." The verse reads, "Wherefore, be keeping in remembrance that at one time you, the Gentiles in the flesh, the ones habitually called Uncircumcision by the so-called Circumcision performed by hand in the flesh."

Now Paul enumerates five things that were true of these uncircumcised Gentiles. The *first* is that they were "without Christ." Expositors says: "It describes their former condition as one in which they had no connection with Christ; in which respect they were in a position sadly inferior to that of the Jews, whose attitude was one of hoping and waiting for Christ, the

Messiah. Their apartness from Christ, their lack of all relation to Him — this is the first stroke in the dark picture of their former heathen life, and the four to which the eye is directed in the subsequent clauses all follow from that." To understand the above most clearly, we should know that the word "Christ" is the English spelling of the Greek word *christos,* which in turn is the translation of the Hebrew word for Messiah. The word "Christ" here is not to be taken in its Christian sense, but in its Jewish one. The point is not that these Ephesians were without Christ as Saviour, but as Gentiles, they had no covenant connection with Him as the Jews had with Him as Messiah.

The *second* thing true of these Ephesians was that they were "aliens from the commonwealth of Israel." We have a participle in the Greek, "alienated from the commonwealth of Israel." Expositors says: "It does not necessarily imply a lapse from a former condition of attachment or fellowship, but expresses generally the idea of being a *stranger* as contrasted with one who is *at home* with a person or an object. The term *politeia* (commonwealth) has two main senses — a *state* or *commonwealth,* and citizenship or the rights of a citizen. The first of these is most in harmony with the theocratic term 'the Israel,' and so it is understood by most. These Ephesians, therefore, had no part in the theocracy, the O.T. constitution under which God made Himself known to the Jew and entered into relation with him."

The *third* thing true of them was that they were "strangers from the covenants of promise." The definite article is in the Greek text. It is, "strangers from the covenants of the promise." Expositors comments: "The word *xenos* (strangers), which has the particular meaning of one who is not a member of a state or city, is used here in a general sense of *foreign* to a thing, having no share in it. The *diathēkai* (covenants) are the covenants with Abraham and the patriarchs. It is obviously the covenants of Messianic significance that are in view. That the Mosaic Law or the Sinaitic Covenant is not in view seems to follow from the mention of the promises; for that covenant was not distinctively of the promise, but is described by Paul as coming in after it and provisionally (Gal. 3:17-19). The 'promise' is the one distinctively so-called, the great Messianic promise given the Hebrew people."

The *fourth* thing true of these Gentiles was that they had "no hope." Expositors says: "It is not only that they had not the hope, the Messianic hope which was one of the distinctions of the Israelite, but that they were utterly without hope. Ignorant of the divine salvation and of Christ in whom it was found, they had nothing to hope for beyond this world."

The *fifth* thing was that they were "without God in the world." Again, Expositors has a helpful comment: "As they were without Christ, and without hope, so were they without God — without the knowledge of the one true and living God and thus destitute of any God. So in Gal. 4:8, Paul speaks of Gentiles like these as *knowing* not God and doing service unto them *which by nature are no gods.*" As to the phrase: "in the world," the same authority says: "The domain of their life was this present evil world, and in it, alienated as it was from God, they had no God."

Translation. *On this account be remembering that at one time, you, the Gentiles in the flesh, the ones habitually called uncircumcision by that which is called circumcision in the flesh made by hand, that you were at that time without Christ, alienated from the commonwealth of Israel and strangers from the covenants of the promise, not having hope and without God in the world.*

(2:13) Vincent says: *"Now,* in contrast with *at that time. In Christ Jesus,* in contrast with alienated from, etc. *Jesus* is added because *the Christ* who was the subject of promise, the Messiah, has come into the world under that personal name. The phrase includes the promised Messiah and the actual Saviour."

Translation. *But now in Christ Jesus you who at one time were far off, have become near by the blood of the Christ.*

(2:14) The intensive use of the pronoun in the Greek text gives us, "For He Himself is our peace." The Greek verb *eirō*

means "to join"; the noun *eirēnē*, refers to the things joined
together. To make peace, therefore, means "to join together
that which is separated." Jew and Gentile, by God's act of selecting the Jewish nation to be the channel through which He
will bring salvation to the lost, had been separated. Now, in
the blood of Christ they in the Church have been joined. This
is the peace spoken of here. Expositors comments: "As most
commentators notice, the emphasis is on the *autos* (intensive pronoun) — 'He and no other.' But there is probably more in it
than that. The selection of the abstract *eirēnēn* (peace), instead
of the simple *eirēnopoios* (peace maker), suggests that not only
'He alone' but 'He in His own Person' made peace. It is not
only that the peace was made *by* Christ and ranks as His achieve-
ment, but that it is so identified with Him that were He away
it would also fail, — so dependent on Him that apart from Him
we cannot have it." The word "our" refers to Jew and Gentile.
In making peace, our Lord made *the* both (Jew and Gentile) one.
The words "the both" are abstract neuter, showing that two
parties or classes are in the apostolic mind.

As to the words, "the middle wall of partition," Vincent says:
"literally, *the middle wall of the fence or hedge*. The wall which
pertained to the fence; the *fact* of separation being emphasized
in *wall*, and the *instrument* of separation in *fence*. The hedge
was the whole Mosaic economy which separated Jew and
Gentile."

Translation. *For He Himself is our peace, the One who made
the both one, having broken down the middle wall of the
partition.*

(2:15) The words "the enmity" follow the words "middle
wall of partition," only the participle separating them, and should
be construed as defining them, namely, "the middle wall which
was the enmity." The enmity was broken down. The law was
abolished. The word "abolished" is *katargeō*, "to render inoperative." The enmity was between Jew and Gentile, the result
of the separating influence of the Mosaic economy. The order
of words in the Greek is, "in His flesh the law of the command-

ments in ordinances having abolished." That is, our Lord
abolished the law by His death on the Cross. Expositors says:
"Farther statement of the way in which Christ by His death on
the Cross removed the separation and the hostile feeling between
Jew and Gentile, namely, by abrogating the dividing law itself.
The law is now introduced, and the term 'the law' is to be taken
in its full sense, not the ceremonial law only, but the Mosaic law
as a whole, according to the stated use of the phrase. This law
is *abolished* in the sense of being rendered inoperative . . . The
law is one of 'commandment-in-decrees.' What is in view is its
character as mandatory, and consisting in a multitude of pre-
scriptions or statutes. . . . The law was made up of commandments and these commandments expressed themselves and operated in the form of ordinances. The word *dogma* (ordinance)
in the N. T. never means anything else than statute, decree,
ordinance."

As to the meaning of the words, "to make in Himself of
twain, one new man," Expositors says: "The new creation and
the new union have their ground and principle *in* Christ. What
was contemplated, too, was not simply the making of *one man*
where formerly there were two, but the making of *one new man*.
The result was not that, though, the separation between them
was removed, the Jew still remained Jew and the Gentile, still
Gentile. It was something new, the old distinctions between
Jew and Gentile being lost in a third order of 'man,' — the
Christian man." The word "make" is not *poieō*, "to make," but
ktizō, "to create." The word "new" is *kainon*, not "new" in time
but "new" in quality. The word "man" is not *anēr*, "a male
individual," but *anthrōpos*, the generic, racial term, speaking of
an individual, here of the new creation made up of male and
female, the mystical body of Christ.

Translation. *The enmity, in His flesh having rendered inoperative the law of the commandments in ordinances, in order
that the two He might create in Himself, resulting in one new
man, making peace.*

(*2:16*) We have here, Expositors says, "a further statement of object, the *kai* (and) continuing and extending it. Only at this point is the prior and larger idea of the reconciliation *to God* introduced, and even now it is in connection with the idea of the reconciliation of Jew and Gentile. . . . In the context, it is true, so far as the relations of Jew and Gentile to each other are dealt with, we have simply the idea of a state of separation into two hostile camps giving place to a state of unity. But in the present clause, the larger truth of a reconciliation *to God* is in view, and this favors the idea of a *restoration* to a condition which had been lost." The verb, *apokatallassō,* because of its prefixed preposition *apo* which gives it the force of *back,* hints at a restoration to a primal unity, that unity being the unity of the human race before God brought in the Jew as a separate and distinct nation, not numbered amongst the other nations. That is, Jew and Gentile in Christ Jesus, restored to a primal unity where there was neither Jew nor Gentile, are now reconciled to God. The simple verb *katallassō,* means "to reconcile those that are at variance." God and the sinner are at variance because of sin. In salvation the believing sinner is brought into a state in which he is yielded and obedient to God, willingly, of his own free will and accord.

Jew and Gentile are reconciled in one body to God. "The reference," Expositors says, "is to the Jews and Gentiles now making one body, compare the 'one body' in I Cor. 10:17; Eph. 4:4; and especially in Col. 3:15. His object was to bring the two long-sundered and antagonistic parties as one whole, one great body, into right relation to God by His Cross." As to the words "having slain the enmity thereby," Alford says that the enmity here refers to that between the sinner and God. The "enmity" of verse 15 is defined in its context as that between Jew and Gentile, for the purpose of God was to reconcile these two. The "enmity" of verse 16 is that between the sinner and God, for His purpose was to reconcile both Jew and Gentile in one body to Himself.

Translation. *And in order that He might reconcile the both in one body to God through the Cross, having put to death the enmity by it.*

(2:17, 18) "Came" is an aorist participle; "having come" in His first Advent, "He proclaimed glad tidings of peace" in His atoning work of salvation on the Cross, "to you (Gentiles) who were far off, and to you (Jews) who were near." The word "preached" is not *kērussō,* "to proclaim," but *euaggelizomai,* "to bring good news."

Expositors says of verse 18, "the verse is a confirmation of the previous statement in the form of an appeal to the experience of those addressed. The fact that we, both of us, are now brought to God through Him is a witness to the truth . . . that Christ came and preached peace to both." The word "access" is the translation of *prosagō,* "to open a way of access." It was used of those who secure for one the privilege of an interview with a sovereign. The French word *entree* exactly translates it. It is by means of the ministry of the Holy Spirit that the saints have *entree* into the presence of God the Father. Note if you will, the Trinity. God the Son provides the way into the Father's presence through the Blood of His Cross, God the Spirit conducts the saint in and presents him, and God the Father is the One into whose presence the believer is brought.

Translation. *And having come, He proclaimed glad tidings of peace to you who were far off, and to you who were near, because through Him we have our entree, the both of us, by one Spirit into the presence of the Father.*

(2:19, 20) In the words "now therefore" (*ara oun*), "Paul brings to their conclusion the statements made in vv. 14-18, and draws from them the natural, comforting inference" (Expositors). The words "strangers and foreigners" are a comprehensive expression including "all who, whether by natural or territorial demarcation, or by the absence of civic privileges, were not citizens." The word "stranger" is *zenos,* "an alien." The word speaks of that which is of a different quality or nature than something else, thus, alien to it. Sinners are aliens to the kingdom of God, having a totally-depraved nature that makes them different, and different in a hostile sense. The word "foreigners" is *paroikos*, from *para*, "alongside," and *oikeō*, "to make one's home." Thus it speaks of one who has a home alongside of someone else. It is used here of one who comes from another country or city and settles in another, but does not rank as a citizen.

Translation. *Now then, no longer are you aliens and foreign sojourners, but you are fellow-citizens of the saints and householders of God, having been built up upon the foundation of the apostles and prophets, there being a chief corner stone, Jesus Christ Himself.*

(2:21, 22) "In whom" refers back to "Jesus Christ." The building, of course, is the Church, the Mystical Body of Christ composed of believers who are brought into salvation during the Church Age which began at Pentecost and ends at the Rapture. The words, "fitly framed together" are the translation of *sunarmologeō*, from *harmos*, "a joint," and *legō*, "to pick out," thus, "to join together," the total meaning being, "to join closely together." It is an architectural metaphor. "Temple" is *naos*, "the inner sanctuary," not *hieros*, "the temple with its porches and outbuildings."

Translation. *In whom the whole building closely joined together, grows into a holy inner sanctuary in the Lord, in whom also you are being built together into a permanent dwelling place of God by the Spirit.*

CHAPTER THREE

(3:1) The words "for this cause" refer back to "the building together of the saints" of 2:20-22. That is, "seeing you are so builded together for a dwelling place of God" (Vincent). Then comes a parenthetical paragraph to verse 13, and the words "for this cause" are resumed. The apostle began his prayer of 3:14-21 in verse one, but between 3:1 and 3:14, we have a digression, the purpose of which is to acquaint the Gentiles with their call and Paul's knowledge of the mystery of Jew and Gentile in one body.

Paul designates himself as "I, Paul, a prisoner of Jesus Christ for you Gentiles." Expositors, quoting Meyer, says: "*egō Paulos* (I, Paul), a solemn and emphatic designation of the writer by himself, expressive rather of his personal interest in them than the consciousness of his authority." The definite article appears before "prisoner," and Expositors says: "The article with *desmos* (prisoner) expresses simply the *character* in which Paul appears at present or the *class* to which he belongs, . . . not his pre-eminence among the Lord's prisoners, as if it meant the prisoner *par excellence* (Meyer), a claim surely which would neither be like Paul nor in harmony with the thought of the paragraph."

He is the prisoner of "the Christ Jesus," the definite article appearing before Christ. Paul's thought is, "the prisoner of the Messiah, who is now called Jesus." The words are in the genitive case, probably, the genitive of originating cause. Paul was one made prisoner by Christ Jesus (Expositors). He is a prisoner "on behalf of you the Gentiles." The same authority explains, "Paul was called specially to be a minister of Christ to the Gentiles (Acts 21:21, 28; 22:21), and his preaching Christ as for the Gentiles equally with the Jews provoked that enmity of the Jews which led to his imprisonment. It was thus for the Gentiles that he was a prisoner; and there is probably also the further thought in the *huper humōn* (on behalf of you) that Paul's imprisonment was to be for their good, helpful to their Christian life, for the idea with which the paragraph closes is that his afflictions were their glory (v. 13)."

Translation. *On this account I, Paul, the prisoner of the Messiah, Jesus, on behalf of you, the Gentiles.*

(3:2, 3) The "if" is *ei ge*. It is a supposition that is taken for granted. The idea is, "if, indeed, as I may assume" (Expositors). Alford translates "assuming that." He says, "The Ephesians *had heard* all this, and St. Paul was now delicately reminding them."

The word "dispensation" is *oikonomia,* made up of *oikos,* "a house" and *nomos,* "law," thus, "the law of the house." The word speaks in general of the oversight, management, or administration one has over something. Paul was given the responsibility of having oversight or management over the grace of God in the sense that he was to administer it in its publicity. He was given the revelation of the grace of God and the responsibility of properly preaching and teaching it. This grace given Paul for the Gentiles, he defines in verse 6.

Then Paul explains his knowledge of this particular grace. It was given him by revelation. The word is *apokalupsis,* "an uncovering, a laying bare." "Mystery" is *mustērion,* "a secret purpose of God which when uncovered is understood by the Spirit-taught believer." The words, "as I wrote afore in few words," refer ostensibly to the contents of 2:11-22 which tie up with the mystery of 3:6.

Translation. *Assuming that you heard of the administration of the grace of God which was given to me for you, that by revelation there was made known to me the mystery even as I wrote above in brief.*

(3:4, 5) "Whereby" is *pros ho, literally,* "toward which," the idea being "agreeably to which," namely to what Paul had written. Expositors offers "in accordance with which." The word "knowledge" is *sunesis*. It is used in the N. T. of mental apprehension. It is defined as "insight depending on judgment and inference." It appears to denote the idea of a critical understanding, the apprehension of the bearing of things. The words "of Christ" are genitive of description, defining the mystery. It is the mystery relating to Christ, the revelation of the long-hidden purpose of God regarding Christ as not for Israel only, but also for the Gentiles (Expositors).

The word "ages" is *genea*, "the period covered by a generation of men," thus, "a generation." The word "other" is *heteros,* "another of a different kind." The expression, "the sons of men," does not refer to O.T. prophets as against those of the N.T., but to men in general, in conformity with the word "generations." The word "as" (*hōs*) "has its proper comparative force." "The *fact* of the revelation made in pre-Christian times to the fathers and the prophets is not questioned. The matter in view is the *measure* or *manner* of the revelation. The *nun* (now) is '*in these Christian times,*' and the aorist 'revealed' defines the fuller revelation as made definitely at a former period of these times" (Expositors).

Translation. *In accordance with which you are able when you read to understand my insight into the mystery of the Christ which in other and different generations was not made known to the sons of men as now it has been revealed to His holy apostles and prophets by the Spirit.*

(3:6) Paul now proceeds to make known the mystery. The words "should be" are *einai*, the infinitive of the verb of being. The translation should read: "that the Gentiles are." The contents of the mystery are a fact, not a purpose. The Gentiles are fellow-heirs with the Jews. They are *sussōma*, "fellow-members," that is, "belonging jointly to the same body." They are "fellow-partakers of the promise." The Gentiles inherit jointly with the Jews the blessings of salvation. They are fellow-members of the same body, the Mystical Body of Christ, which is a new creation, in which the line of separation between Jew and Gentile is broken down. They are fellow-partakers of the promises which are in Christ Jesus. The best Greek texts include the name "Jesus," which makes all the difference in the world. If it were not there, Paul would be saying that the Gentiles were fellow-partakers of the Jewish Messianic promises, which is not true. Israel will yet be brought back into fellowship with and service to God in the Millennium. The addition of the name "Jesus" refers the name "Christ" to the "Anointed" of God who became the Saviour at the Cross. Any promises in Him that are not distinctly Messianic and Jewish, are the promises referred to here.

The Scofield Bible has a valuable note: "That the Gentiles were to be saved was no mystery (Rom. 9:24-33; 10:19-21). The mystery 'hid in God' was the divine purpose to make of Jew and Gentile a wholly new thing — 'the Church, which is His (Christ's) body,' formed by the baptism with the Holy Spirit (I Cor. 12:12, 13) and in which the earthly distinction of Jew and Gentile disappears (Eph. 2:14, 15; Col. 3:10, 11). The revelation of this mystery, which was foretold but not explained by Christ (Mt. 16:18), was committed to Paul. In his writings alone we find the doctrine, position, walk, and destiny of the Church."

Translation. *That the Gentiles are fellow-heirs, and belong jointly to the same body, and are fellow-partakers of His promise in the glad tidings.*

(3:7, 8) The word "minister" is *diakonos,* "a servant seen in his activity." Our word "deacon" comes from this Greek word. The Greek word refers to one who serves. The word "minister" is misleading, since it is the technical word used today to designate the pastor of a church. Paul merely meant that he became one who ministered the gospel, served God in that capacity.

"The gift of the grace of God" is "the gift *consisting in* the grace, and the particular grace in view is the *office of the apostleship* or *the ministry to the Gentiles*" (Expositors).

This gift of the apostleship was "according to the working of His power." Vincent says: "The gift was bestowed in accord-

ance with that efficiency which could transform Saul the perse-
cutor into Paul the apostle to the Gentiles." Expositors says:
"The thought of the dignity of the office he had received at the
cost of such grace and power at once evokes the sense of his own
utter unworthiness, to which he gives stronger expression here
than even in I Cor. 15:9, or II Cor. 12:11." The words "less
than the least" are *elachestoteros,* a comparative formed on a
superlative; literally, "more least" than all the saints.

The word "unsearchable" is *anexichniaston,* from *exichniazō.*
"to trace out," and Alpha privative which negates the word,
making it mean, "that which cannot be traced out." The riches
of Christ here "are the riches that Christ has or which are in
Him. The *ploutos* (wealth) thus contained in Christ is the
whole wealth of the salvation He bestows; and this is 'unsearchable' not in the sense of *inexhaustible,* but rather in that of
unfathomable, 'past finding out,' such as cannot be fully compre-
hended by men" (Expositors).

Translation. *Of which I became one who ministers according to the gift of the grace of God which (grace) was given to
me according to the operative energy of His power; to me, the
one who is less than the least of all saints there was given this
grace, to the Gentiles to proclaim the glad tidings of the wealth
belonging to the Christ.*

(3:9) "To make see" is *phōtizō,* "to bring to light." The
word "all" is rejected by the Nestle and the Westcott and Hort
texts. "Fellowship" is *oikonomia,* "administration, dispensing
technique, stewardship." It was given to Paul to bring to light
the arrangement, the way this mystery was administered, namely,
the admission of the Gentiles on equal terms with the Jews.
"World" is *aiōn,* "an age." This mystery was formed *before*
the ages of time began, and kept secret since they started.
"Through Jesus Christ" is a rejected reading.

Translation. *And to bring to light what is the administration
of the mystery which has been kept covered up from the beginning of the ages in the God who created the all things.*

(3:10)   The words "to the intent" reach back to verses 8 and 9.   Vincent says: "Grace was given me to preach Christ and to enlighten men as to the long-hidden mystery of the admission of the Gentiles, *in order that now, etc.*"   The principalities and powers are the holy angels.   Alford says: "For this sublime cause the humble Paul was raised up — to bring about — he, the least worthy of the saints, — that to the heavenly powers themselves should be made known, by means of those whom he was empowered to enlighten, etc."   "Might be known" is *gnōrizō,* "to make known."   "By" is *dia,* "through the intermediate agency of."   "Manifold" is *polupoikilos,* "much — variegated, marked with a great variety of colors."   The Church thus becomes the university for angels, and each saint a professor. Only in the Church can the angels come to an adequate comprehension of the grāce of God.   They look at the Church to investigate the mysteries of redemption.   I Peter (1:12) speaks of the things which the angels have a passionate desire to stoop down and look into, like the golden cherubim that overshadow the Mercy Seat, ever gazing upon the sprinkled blood that is upon it.   The preposition *para,* "beside," is prefixed to the verb "stoop down," which speaks of the angels as spectators viewing the great plan of redemption from the side lines, not being participants in it.

Translation.   *In order that there might be made known now to the principalities and powers in the heavenly places, through the intermediate agency of the Church, the much variegated wisdom of God.*

(3:11, 12)   The words "eternal purpose" are *prothesin tōn aiōniōn,* "the purpose of the ages," but rendered best in English by the word "eternal."   Alford says: "The genitive is apparently one of time, as when we say, 'it has been an opinion of years': the duration all that time giving the *aiōnes* (ages) a kind of possession.   If so, the sense is best given in English by 'eternal.'"   "Purposed" is *poieō,* "to do, to carry into effect."   "Boldness" is *parrēsia,* "freedom of speech, unreservedness of speech." "Access" is *prosagōgē,* "entree"; Thayer defines, "that friendly relation to God whereby we are acceptable to Him and have assurance that He is favorably disposed towards us." "Confidence" is *pepoithēsis*, from *peithō*, "to persuade." It comes from the perfect participial form which refers to a past process of being completely persuaded, with the present result that we are in a confirmed and settled state of utter confidence. The words, "faith of Him," Vincent renders, "faith in Him."

Translation. *According to the eternal purpose which He carried into effect in the Christ, Jesus our Lord, in whom we are having our freedom of speech and entree in perfect confidence through faith in Him.*

(3:13) The word "wherefore" refers back to verses 1-12, where "the dignity of the office committed to Paul and its significance," (Expositors) is spoken of. "Because the great trust of the apostleship among the Gentiles is what he has declared it to be for himself and for them, he puts this request before them . . . . Paul himself rejoiced in his tribulations (II Cor. 12:5, 10; Col. 1:24, etc.), . . . but he might have cause enough to be apprehensive that these converts might not all view painful things as he did" (Expositors). The word "faint" is *egkakeō*, "to lose courage, become faint of heart." Expositors says: "Paul's tribulations were endured in their behalf, and were of value for them. The greater the office of the sufferer, the more did the afflictions which he was content to endure for them redound to their honor; and the better this was understood by them, the less should they give way to weakness and discouragement." "I desire" is *aiteō*, "to ask," and in the middle voice as it is here, "to ask for one's self, in one's own interest."

Translation. *Wherefore, I am asking in my own interest, that you do not lose heart by reason of my tribulations on your behalf which are of such a nature as to be your glory.*

(3:14, 15) The words, "for this cause," go back to the same words in 3:1 which themselves go back to the thought of Jew and Gentile becoming one body in Christ, and this body growing into a holy inner sanctuary for the dwelling-place of God. On account of this, Paul says, "I bow my knees." Expositors says, "The thought of the new relations into which the Ephesians had been brought by grace toward God and toward the Jews — the reconciliation of the Cross, peace effected where once there was only enmity, the place given them in the household of God gave Paul cause for prayer in their behalf." The expression, "I bow my knees," Calvin says, was "a simple, natural figure for *prayer, earnest* prayer — not as if Paul actually knelt as he wrote." "Unto" is *pros,* which means "facing." It speaks of the consciousness which Paul had when praying that he was directing his prayer to God who was listening while he prayed. "Of whom" is *ex hou,* literally "out from whom," thus, as Vincent puts it, "after whom." The source of the naming was the Father. It is not "the whole family," but "every family," *pas* being used without the article. The translation therefore reads, "after whom every family in heaven and upon earth is named." Expositors says: "The sense, therefore is 'the Father, from whom all related orders of intelligent beings, human and angelic, each by itself, get the significant name of *family, community.'* The various classes of men on earth, Jew, Gentile, and others, and the various orders of angels in heaven, are related to God, the common Father, and only in virtue of that relation has any of them the name of *family.*" But we must be careful here to note that the fatherhood of God over all created intelligences is in the sense of Creator, as in Paul's word to the Athenians, "We are the offspring of God," not at all in the sense of salvation where only saved individuals are children of God. The words "of our Lord Jesus Christ," are rejected by Nestle and by Westcott and Hort.

Translation. *On this account I bow my knees to the Father from whom every family in heaven and on earth is named.*

(3:16) Paul prays that "God might grant to you (the Ephesian saints) according to the measure of His glory, with power to be strengthened through His Spirit (this strengthening entering) into the inner man." "The glory is the whole *revealed perfections* of God, not merely His *grace* and *power* . . . The measure of the gift for which Paul prays on behalf of the

Ephesians is nothing short of those perfections of God which are revealed now in their glorious fulness and inexhaustible wealth" (Expositors).

The preposition "in" is *eis,* "unto," and is a preposition of motion. "The strengthening was to take effect by means of *power imparted* or infused, and this impartation of power was to be made through the Spirit of God *into the inward man.* The 'inward man' is viewed here as the *recipient,* that into which the strengthening was to be poured, or the *object towards* which the gift was directed" (Expositors). The inward man refers here to the personal, rational self, the moral I, the essence of the man which is conscious of itself as a moral personality (Expositors, Vincent). Paul is here speaking of the fulness of the Holy Spirit. The reader is urged to study the author's work on that subject in his book *Riches from the Greek New Testament.*

Translation. *That He would grant to you according to the wealth of His glory, with power to be strengthened through the Spirit into the inward man.*

(3:17-19) The purpose of the strengthening by the Spirit is now given, "that Christ may dwell in your hearts." The personal presence of the Lord Jesus in the heart of the believer is not in view here. That is taken for granted. The word "dwell" is *katoikēsai,* made up of *oikeō,* "to live in as a home," and *kata,* "down," thus "to settle down and be at home." The tense is aorist, showing finality. The expanded translation is; "that Christ might finally settle down and feel completely at home in your hearts." Dr. Max Reich once said in the hearing of the writer, "If we make room for the Holy Spirit, He will make room for the Lord Jesus." That is, if the saint lives in conscious dependence upon and yieldedness to the Holy Spirit, the Holy Spirit will make room for the Lord Jesus in the heart and life of the saint by eliminating from his life things that are sinful and of the world, and thus enable the saint to make the Lord Jesus feel completely at home in his heart. Wonderful condescension of heaven's King, to be content to live in a believer's heart and have fellowship with him.

This at-home-ness of the Lord Jesus in the heart of the saint is "through faith in your hearts." This faith is in the Lord Jesus for the fulness of the Holy Spirit. Our Lord says, "If a certain one is thirsting, let him be coming to Me and let him be drinking. The one who places his trust in Me, even as the scripture said, rivers out from his inmost being will flow, of water that is living" (John 7:37, 38). And John adds in explanation, "But this He spoke concerning the Spirit whom those who believed on Him were about to be receiving, for not yet was the Spirit *given,* because Jesus was not yet glorified." This trust here is not a trust in the Lord Jesus as Saviour, but, having believed on- Him as Saviour, the saint is now to believe on Him as the One who fills with the Spirit, or grants the fulness of the Spirit, as Paul puts it in his prayer here.

The words, "being rooted" and "grounded," are perfect tense participles in the Greek text. They are the result of the strengthening by the Spirit and the consequent at-home-ness of the Lord Jesus in the believer's heart and His fellowship with him. The word "rooted" has the idea of securely settled, and "grounded," that of deeply founded. Love here is that love which the Holy Spirit produces and with which He floods the heart of the yielded saint. This inner spiritual condition of heart enables the saint "to comprehend" (v. 18) and "to know" (v. 19).

He will be able to comprehend. "Able" is *exischuō,* "to be eminently able, to have full strength." "Comprehend" is *katalambanō.* The word "comprehend" conveys to the English reader the idea of "understand." The Greek word means "to lay hold of so as to make one's own, to seize, take possession of." One could translate "apprehend," in the sense of mentally grasping some idea or truth. The words "with all saints" indicate that this spiritual capacity is not limited to a few select saints, but is the common property of all those saints who are the recipients of the strengthening fulness of the Holy Spirit, which latter is the result of their faith in the Lord Jesus for that very blessing.

Paul prays that the saints might apprehend, not merely comprehend. One might be able to understand something without having a grasp of the full implications of that thing. Paul is talking about the latter here. The words "breadth, length, depth, and height" have no particular significance except to give the general idea of the vastness of the love of Christ. This love is His love for us, not ours for Him, which latter interpretation is out of the question.

The words "to know" are the translation of *ginōskō* which speaks of knowledge gained by experience. The apprehension of verse 18 is conceptual knowledge. In verse 19, this conceptual knowledge passes into experiential knowledge as the saint experiences in his life that comprehension of the love of Christ for him in the sphere of his earthly life.

This love of Christ, Paul says, "passeth knowledge." Expositors translates, "the knowledge surpassing love of Christ." The word "surpassing" is a participle of *huperballō*, "to throw over or beyond, to transcend, exceed, excel." This love surpasses knowledge, *gnōsis*, "experiential knowledge." That is, no matter how much the saint experiences of the love of Christ, yet there are oceans of love in the great heart of God that have not been touched by his experience. One is reminded of the words of that saint of old who penned the following lines on the walls of his cell regarding the love of God; "Could we with ink the ocean fill, and were the skies of parchment made; were every stalk on earth a quill, and every man a scribe by trade; to write the love of God above, would drain the ocean dry; nor could the scroll contain the whole, though stretched from sky to sky."

The saints are to have an experiential knowledge of the love of God "in order that ye might be filled with all the fulness of God." "With" is *eis* in the Greek text, which is better rendered "to" or "unto," "to the measure or standard of." Vincent says: *"Fulness of God* is the fulness which God imparts through the dwelling of Christ in the heart; Christ, in whom the Father was pleased that all the fulness should dwell (Col. 1:19), and in whom dwelleth all the fulness of the Godhead (Col. 2:9)."

Translation. *That the Christ might finally settle down and feel completely at home in your hearts through the faith, in love having been firmly rooted and grounded in order that you may be able to grasp with all the saints what is the breadth and width and height and depth, and to know experientially the experiential-knowledge-surpassing love of the Christ in order that you may be filled up to the measure of all the fulness of God.*

(3:20, 21) In this doxology, we have two descriptions of God, one, a general one, the other, one that is specific and has to do with believers. The first characterizes Him as One who is able to do *huper panta,* literally, "above all things," thus, "in a measure exceeding all things, beyond all things." The second speaks of Him as able to do *huperekperissou.* The word is made up of *perissos,* "exceeding some number or measure, over and above, more than necessary," *ek,* which is perfective in force here, intensifying the already existing idea in the verb, here adding the idea of exhaustlessness, and *huper,* "above." The compound word is a superlative of superlatives in force. It speaks of the ability of God to do something, that ability having more than enough potential power, this power exhaustless, and then some on top of that. Thus, Paul says that God is able to do super-abundantly above and beyond what we ask or think, and then some on top of that. The word "ask" is *aiteō,* "to ask that something be given"; it is a request of the will. The verb here is in the middle voice, "to ask for one's self or in one's own interest." "Think" is *noeō,* "to consider." The power (*dunamis*) that is putting forth energy in us (*energeō*), is the operation of the Holy Spirit in His work of sanctification. God is able to do for us and answer our prayers according to the efficiency, richness, and power of the working of the Spirit in our lives. This latter is determined by the yieldedness of the believer to the Holy Spirit. Thus, the saint determines what God is able to do for him. In His inherent ability, there is no limit to what God can do in and through the saint. But the saint limits the working of God in and through him by the degree of his yieldedness to the Spirit.

"Unto Him" refers to God the Father. The definite article appears before "glory." It is the glory due Him. This glory is to be given Him "in the Church," "the domain in which the praise that belongs to Him is to be rendered Him" (Expositors). "By Christ Jesus" is *en* Christ Jesus, locative of sphere. It is "in the Church and in Christ Jesus." "The idea is that praise is to be given to God, and His glorious perfections shown forth both in the Church which is the body, and in Christ who is the Head — in the Church as chosen by Him, and in Christ as given, raised, and exalted by Him" (Expositors). The words, "throughout all ages, world without end," are literally, "unto all the generations of the age of the ages"; Expositors says, "Another of these reduplicated expressions by which the mind of man working with the ideas of time, labors to convey the idea of the eternal."

Translation. *Now to the One who is able to do beyond all things, superabundantly beyond and over and above those things that we are asking for ourselves and considering, in the measure of the power which is operative in us, to Him be the glory in the Church and in Christ Jesus into all the generations of the Age of the Ages. Amen.*

CHAPTER FOUR

(4:1-3)   We come now to an important dividing point in this letter.   The first three chapters contain doctrine, the last three, exhortation.   This is the proper order, for only in doctrine can one see the sweet reasonableness of the exhortations, and obtain the necessary power and technique to obey them.   In brief, God says in chapters 1-3, "I have made you a saint."   In chapters 4-6, He says, "Now, live a saintly life."

"Beseech" is *parakaleō*, "I beg of you, please."   Paul might have used his apostolic authority.   But, instead, he pleads. "Therefore" reaches back to all the blessings and exalted positions in salvation which the saints enjoy (ch. 1-3), and reaches ahead to the obligations which such privileges put upon the saints.   Paul designates himself as the prisoner in the Lord.   "In" is *en,* followed by the locative of sphere.   He was the prisoner in the sphere of the Lord.   Expositors says, "It expresses the *sphere* within which his captivity subsisted or the *ground* of that captivity.   He was a prisoner because of his connection with Christ, the Lord, and for no other reason.   As in chapter 3, so here the idea of the dignity of his office seems to lie behind the mention of his imprisonment.   He designates himself 'the prisoner in the Lord,' not with a view to stir the *sympathy* of the readers, and enforce his exhortation by an appeal to feeling, but as one who could rejoice in his sufferings and speak of his tribulations as their 'glory' (3:13; Gal. 6:17)."   The Greek order of words is as follows: "I beg of you, please, therefore, I, the prisoner in the Lord."   "Walk" is *peripateō,* "to walk about," thus, "to conduct one's self, to order one's behavior." "Worthy" is *axiōs,* an adverb, meaning "in a manner worthy of." The adjective form means, "having the weight of (weighing as much as) another thing."   Thus, Paul exhorts the Ephesian saints to see to it that their Christian experience, the Christian life they live, should weigh as much as the profession of Christianity which they make. In other words, they are to see to it that they practice what they preach, that their experience measures up to their standing in grace. The words, "the vocation wherewith ye are called," are literally, "the calling with which you were called." "Calling" (vocation in A.V.) is *klēsis*. The verb refers to that divine summons into salvation which God gives a sinner, in which he is constituted willing to accept the salvation offered. It speaks of that effectual call into salvation which God in sovereign grace extends to a sinner. In Hebrews 3:1, the writer speaks of the recipients as partakers of the heavenly calling, "the calling whose origin, nature, and goal are heavenly" (Cremer). The word "calling" in English sometimes means "occupation" as, "His calling was that of a shoemaker." But it is not so used here. Paul's thought is that sinners were called into salvation and made saints. They are to be obedient to that heavenly calling or summons to be saints, and live saintly lives.

This Christian behavior is to be accompanied by "all lowliness," that is, "all possible lowliness, every kind of lowliness," not, "the sum total of lowliness." The word is *tapeinophrosunē*, which in pagan Greek meant only abject servility, slavishness, a grovelling, mean-spirited disposition, but in the N.T. has been glorified in its meaning. Trench says of this word: "The Christian *lowliness* is no mere modesty or absence of pretension, nor yet a self-made grace. The making of ourselves small is pride in the disguise of humility. But the esteeming of ourselves small, inasmuch as we are so, the thinking truly, and because truly, therefore, lowlily of ourselves." The word is used in an early secular manuscript of the Nile River at its low stage, "It runs low." Expositors defines it: "the lowliness of mind which springs from a true estimate of ourselves — a deep sense of our own moral smallness and demerit." "Meekness" is *prautētos*. Trench defines it as follows: "It is an inwrought grace of the soul, and the exercises of it are first and chiefly toward God. It is that temper of spirit in which we accept His dealings with us as good, and therefore without disputing. This meekness before God is also such in the face of man."

"Longsuffering" is *makrothumia*. Trench, contrasting this word "longsuffering" with *hupomonē* (patience) says: *"Makrothumia* (longsuffering) will be found to express patience with respect of persons, *hupomonē,* patience in respect of things. The man who is longsuffering, is he who, having to do with injurious persons, does not suffer himself easily to be provoked by them, or to blaze up in anger (II Tim. 4:2). The man who is patient (*hupomonē*) is the one who under a great siege of trials, bears up and does not lose courage." "Forbearing" is *anechō,* "to hold up, to sustain, to bear with equanimity, to bear with, endure." This is in explanation of *makrothumia* (longsuffering).

We are to bear with one another "in love." It is in the sphere of the love that God the Holy Spirit produces in the heart of the yielded believer (Gal. 5:22), that we are to be patient with each other as misunderstandings arise, as cutting words are said, as unkind actions are done. The love shown at Calvary was a forgiving love. Ours should be the same.

The words, "endeavoring to keep the unity of the Spirit in the bond of peace," are a further description of the mutual forbearance which is spoken of in the previous verse. "Endeavoring" is *spoudazō,* "to take care, make haste, do one's best." It speaks of a determined effort. It has the idea of exertion in it. "Keep" is *tēreō,* "to keep by guarding, to guard by exercising watchful care." It speaks of guarding something which is in one's possession. "Unity" is *henotēs,* "unanimity, agreement." It is the unanimity or agreement among Christians that is the product of the Holy Spirit. "Bond" is *sundesmos,* "that which binds together." "Of peace" is genitive of description, defining this binding factor. Peace is the binding factor which will preserve the unity which the Spirit has produced. "Peace" is *eirēnē,* "that which is bound together." Expositors says: "The unity, therefore, which is wrought among these Ephesians by the Spirit of God will be theirs in so far as they make peace the relation which they maintain one to another, or the bond in which they walk together."

Translation. *I beg of you, please, therefore, I, the prisoner in the Lord, order your behavior in a manner worthy of the summons with which you were called, with every lowliness and meekness, with longsuffering, bearing with one another in love, doing your best to safeguard the unanimity of the Spirit in the bond of peace.*

(4:4-6) Vincent gives us the connection between what has preceded and these verses. "The connection with the preceding verses is as follows; "I exhort you to *unity,* for you stand related to the *Church,* which is *one body* in Christ; to the *one Spirit* who informs it; to the *one hope* which your calling inspires; to the *one Lord,* Christ, in whom you believe with *one common faith,* and receive *one common sign* of that faith, baptism. Above all, to the *one God,* and *Father.*" Expositors says, "It is a positive statement, . . . giving the objective ground or basis in fact on which the walk in lowliness, meekness, longsuffering, and loving forbearance is urged, and of which it should be the result."

The body is the invisible Church, the Mystical Body of Christ composed of believers saved between Pentecost when the Church was formed and the Rapture when the Church will be caught out of this earth and taken to heaven. The Spirit is the Holy Spirit. The hope of our calling is "the hope which is characteristic of God's call to salvation, and is engendered by it" (Vincent). "Faith" is not the Christian Faith as a system of doctrine and its respective responsibilities. It refers to the principle of faith by means of which all the saints enter into salvation. "One baptism" is *hen baptisma.* Why should all the other words be translated, and this alone be transliterated? Why should the A.V. and commentators transliterate the word, interpreting the Greek word as referring to the rite of water baptism when the entire context is supernatural, even to the faith exercised by the believer in appropriating salvation? The words translated are "one placing into." That is, in response to our act of faith, we were placed by the Holy Spirit into the Body of which Christ is the Head. This is one of the unities vitally related to our salvation, and upon which Paul bases his plea for unity in the Church. There was and is one common placing into the Body of Christ.

Translation. *One body and one Spirit, even as also you were called in one hope of your calling, one Lord, one faith, one placing into, one God and Father of all, the One above all and through all, and in all.*

(4:7) Vincent says: "From the Church as a whole, he passes to its individual members. In the general unity, the individual is not overlooked, and unity is consistent with variety of gifts and offices." Expositors comments: "The article defined *charis* (grace) as *the* grace of which the writer and his fellow-believers had experience, which they knew to have been given them, and by which God worked in·them. What is given is not the *charisma* (extraordinary powers such as special gifts) but the *charis* (grace), the subjective grace that works within and shows itself in its result — the *charism,* the gracious faculty or quality. The emphasis is on the *hekastōi* (to each one), and the *de* (but) is rather the *adversative* particle than the transitional. It does not merely mark a change from one subject to another, but sets *the each* over against the *all,* and this in connection with the injunction to keep the unity of the Spirit. God's gracious relation to *all* is a relation also to each *individual.* Not one of them was left unregarded by Him who is the God and Father of all, but each was made partaker of Christ's gift of grace, and each, therefore stands pledged to do his part toward maintenance of unity and peace."

This grace which is in the form of the enabling and empowering of the Holy Spirit, is given the saint "according to the measure of the gift of Christ." Expositors explains as follows: "Each gets the grace which Christ has to give, and each gets it in the proportion in which the Giver is pleased to bestow it; one having it in larger measure and another in smaller, but each getting it from the same Hand and with the same purpose." We must be careful to note that this grace has to do with the exercise of special gifts for service, not the grace for daily living. The former is limited, and is adjusted to the kind of gift and the extent to which the Holy Spirit desires to use that gift in the believer's service. The latter is unlimited and subject only to the limitations which the believer puts upon it by a lack of yieldedness to the Spirit. The context here, (4:11, 12), is one of service, not of general Christian experience.

Translation. *But to each one of us there was given the grace in the measure of the gift of the Christ.*

(4:8) From the subject of the general enabling grace of God given to all saints for service, Paul turns to gifts which He gives to men. The word here is not *charisma*, referring to special gifts such as the gifts noted in I Cor. 12:4-11, but *doma*, a general term for that which is given. These gifts are the gifted men mentioned in 4:11. Christ gave these gifts to the Church when He ascended to Heaven. But in order to ascend to Heaven and give these gifts to the Church, He had to lead captivity captive. Who are these captives?

He led these individuals captive in His ascension. But what ascension? Was it His ascension from Olivet after His forty day post-resurrection ministry? Or, was it His ascension on the first day of the week, straight from the resurrection tomb (John 20:17)? In the former instance, the Shekinah Glory Cloud was God's official chariot of protection through the principalities and powers in the lower atmosphere, the demons. In His ascension from the Easter morning tomb, there is no record of such a cloud. Fulfilling the type of the priest on the Day of Atonement in which the latter after sacrificing the animal at the Brazen Altar, and passing through the Court and the Holy Place into the Holy of Holies, sprinkled the blood on the Mercy Seat, thus, completing the typical atonement, our Lord was on His way from the Cross through the heaven of the clouds and of the stars, into Heaven itself, to present Himself in the Holy of Holies as High Priest, having shed His blood on the Cross, com-

pleting the atonement by His presence in the heavenly Holy of
Holies in a bloodless human body, proof of the fact that He had
paid for sin with His own blood (Heb. 9:11-15, 24-28).

But to go from earth to Heaven, He had to pass through the
territory of Satan and his demons in the air (Heb. 4:14, passed
through (*dia*) the heavens). Satan tried to keep our Lord from
going to the Cross. He tried to keep Him in the tomb. Unsuc-
cessful in these attempts, he tried to keep Him from completing
the atonement by barring His progress through the air. Concerning this battle our Lord had with the demons, Paul speaks
in Col. 2:15. The principalities and powers are the demons of
Ephesians 6:12. The word "spoiled" is *apekduomai*, "wholly to
strip off from one's self for one's own advantage." *Endunō*
means "to put on," as a garment. Thus, *apekduomai* means "to
strip off from one's self" that with which one is clothed. Our
Lord, in going through the kingdom of Satan in the air, was
opposed by the demons who attempted to keep Him from completing the atonement by presenting Himself as High Priest in
Heaven. He stripped off and away from Himself, the demons
who in attempting to impede His progress, would cling to His
Person.

The words "made a show of," are the translation of *deigmatizō*, "to make a display of, exhibit." "Openly" is *parrēsia*,
"boldly." "Triumphing" is *thriambeuō*, "to celebrate a triumph."
It was used among the Romans of a triumphal procession, such
as that of a victorious general home from the wars, leading his
captives and booty in a procession through the streets of Rome.
Here our Lord leads the demons whom He has stripped off and
away from Himself, in a triumphal procession through the air.
The translation reads, "Having stripped off and away from Himself the principalities and authorities, He made a display of them
in boldness, leading them in a triumphal procession in it."

Translation. *Wherefore He says, Having ascended on high,
He led away captive those taken captive, and gave gifts to men.*

(4:9, 10) The contents of these verses "are parenthetical,
showing what the ascension of Christ presupposes. By descend-

ing into the depths and ascending above all, He entered upon His function of filling the whole universe, in virtue of which function He distributes gifts to men. . . . His ascent implies a previous descent" (Vincent). The words "lower parts of the earth," Vincent says, refer to the under world. "The reference is to Christ's descent into Hades" (Vincent). Our Lord, between His death on the Cross and His resurrection from the tomb, went to two places in the unseen world. Peter says: "For Christ also once for all died for sins, a just Person in behalf of unjust persons, in order that He might provide for us an *entree* into the presence of God, having been put to death on the one hand with respect to the flesh, but made alive on the other hand with respect to the spirit (His human spirit), in which spirit also to the imprisoned spirits proceeding, He made a proclamation, to those who were non-persuasible aforetime when the longsuffering of God waited in the days of Noah while the ark was being gotten ready" (I Peter 3:18-20). This place is called *Tartarōsas,* the prison house of the fallen angels (II Peter 2:4). What He proclaimed to them is not specifically stated. The verb "preached" is not *euaggelizomai,* "to preach the gospel," but *kērussō,* "to make a proclamation." The other place He went to was the place for departed human beings, called "Paradise" (Luke 23:43) or "Abraham's Bosom" (Luke 16:22). He, as the Man Christ Jesus, went to the place of the righteous dead.

Translation. *Now, the fact that He ascended, what is it except that also He descended into the nether parts of the earth. The One who descended, Himself is also the One who ascended above all the heavens, in order that He might fill all things.*

(4:11, 12) In verse 11, Paul identifies the gifts spoken of in verse 7. They are gifted men, given to the Church. There is an intensive pronoun in the Greek text. "He Himself gave," and no other. He gave some saints as apostles. The word speaks in a primary sense of the twelve apostles, and in a secondary sense, of those who proclaim the Word of God today. "Prophets" refers, not to those who foretell the future, but to preachers and expounders of the Word. Evangelists are the travelling missionaries both in home and foreign lands. The word "pastor" is *poimēn,* "a shepherd." The words "pastors" and "teachers" are in a construction called Granvill Sharp's rule which indicates that they refer to one individual. The one who shepherds God's flock is also a teacher of the Word, having both the gifts of shepherding and teaching the flock. God's ideal pastor is one who engages in a didactic ministry, feeding the saints on expository preaching, giving them the rich food of the Word.

These gifted men are given the Church "for the perfecting of the saints." The word "perfecting" is *katartizō,* "to equip for service." These gifted men are to specialize in equipping the saints for "the work of the ministry," that is, for ministering work, in short, Christian service. This is in order that the Body of Christ, the Church, might be built up, by additions to its membership in lost souls being saved, and by the building up of individual saints.

Translation. *And He Himself gave some, on the one hand, as apostles, and on the other hand, as prophets, and still again some as bringers of good news, and finally, some as pastors who are also teachers, for the equipping of the saints for ministering work, with a view to the building up of the Body of Christ.*

(4:13) "Till" is *mechri,* "as far as, unto, until." Expositors says: "The statement of the great object of Christ's gifts and provision made by Him for its fulfillment is now followed by a statement of the *time* this provision and the consequent service are to last, or the point at which the great end in view is to be realized. It is when the members of the Church have all come to their proper unity and maturity in their Head. . . . Paul gives no clear indication of the *time,* and it may be, therefore, that he has in view only the goal itself and the attainment of it at whatever time that may take effect." "Come" is *katantaō,* "to arrive at, to attain to." "In" is *eis,* "into, unto." It is a goal to be striven after; translate, "until we all attain to the unanimity of the faith." The faith here is faith as exercised in Christ. It is the oneness of faith in Christ. Alford asks: "Have not all Christians the same faith? No doubt they have as regards its substance, but not as regards its clearness and purity; because the object of faith may be diversely *known,* and knowledge has ever such a powerful influence on faith. Therefore, he adds to this unity of faith, 'and of the knowledge of the Son of God'; true and full unity of faith is then found, when all thoroughly know Christ, the object of faith, alike, and that in His highest dignity as the Son of God." The word "knowledge" is *epignōsis,* "full knowledge, precise and correct knowledge." "Perfect" is *teleios,* "mature, complete, full grown." Expositors says: "The state at which unity is lacking is the stage of immaturity; the stage in which oneness in faith and knowledge is reached, is the state of mature manhood in Christ." The words "mature man," refer to the individual believer. The apostle has in mind the spiritual maturity of each saint. The words, "unto the measure of the stature of the fulness of Christ," further define what Paul means by the mature saint. The expression "the fulness of Christ," refers to the sum of the qualities which make Christ what He is. These are to be imaged in the Church (1:23), and when these are in us we shall have reached our maturity and attained to the goal set before us. Thus the whole idea will be this — 'the measure of the age, or (better) the stature, that brings with it the full possession on our side of that which Christ has to impart — the embodiment in us the members, of the graces and qualities which are in Him the Head.'" The term, "spiritual maturity," as applied to a Christian, is ever a relative one, not an absolute one. Paul, in Phil. 3:12 disclaims absolute spiritual maturity, while in 3:15, he claims relative maturity of Christian experience. This process of conforming the saint to the image of Christ begins in this life in the work of the Spirit in sanctification and is never completed in eternity, for the finite can never equal the infinite nor even remotely approach to it. Christ's perfections are so wonderful that the saints will ever bear but a dim reflection of them. This is the distance between finiteness and infinity.

Translation. *Until we all attain to the unity of the faith and of the experiential, full, and precise knowledge of the Son of God, to a mature man, to the measure of the stature of the fulness of the Christ.*

(4:14) "Children" is *nēpios,* literally, "that which does not talk," thus, "an infant, a little child." It is the opposite of *teleios,* "mature." "Tossed to and fro" is *kludōnizō,* a nautical term meaning, "to be tossed by the waves," metaphorically, "to be agitated mentally," like the waves. "Carried about" is *peripherō,* "to carry around." The verb has the idea of carrying about in circles. "Doctrine" is *didaskalia,* "teaching." Vincent says, "The different teachings of philosophers or of religious quacks are represented as winds, blowing the unstable soul in every direction." "Sleight" is *kubeia,* literally, "dice-playing." Expositors says: "It is in the character, not of *gamesters,* but *deceivers* that the false teachers are immediately presented. This 'sleight of men' is in contrast with 'the faith and the knowledge *of Christ,*' or it may be with the pure, sure word of God by which the faith and knowledge of the Son of God came."

"Cunning craftiness" is *panourgia,* "cunning, knavishness, treacherous deceitfulness." The words, "whereby they lie in wait to deceive," resolve themselves into the following: "Lie in wait" is *methodeia,* "a deliberate planning or system." Our word "method" comes from this Greek word. Expositors offers the translation, "in craftiness, furthering the scheming, deceitful art which has for its result the false way of life that strays fatally from the truth."

Translation. *In order that no longer we may be immature ones, tossed to and fro and carried around in circles by every wind of teaching in the cunning adroitness of men, in craftiness which furthers the scheming deceitful art of error.*

(4:15, 16) "Speaking the truth" is *alētheuō,* which Expositors translates as "truthing it." Vincent offers, "being or walking in truth." Alford says: "*Commit* here means merely to *speak the truth,* as the whole matter dealt with is more general . . . The verb has the widest sense of being true. . . . It is almost impossible to express it satisfactorily in English." He offers, "followers of truth," but not in the sense of searchers after truth.

The phrase "in love" qualifies "speaking the truth." Alford says: " 'In love' is added, as the element in which the Christian 'speaking the truth' must take place; it is not and cannot be a 'speaking the truth' at all hazards — a fiat truthfulness: but must be conditioned by love: a true-seeking and true-being with loving caution and kind allowance — not breaking up, but cementing brotherly love by walking in truth."

"Into" is *eis,* and the latter should be rendered "unto." We are to grow unto Him. "This means," Expositors says, "more than that we are to grow into *resemblance* to Him, or that our growth is to be according to His *example.* It means that as He is the source *from* which the grace or power comes that makes it possible for us to grow, He is also the *object* and goal to which our growth in its every stage must look and is to be directed." "Which" is *hos,* the masculine relative pronoun, and should be rendered "who."

Paul uses the analogy of a human head and a human body to illustrate the relation of the Lord Jesus as the Head to His Body, the Church, each saint being a member of that body. He as the Head is the source of growth and well-being of each member. "Fitly joined together" is in the Greek text a present participle. This process is still going on. The word is *sunarmologeō,* "to join closely together." "Compacted" is *sunbibazō,* "to cause to coalesce, to unite or knit together." This is also a present participle, speaking of a process going on. So far we have, "From whom as a source, all the body being constantly joined closely together and growing constantly together." This process in which the members of the Body of Christ are being joined closely together and are growing together in a vital, organic union, is brought about "by that which every joint supplieth." "By" is *dia,* the preposition of intermediate agency. The Greek here is "through the intermediate agency of every joint of supply." That is, the joints of supply are the bonds that bind the members of the Body together, and are the channels through which the source of supply of life from the Head, Jesus Christ, is brought to the various members, this divine energy joining closely together the members and causing them to grow into an organic union.

The entire Body composed of individual saints, constantly being more closely joined together and constantly growing together into an organic union through the life of the Head flowing through the bands of supply that join its members together, does so "according to the measure of every part." The words "effectual working" are the translation of *energeia,* "working, efficiency." The word speaks of power in exercise, operative power. "According to" is *kata,* "down." The word speaks of control, domination. "Measure," is *metron,* "an instrument for measuring, a vessel for receiving and determining the quantity of things, determined extent, portion measured off." The life of the Head flowing through the bands of supply, is constantly joining together and causing to grow together the individual members, this process being controlled or dominated by the operative energy put forth, the volume or strength of this operative energy coming from the Head of the Body, being determined by the capacity of each part to hold and allow to operate in him or her. That is, the degree to which this life of the Head flowing through the members operates, joining the members of the Body more closely together into a more compact organic union, is determined by the individual saint's fellowship with the Lord and with his fellow saints. This more compactly built Body will show in the closer ties of Christian love and brotherhood as exhibited by the saints in their Christian experience.

This "maketh increase of the body unto the edifying of itself in love." "Increase" is *auxēsis,* "growth, increase." "Edifying" is *oikodomē,* "building up, the act of building up," the promoting of Christian wisdom, piety, holiness, etc."

Expositors sums it up by saying, "The idea appears to be that the body is fitly framed and knit together by means of the joints, every one of them in its own place and function, as the points of connection between member and member, and the points of

communication between the different parts and the supply which
comes from the Head. The joints are the constituents of union
in the body and the media of the impartation of the life drawn
by the members from the head."

Translation. *But speaking the truth in love, may grow up
into Him in all things, who is the Head, Christ, from whom all
the body constantly being joined closely together and constantly
being knit together through every joint of supply according to
the operative energy put forth to the capacity of each part,
makes for increased growth of the Body resulting in the building
up of itself in the sphere of love.*

(4:17) "Therefore" resumes the exhortation of 4:1-3. "This"
(*touto*) refers to the words of exhortation which follow. "Tes-
tify" is *martureō*, which is used of a solemn declaration, protest,
or injunction of the nature of an appeal to God. In the words,
"in the Lord," the writer is seen "identifying himself with Christ
and giving the exhortation as one made by Christ Himself"
(Expositors). "Walk" is *peripateō*, "to conduct one's self, order
one's behavior." "Vanity" is *mataios*, "that which is in vain,
aimless, resultless, futile." The word speaks of want of attainment. "Mind" is *nous*, not merely the intellectual faculty or
understanding, but also the faculty for recognizing moral good
and spiritual truth. Expositors says: "It is a description of
the walk of the heathen world generally — a walk moving within
the limits of intellectual and moral resultlessness, given over to
things devoid of worth or reality."

Translation. *This, therefore, I am saying and solemnly declaring in the Lord, that no longer are you to order your behavior as the Gentiles order their behavior in the futility of their
mind.*

(4:18) "Darkened" is the perfect participle of *skotoō*, "to
darken or blind the mind." The perfect tense speaks of a process
completed in past time having present results. Paul uses the
perfect tense here to show the finished and permanent result
of the blinding of the mind by sin. "Understanding" is *dianoia*,
"the mind as the faculty of understanding, feeling, desiring."

The translation reads; "being those who have been permanently blinded with respect to the mind."

"Alienated" is *apallotriō,* "to be estranged," used of those who have estranged themselves from God. It means also, "to shut out from one's fellowship and intimacy." Expositors says: "Being in a state of moral darkness, they also become alienated from the true life." The life of God is the life that God has in Himself and that which He imparts to the believing sinner. "Ignorance" is *agnoia,* which Expositors says "is not a term merely of intellect. It denotes an ignorance of divine things, a want of knowledge that is inexcusable and involves moral blindness (Acts 3:17, 17:30, I Peter 1:14). It is further defined here not simply as 'their ignorance,' but as an ignorance 'being in them' — surely a phrase that is neither tautological nor without a purpose, but one that describes their ignorance in respect to its *seat.* Their alienation had its cause, not in something external, casual, or superficial, but *in themselves,* — in a culpable ignorance in their own nature or heart."

The word "blindness" is *pōrōsis,* "hardness." The word is formed from *pōros,* "hard skin or induration." It means literally "the covering with a callous." The word occurs in Mark 3:5; Romans 11:25, and here, and is used of mental or moral hardening. These Gentiles were alienated from God through their culpable moral and spiritual ignorance and through the hardening of their hearts.

Translation. *Being those who have had their understanding darkened, who have been alienated from the life of God through the ignorance which is in them, through the hardening of their hearts.*

(4:19) "Who" is *hoitines,* a relative and indefinite pronoun showing character or nature, "who are of such a nature that." "Being past feeling" is *apalgeō,* a participle in the perfect tense. The word means, "to cease to feel pain or grief, to become callous, insensible to pain, apathetic." Expositors says: "It expresses the condition, not of *despair* merely, but of moral insensibility, 'the deadness that supervenes when the heart has ceased

to be sensible to the stimuli of the conscience' (Ellicott)." "Have
given themselves over" is *paradidōmi,* literally, "to give alongside." Today we would say, "sell down the river." The verb
means "to give into the hands of another, to betray, to hand
over, give one's self up, present one's self." "Lasciviousness" is
aselgeia, "wanton lawless insolence." The *aselgeia* person is one
who acknowledges no restraints, who dares whatsoever his
caprice and wanton petulance may suggest. "Wantonness" is
the best word to describe it. The word speaks of a complete
surrender of self.

"To work" is *eis ergasian,* literally, "to a working." Vincent
says, "In Acts 19:25, used of *a trade.* Not precisely in this sense
here, yet with a shade of it. They gave themselves up as to the
prosecution of a business. The *eis,* 'unto,' is very forcible."
"All uncleanness" is *akatharsias pasēs,* "every kind of uncleanness," moral uncleanness in the widest sense. "*With greediness*
describes the condition or frame of mind in which they wrought
the uncleanness" (Expositors). The Greek word means "greed,
covetousness."

Translation. *Who, being of such a nature as to have become
callous, abandoned themselves to wantonness, resulting in a performing of every uncleanness in the sphere of greediness.*

(4:20, 21) The "ye" (*humeis*) is emphatic. It is, "As for
you, in contradistinction to the Gentiles yet unsaved." The Greek
order of words is, "But as for you, not thus did you learn the
Christ." The aorist tense marks a specific time. It was at
their conversion. Vincent says: "The phrase *learn Christ* occurs
nowhere else. *Christ* does not stand for *the doctrine of Christ;*
but Christ is the subject of His own message." Expositors says:
"Nor can it be taken to mean '*learned to know Christ.*' Christ
must be taken as the object of the learning, and the form 'the
Christ,' especially looking to the following 'Jesus' (v. 21), probably indicates that the official sense is in view here. . . . The
Christ, the Messiah. He personally — that was the contents of
the preaching which they heard, the *sum* of the instruction they
received and the knowledge they gained then."

"If so be" is *ei,* a particle of a fulfilled condition. The A.V. translates as if it were *ean,* the conditional particle of a hypothetical case. This particle *ei* is used with the indicative mode which implies the truth of the supposition. The translation should read: "If as is the case." They *had* heard. Expositors says: "The point, therefore, is this — 'if, as I take it to be the fact, it was He, the Christ, that was the subject and the sum of the preaching which you heard then.'"

"By Him" is *en autōi,* "in Him." It is, "in Him you were instructed." Expositors says: "*en autōi* (in Him) is not to be reduced to 'by Him,' or 'about Him,' or 'in His name,' but has its proper sense of 'in Him.' The underlying idea is that of union with Christ. The 'taught,' therefore, refers probably to instructions subsequent to those which were given them at their first hearing. It was in *fellowship* with Christ that they received these instructions."

Vincent comments on the words "as the truth is in Jesus." "*As* corresponds with *not so.* Ye did not in such a manner learn Christ if ye were taught in such a manner as is truth, etc. Render, as Rev., *as truth is in Jesus.* Sehaff paraphrases: 'If you were taught so that what you received is true as embodied in the personal Saviour.' 'Taught in the lines of eternal fact and spiritual reality which meet in Him' (Moule). *Jesus* is used rather than *Christ;* the historical rather than the official name. The life of Christianity consists in believing fellowship with the historic Jesus, who is the Christ of prophecy."

Translation. *But as for you, not in this manner did you learn Christ, since indeed, as is the case, you heard, and in Him were taught just as truth is in Jesus.*

(4:22-24) "That ye put off, etc." gives the purport of the instruction given. Connect with "were taught." The connection is, "ye were taught that ye put off, etc." The word "old" is *palaios,* "old in the sense of worn out, decrepit, useless." "Man" is *anthrōpos,* the racial term, not *anēr,* a male individual. The word refers to the individual self. The expression "the old man" therefore refers to the unsaved person dominated by the totally depraved nature. The expression, "put off," is a figure taken from the putting off of garments. Paul, in Romans 6:6 says: "Knowing this, that our old man (that person we were before we were saved) was crucified with Him in order that the physical body which before salvation was dominated by the totally depraved nature, might be rendered inoperative in that respect, to the end that no longer are we rendering an habitual slave's obedience to sin" (translation plus paraphrase). It was in our identification with Christ in His crucifixion that *potentially* we put off the old man, and we did so *actually* at the moment we were saved.

This act of putting off this old man had to do with the "former conversation." The word "conversation" is obsolete English for "manner of life." This old man is described as "corrupt according to the deceitful lusts." "Is corrupt" is a present participle. The idea is, "which is being corrupted." It speaks of the progressive condition of corruption which characterized the old man. The unsaved person is thus subject to a continuous process of corruption which grows worse as time goes on. This process of corruption is "according to the deceitful lusts." "Lusts" is *epithumia,* "a craving, a passionate desire," good or evil according to the context. Here it is evil cravings. This process of corruption is dominated or controlled by the passionate desires of deceit, deceit being personified. All this, the believing sinner put off when he was saved.

The second point in the teaching they received was that in their Christian experience they are being renewed in the spirit of their mind. "Renewed" is *ananeoō,* "to be renewed, to be renovated by inward reformation." "And" is *de,* a particle which here is transitional or continuative. They have put off the old man. Moreover, they are being renewed in the spirit of their minds. And they have put on the new man. Upon the basis of these three facts, Paul commences his exhortations in 4:25 with "wherefore, speak every man truth etc." The renewal is, of course, accomplished by the Holy Spirit.

The word "spirit" refers to the individual's human spirit, that part of him which gives him God-consciousness, that makes him a moral agent. Vincent comments: "The apostle's object is to set forth the moral self-activity of the Christian life. Hence *pneuma* (spirit) is here the higher life-principle in man by which the human reason, viewed on its moral side — the organ of moral thinking and knowing is informed. The renewal takes place, not in *the mind*, but in *the spirit* of it. 'The change is not in the mind psychologically, either in its essence or in its operation; and neither is it in the mind as if it were a superficial change of opinion on points of doctrine or practice: but it is in the spirit of the mind; in that which gives mind both its bent and its material of thought. It is not simply in the spirit as if it lay there in dim and mystic quietude; but it is in the spirit of the mind; in the power which, when changed itself, radically alters the entire sphere and business of the inner mechanism' (Eadie)."

The third fact in the teaching is that they "put on the new man." The word "new" is *kainos*, not new in point of time, which would be *neos*, but new in point of quality, new in quality as opposed to the old in the sense of outworn, marred through age, which latter designations refer to the old man. "Man" is again *anthrōpos*, the individual. Since the old man refers to the unsaved person dominated by the totally depraved nature, the new man refers to the saved person dominated by the divine nature. This new man "after God is created in righteousness and true holiness." This is what Paul has reference to when he says, "Therefore if any man be in Christ, he is a new creation" (II Cor. 5:17). "After God" is *kata theon*, "according to what God is in Himself," that is, created after the pattern of what God is. The expression "true holiness" could better be rendered, "holiness of truth," "truth" being personified and being opposed to the "deceit" of verse 22 which was also personified.

Translation. *That you have put off once for all with reference to your former manner of life the old man which is being corrupted according to the passionate desires of deceit; moreover*

that you are being constantly renewed with reference to the
spirit of your mind; and that you have put on once for all the
new man which after God was created in righteousness and holi-
ness of truth.

(4:25)   At this point we will take a little time out to look
at the construction of this large section.   In chapters 1-3 Paul
presents doctrine.   He shows the exalted position to which the
believing sinner was raised in Christ Jesus.   In chapters 4-6 he
presents exhortation which is based upon the doctrine, which
latter demonstrated the sweet reasonableness of the exhortation
and the ability of the saint to obey it.   In 4:1-3, the apostle
starts his hortatory section with general exhortations.   In 4:4-16,
he speaks of the gifted men given the Church by God whose
ministry should help the saints obey the exhortations.   In 4:17-
25, Paul shows the tremendous change wrought in the believing
sinner.   Now, upon this latter basis consisting of three points,
first, they put off the old man, *second,* they are being renewed
in the inner man, and *third,* they have put on the new man, he
presents the detailed exhortations beginning in verse 17.

Therefore, since all this is true of you, "putting away lying,
speak every man truth with his neighbor."   "Putting away
lying" is in the Greek text an aorist participle, and an article and
noun in the accusative case.   The translation reads, "having put
off once for all the lie."   In putting off once for all the old man,
they put off the habit of lying which was part of that old man.
In view of the fact that they have done that, they are exhorted
to speak truth, each one to his neighbor.   The reason for this
exhortation is that they are members of one another.   Expositors says: "Reason for this practice of truth — a reason drawn
not from the common conceptions of duty or social weal, but from
the profound Christian idea of union one with another through
union with Christ.   As in the human body each member is *of*
the other in connection and *for* the other in service, so in the
spiritual body of which Christ is the Head, the members belong
one to another and each serves the other."

Translation. *Wherefore, having put off the lie once for all, be speaking truth each with his neighbor, because we are members belonging to one another.*

(4:26) There are three words for "anger" in the Greek New Testament. *Thumos* speaks of a turbulent commotion, the boiling agitation of the feelings, passion, anger forthwith boiling up and soon subsiding, which is forbidden in Ephesians 4:31. *Parorgismos,* translated "wrath" in 4:26, is also forbidden. It refers to anger that is accompanied by irritation, exasperation, embitterment. *Orgē* is an anger which is an abiding and settled habit of the mind that is aroused under certain conditions. This is the anger spoken of in the words, "be ye angry." Trench says: "Under certain conditions, *orgē* (anger) is a righteous passion to entertain. The Scripture has nothing in common with the Stoic's absolute condemnation of anger. It inculcates no apathetic attitude, but only a moderation, not an absolute suppression of the passions which were given to man as winds to fill the sails of his soul, as Plutarch excellently puts it. When guided by reason, anger is a right affection, so the Scripture permits it, and not only permits, but on fit occasion demands it. . . . There is a 'wrath of God' (Matt. 3:7, Rom. 12:19); who would not love good unless He hated evil, the two being so inseparable, that either He must do both or neither; a wrath also of the merciful Son of Man (Mk. 3:5); and a wrath which righteous men not merely may, but, as they are righteous, must feel; nor can there be a surer or sadder token of an utterly prostrate moral condition than the not being able to be angry with sin — and sinners. 'Anger,' says Fuller, 'is one of the sinews of the soul; and he that wants it hath a maimed mind, and with Jacob sinew-shrunk in the hollow of his thigh, must needs halt. Nor is it good to converse with such as cannot be angry.' 'The affections' as another English divine has said, 'are not, like poisonous plants, to be eradicated, but as wild, to be cultivated.' St. Paul is not therefore, as so many understand him, condescending to human infirmity, and saying, 'Your anger shall not be imputed to you as sin, if you put it away before nightfall,' but rather, 'Be ye angry, yet in this anger of yours suffer no sinful element to mingle; there is that which may cleave even to a righteous anger, the *parorgismos,* the irritation, the exasperation, the embitterment which must be dismissed at once, that so, being defecated (purified) of this impurer element which mingled with it, that only may remain which has a right to remain."

The words, "be ye angry," are a present imperative in the Greek text, commanding a continuous action. This *orgē,* this abiding, settled attitude of righteous indignation against sin and sinful things, is commanded, together with the appropriate actions when conditions make them necessary. But the exhortation "and sin not" is provided as a check and restraint. It is, "stop sinning." Expositors says: "A righteous wrath is acknowledged in Scripture as something that not only *may* but *ought* to be, and is seen in Christ Himself (Mk. 3:5). So Paul speaks here of an anger that is approvable and to be enjoined, while in 'and sin not' he forbids only a particular form or measure of anger. As the following clause suggests, even a righteous wrath by over-indulgence may pass too easily into sin."

In the words, "Let not the sun go down upon your wrath," the word "wrath" is *parorgismos,* anger that is mingled with irritation, exasperation, and embitterment. Such anger is forbidden. In Ephesians 6:4, "Provoke to wrath" is our word *parorgizō,* the verbal form of *parorgismos.* This kind of anger is forbidden, and if indulged in must be checked and surrendered without delay.

Translation. *Be constantly angry with a righteous indignation, and stop sinning. Do not allow the sun to go down upon your irritated, exasperated, embittered anger.*

(4:27) "Neither give place" is in a construction in Greek which forbids the continuance of an action already going on. It is literally, "And stop giving place." "Place" is *topos,* "any portion of space marked off from the surrounding territory." Here it is used in the sense of "opportunity, power, occasion for acting."

Translation. *And stop giving an occasion for acting (opportunity) to the devil.*

(4:28) The Greek is, "The one who is stealing, let him no longer be stealing." That sin was still being committed by the members of the Ephesian church. Expositors says: "Stealing was not wholly condemned by ancient heathen opinion. It was even allowed by the Lacedaemonians. It was a vice into which the recently converted living in the old pagan surroundings, especially when unemployed, might all too readily slip. It has been thought strange, scarcely credible indeed, that professing Christians in these Asiatic churches would have given way to thieving. But the Epistles bear witness to the existence of grosser offences against morality in the churches." Paul now offers a corrective to stealing, in the words, "but rather let him be laboring, working with his own hands that which is good, in order that he may be having wherewith to be sharing with the one who is having need."

Translation. *The one who is stealing, let him no longer be stealing, but rather let him be laboring, working with his own hands that which is good, in order that he may be having wherewith to be sharing with the one who is having need.*

(4:29) The Greek order is, "every word that is corrupt, out of your mouth let it not proceed." Expositors says: "*pas* (every) . . . *mē* (no), the well-known Hebraistic form, the negative attaching itself to the verb, means 'non-utterance' — let that be for every word." The word "communication" is *logos*, "a word," here in the sense of "a saying, utterance, speech." "Corrupt" is *sapros*, "rotten, worn out, unfit for use, worthless, bad." Paul goes on; "Every word that is corrupt, out of your mouth let it not be proceeding, but whatever is good, suitable for the use of edification with respect to the need, and this, in order that it may impart grace to those who are hearing." "Grace" is *charis*, the N.T. word for God's grace in salvation. Here it refers to the spiritual blessings and benefits that will accrue to the hearers from the gracious words of the speaker.

Translation. *Every word that is rotten and unfit for use, out of your mouth let it not be proceeding, but whatever is good, suitable for edification with respect to the need, in order that it may impart grace to the hearers.*

(4:30) The Greek has it, "And stop grieving the Spirit, the Holy Spirit of God." Expositors says: "This is not a general exhortation, but one bearing, as the 'and' indicates, particularly on the preceding injunction. The utterance of evil or worthless words is repugnant to the holiness of the Spirit, and is to be refrained from as calculated to grieve Him. The injunction is made more solemn by the designation as 'the Holy Spirit' and 'the Spirit of God.' The Spirit is here seen as capable of feeling, and so as personal. In Isaiah 63:10 we have a similar idea, following the statement that Jehovah was *afflicted* in all His people's afflictions. These terms, no doubt, are anthropopathic, as all terms which we can use of God are anthropomorphic and anthropopathic. (Gentle reader, these two enormous words mean "a representation or conception of God under human form or with human attributes." K.S.W.) But they have reality behind them, and that as regards God's *nature* and not merely His acts. Otherwise we should have an unknown God and One who might be *essentially* different from what we are under the mental necessity of thinking Him to be. What love is in us points *truly,* though tremulously, to what love is in God. But in us love, in proportion as it is true and sovereign, has both its *wrath-side* and its *grief-side;* and so must it be with God, however difficult for us to think it out."

The word "whereby" is *en hōi,* literally "in whom." The Holy Spirit is Himself the seal that God has placed in us. Please turn back to our comments on 1:13 for the significance of a seal and its application with reference to the Spirit as a seal. He is the seal, indicating that the transaction whereby the Son of God paid the penalty of human sin at the Cross is a finished transaction, and that God owns us as His property by right of purchase, also that because of the two preceding facts the saints are secure in salvation "unto the day of redemption," that is, with a view to the day (at the Rapture) when our physical bodies will be glorified. The Holy Spirit is the seal God places upon the saints which guarantees all this.

Translation. *And stop grieving the Spirit, the Holy Spirit of God, in whom you were sealed with a view to the day of redemption.*

(4:31) "Bitterness" is *pikria,* "resentfulness, harshness, virulence," "All" is *pasa,* "all manner of." "Wrath" here is *thumos,* "a violent outbreak of anger, anger forthwith boiling up and soon subsiding again." "Anger" is *orgē,* the word used in 4:26 of legitimate anger, namely, righteous indignation. But here, Vincent says: "What is commanded in verse 26 is here forbidden, because viewed simply on the side of human passion." "Clamor" is *kraugē,* "the outcry of passion, the outward manifestation of anger in vociferation or brawling." "Evil speaking" is *blasphēmia,* slanderous and injurious speech." "Put away" is *airō,* "to bear away what has been raised, to carry off, to take away."

Translation. *All manner of harshness and violent outbreaks of wrath and anger and brawling and slanderous speech, let it be put away from you together with all manner of malice.*

(4:32) "Be" is *ginomai* "to become." Expositors says: "The idea is that they had to abandon one mental condition and make their way, beginning there and then, into its opposite." "Kind" is *chrēstos,* "benevolent, gracious, kind," opposed to "harsh, hard, bitter, sharp." "Tenderhearted" is *eusplagchnos,* "compassionate, tenderhearted." "Forgiving" is not *aphiēmi,* the word usually used when God forgives our sins, which word means "to put away," God forgiving our sins in the sense that He in the Person of His Son bore them on the Cross, paying the penalty, satisfying the just demands of His law, but *charizomai,* "to do a favor to, do something agreeable or pleasant to one, to show one's self gracious, benevolent, to forgive in the sense of treating the offending party graciously." The same word is used of God here forgiving us in Christ. The translation should not be "for Christ's sake," but "in Christ." The Greek is *en Christōi,* "in Christ." It is "the God who forgives, being the God who manifests Himself and acts *in* the suffering, reconciling Christ" (Expositors). It is the God who forgives in the sphere of Christ in that His forgiveness is made possible from the point of the law, through the atonement. "Even as" is *kathōs,* "according as, just as, in the degree that, seeing that"; Alford says, "argument from His example whom we ought to resemble — also from mingled motives of justice and gratitude."

Translation. *And be becoming kind to one another, tender-hearted, forgiving each other even as and just as also God in Christ forgave you.*

CHAPTER FIVE

(5:1, 2) "Be" is *ginomai,* "to become." "Followers" is *mimētai,* "imitators." Our word "mimick" comes from this Greek word. Expositors says: "The loftiest and most exalting endeavor that can possibly be set before man, proposed to us by Christ Himself (Matt. 5:45, 48)." "Dear children" is *tekna agapēta,* "children beloved." "As" is *hōs;* "the comparative particle points to the *manner* or *character* in which the *imitation* is to be made good, and indicates at the same time a *reason* for it. They are children of God, experiencing His love. Children should be like the father, and love should meet love" (Expositors). "Walk in love" is "be constantly ordering your behavior within the sphere of love." This love is the *agapē* love which God is, which God exhibited at the Cross, which Paul analyzes in I Corinthians 13, and which is the fruit of the Spirit in the yielded saint. The saint is to order his behavior or manner of life within the sphere of this divine, supernatural love produced in his heart by the Holy Spirit. When this love becomes the deciding factor in his choices and the motivating power in his actions, he will be walking in love. He will be exemplifying in his life the self-sacrificial love shown at Calvary and the Christian graces mentioned in I Corinthians 13. "Hath given Himself" is *paredōken heauton,* "gave Himself up"; a "statement of the act in which Christ's love received its last and highest expression, namely, the surrender of Himself to death" (Expositors). "For us" is *huper hēmōn. Huper* is the great preposition of substitutionary atonement in the N.T., and means, "instead of, in behalf of." It does not merely mean that Christ died for us, for our benefit, but He died instead of us, in our place. He substituted for us, receiving the full impact of the divine wrath against sin. "Offering" is *prosphoran,* from *prospherō,*

119

"to carry to." It is used of the blood offerings of the Levitical system (Heb. 10:8). Our Lord fulfilled these by becoming an offering for sin on the Cross. "Sacrifice" is *thusia*, from *thuō*, "to kill a sacrificial victim, to immolate, to sacrifice." Thus, again, our Lord is spoken of in O.T. terminology as a sacrifice, the fulfillment of the O.T. sacrifices which were in the form of animals killed and then offered on the Brazen Altar. He offered Himself as a sacrifice to God in full payment of the debt of sin which we as sinners owed, and which the violated law demanded. "A sweetsmelling savour" is *eis osmēn euōdias,* literally, "for a savour of a sweet smell," or, "for an odor of a sweet smell."

Translation. *Be becoming therefore imitators of God, as children beloved, and be ordering your behavior within the sphere of love, even as Christ also gave Himself up in our behalf and in our stead as an offering and a sacrifice to God for an odor of a sweet smell.*

(5:3, 4) The Greek order of words is, "But fornication and uncleanness, every kind of it." Expositors says: "*De* (but) carries the exhortation over to a prohibition expressed in the strongest terms, which is levelled against one of the deadliest and most inveterate temptations to which Gentile Christians were exposed. The term *porneia* (fornication) is to be taken in its proper sense and is not to be restricted to any one particular form — the license practiced at heathen festivals, concubinage, marriage within prohibited degrees, or the like. The moral life of the Graeco-Roman world had sunk so low that, while protests against the prevailing corruption were never entirely wanting, fornication had long come to be regarded as a matter of moral indifference, and was indulged in without shame or scruple, not only by the mass, but by philosophers and men of distinction who in other respects led exemplary lives." The word *porneia* was used of illicit sexual intercourse in general.

The word "or" (*ē*) Vincent says, "sets this sin emphatically by itself." The word "covetousness" is *pleonexia,* "greedy desire to have more, avarice." "Not once" is *mēde,* "not even." Expositors says: "The strong negative *mēde* gives it this force

— 'Not to speak of doing such a thing, let it not be even so much as mentioned among you.'" Commenting on "as becometh saints," the same authority says: "The position of sainthood or separation to God, in which the gospel places the Christian, is so far apart from the license of the world as to make it utterly incongruous even to speak of the inveterate sins of a corrupt heathenism."

"Filthiness" is *aischrotēs,* "obscenity, shameless, immoral conduct." "Foolish talking" is *mōrologia,* from *mōros,* "foolish" in the sense of the lack of forethought and wisdom, impious, godless, because such a man neglects and despises what relates to salvation, and *logos,* "a word, speech." Vincent says: "Talk which is both foolish and sinful. It is more than random or idle talk." "Words obtain a new earnestness when assumed into the ethical terminology of Christ's school. Nor, in seeking to enter fully into the meaning of this one, ought we to leave out of sight the greater emphasis which the words *fool, foolish, folly* obtain in Scripture than elsewhere they have or can have. There is the positive folly as well as the negative to be taken account of, when we are weighing the force of *mōrologia*: it is that *talk of fools* which is foolishness and sin together (Trench)." "Jesting" is *eutrapelia.* Vincent says: "Only here in the N.T. From *eu,* 'well' or 'easily,' and *trepō,* 'to turn.' That which easily turns and adapts itself to the moods and conditions of those with whom it may be dealing at the moment. From this original sense of *versatility* it came to be applied to *morals,* as *time-serving,* and to *speech* with the accompanying notion of *dissimulation.* Aristotle calls it *chastened insolence.* The sense of the word here is *polished* and *witty speech as the instrument of sin;* refinement and versatility without the flavor of Christian grace. 'Sometimes it is lodged in a sly question, in a smart answer, in a quirkish reason, in shrewd intimation, in cunningly diverting or cleverly retorting an objection: sometimes it is couched in a bold scheme of speech, in a tart irony, in a lusty hyperbole, in a startling metaphor, in a plausible reconciling of contradictions, or in acute nonsense. . . Sometimes an affected simplicity, sometimes a

presumptuous bluntness giveth it being. Its ways are unaccount-
able and inexplicable, being answerable to the numberless rovings
of fancy and windings of language' (Barrow)." "Convenient"
is *anēkō*, and in the perfect tense. The word means "befitting,
seemly."

Translation. *But fornication and uncleanness, every kind of
it, or covetousness, let it not be even named among you, just as
it is befitting to saints; and obscenity and foolish talking or
ribaldry, which things have not been seemly or fitting, but rather
giving of thanks.*

(5:5) "Ye know" is *iste ginōskontes*, "ye are knowing, recognizing." The Revision gives "ye know of a surety." Expositors translates, "ye know, being aware that." The word "know"
is *oida* which speaks of absolute, beyond the peradventure of a
doubt knowledge, a knowledge that is self-evident. The word
translated above, "recognizing," is *ginōskō* which speaks of
knowledge gained by experience. Paul reminds the Ephesian
saints that they are absolutely convinced of the truth of the facts
which he is about to call to their attention. "Whoremonger" is
pornos, "a man who prostitutes his body to another's lust for
hire, a male prostitute, a man who indulges in unlawful sexual
intercourse, a fornicator." "Unclean" is *akathartos*, used in a
moral sense, "unclean in thought or life." "Covetous" is
pleonektēs, "one eager to have more," especially what belongs
to others, "greedy of gain." "Idolator" is *eidōlolatrēs*, "a worshipper of false gods, a covetous man as a worshipper of Mammon."

Translation. *For this you know absolutely and experientially,
that every whoremonger or unclean person or covetous person
who is an idolator, does not have an inheritance in the kingdom
of the Christ and of God.*

(5:6) "Vain" is *kenos*, "empty, hollow." These words were
empty, hollow, without the substance of truth or reality. They
were "plausible, but devoid of truth, and employed to palliate
heathen vices" (Vincent). Expositors says: "The expression
is a general one, applying to all who sought by their sophistries

to palliate the vices in question or make them appear to be no vices. These would be found mostly (though by no manner of necessity exclusively) among the heathen, especially among such Gentiles as heard the truth and remained unbelieving." "These things" refers back to the sins mentioned in the previous verse. The word "children" is *huios*, "sons," a Hebraism, calling a person having a certain quality, a son of that quality.

Translation. *Let no one keep on deceiving you by means of empty words, for because of these things there comes the wrath of God upon the sons of the disobedience.*

(5:7-10) "Be" is *ginomai* "to become." Vincent says that "it is a warning against lapsing into old vices." "Partakers" is *sunmetochos* from *metechō*, "to hold with" another, and *sun* "with," the compound word meaning, "partaking together with one." The prohibition is that the saints should not participate with the sons of disobedience in the vices mentioned in verse 5. The prohibition is in the present imperative with the negative *mē*, "Stop therefore becoming joint-partakers with them."

The reason for not lapsing into their former sins is seen in the words, "for you were at one time darkness." The verb "were" is in the emphatic position. The sense is, "You *were*. So do not again become darkness." The word "light" is *phōs*, referring to light itself, not a mere lamp. Expositors says: "The completeness of the change is indicated again by the use of the abstract term — so possessed and penetrated were they by that truth that they could be described not simply as *enlightened* but as themselves now *light*. And this 'in the Lord,' for it was in virtue of their fellowship with Christ that this new apprehension of things came to them, transforming their lives."

"Walk" is *peripateō*, "to order one's behavior, to conduct one's self." Present imperative in form, the verb commands an habitual action; "Be habitually conducting yourselves as children of light." The word "children" is *teknon*, "a born one," a child looked upon in his birth relationship to the one who bore it. The admonition is to those who are children of God, thus light in the Lord, thus, children of light. Expositors comments: "If these Ephesians were now 'light in the Lord,' it was not for themselves only but for others. They were called to live a life beseeming those to whom Christian enlightenment and purity had become their proper nature."

The Nestle and the Westcott and Hort texts have "light" rather than "spirit." The fruit of the aforementioned light is a figurative expression, speaking of the moral results of the light, of its products as a whole. "Goodness" is *agathōsunē*, "goodness" in the sense of "active goodness, beneficence."

"Proving" is *dokimazō*, "to put to the test for the purpose of approving, and having found that the thing tested meets the specifications laid down by the test, then to place one's sanction or approval on the thing or person tested." "Acceptable" is *euareston*, "well-pleasing."

Translation. *Stop therefore becoming joint-participants with them; for you were at one time darkness, but now light in the Lord. As children of light be habitually conducting yourselves; for the fruit of this light is in the sphere of every beneficence and righteousness and truth, putting to the test and then approving what is well-pleasing to the Lord.*

(5:11, 12) "Fellowship" is *sunkoinōneō*, "to become a partaker together with others." The word refers to a joint-participation between two or more individuals in a common interest and a common activity. "Reprove" is *elegchō*, "to reprove or rebuke so as to bring out conviction or confession of guilt." Trench says that the word "implies not merely the charge, but the truth of the charge, and further the manifestation of the truth of the charge; nay, more than all this, very often also the acknowledgment, if not outward, yet inward, of its truth on the part of the accused; it being the glorious prerogative of the truth in its highest operation not merely to assert itself, and to silence the adversary, but to silence him by convincing him of his error."

Alford explains verse 12 as follows: "The connection seems to be, 'reprove them — this they want, and this is more befitting you — for to have the least part in them, even in speaking of them, is shameful.'" He quotes Klotz, "the connection being, 'I mention not, and you need not *speak of,* these deeds of darkness, much less have any fellowship with them — your connection with them must only be that which the act of *reproof* necessitates.'" Expositors explains: "The secrecy of the works in question is the reason why they require to be openly reproved; and the point is this — the heathen practice in secret, vices too abominable even to mention; all the more is the need of open rebuke instead of silent overlooking or connivance (Meyer, Ellicott, etc.)."

Translation. *And stop having fellowship with the unfruitful works of this darkness, but rather be rebuking them so as to bring out confession and conviction, for concerning the things done in secret by them, it is shameful to be speaking.*

(5:13) "All things" is *ta panta,* "the all things," that is, the secret sins just mentioned, the Greek article pointing back to these. "That are reproved" is a present participle in the Greek text, "being reproved," or "when they are reproved." "Made manifest" is *phaneroō,* "to make visible or known what has been hidden or unknown." "Doth make manifest" is passive voice in Greek text, "is made manifest." Thus, "everything that is made manifest is light." Vincent comments: "A general proposition, going to show that manifestation can come only through light. Whatever is revealed in its true essence by light is of the nature of light. It no longer belongs to the category of darkness. Manifestation is a law of good and evil alike. That which is of the truth *seeks* the light and *cometh* to the light. That which is evil avoids the light and loves darkness better than light, but none the less is brought to the light and appears in its own light."

Translation. *But all the aforementioned things when they are reproved by the light are made visibly plain, for everything that is being made plain is light.*

(5:14) The words, "he saith," are sometimes used by Paul as a formula referring to what God has said. The source of the quotation is a moot question, whether a combination of some texts in the O.T., or the words of some ancient hymn. As to its connection with what precedes, Expositors has a helpful note:

"The passage is introduced in connection with the reference to the effects of a faithful 'reproof' and under the impression of the figure of the *light*. It takes the form of an appeal to wake out of the pagan condition of sin, described by the two-fold figure of *sleep* and *death,* and of a promise that then Christ will shine upon the sinner with the saving light of His truth. The quotation comes in relevantly, therefore, as a further enforcement both of the need for the *reproof* which is enjoined, and of the good effects of such a *reproof* faithfully exercised." The words "give light," are the translation of *epiphauskō,* "to shine upon." Thayer comments as follows: "Christ will pour upon thee the light of divine truth as the sun gives light to men aroused from sleep."

Translation. *Wherefore He says: Be waking up, the one who is sleeping, and arise from the dead, and there shall shine upon you, Christ.*

(5:15, 16) "See" is *blepō,* "to discern mentally, observe, perceive, consider, contemplate, look to in the sense of taking care, take heed." "Circumspectly" is *akribōs,* "exactly, accurately, carefully." "Walk" is *peripateō,* "to order one's behavior, to conduct one's self." The translation reads, "Be constantly taking heed how accurately you are conducting yourselves." That is, see to it that your conduct is accurate with respect to the demands of the Word of God. It is like a motorist accurately following on the right side of the center line dividing traffic. "Fools" is *asophos,* "the unwise"; "wise," *sophos* "the wise." "Redeeming" is *exagorazō,* "to buy up." In the middle voice as it is used here, it means, "to buy up for one's self or one's advantage." Metaphorically, it means, "to make a wise and sacred use of every opportunity for doing good," so that zeal and well-doing are as it were the purchase-money by which we make the time our own" (Thayer). "Time" is not *chronos,* "time as such," but *kairos,* "time as regarded in its strategic, epoch-making, seasonable, opportune seasons." The idea is not to make best use of time as such, which is what we should do in the sense of not wasting it, but of taking advantage of the opportunities that present themselves. "Evil" is not *kakos,* "evil in the abstract," but *ponēros*, "evil in active opposition to the good, pernicious."

Translation. *Be constantly taking heed therefore how accurately you are conducting yourselves, not as unwise ones but as wise ones, buying up for yourselves the opportune time, because the days are pernicious.*

(5:17) "Unwise" is *aphrōn*, "without reason, senseless, foolish, stupid, without reflection or intelligence, acting rashly." "Understanding" is *suniēmi*, "to set or bring together, to put the perception with the thing perceived, to set or join together in the mind," thus, "to understand." The word speaks of reflective thinking. The verb is present imperative in a prohibition, forbidding the continuance of an action already going on. *Ginomai* is the verb, meaning "to become."

Translation. *On this account stop becoming those who are without reflection or intelligence, but be understanding what the will of the Lord is.*

(5:18-20) "Be drunk" is *methuskō*, "to get drunk, become intoxicated." Wycliffe translates, "be filled." Vincent says: "A curious use of the word occurs in Homer, where he is describing the stretching of a bull's hide, which in order to make it more elastic, is *soaked* (*methuskō*) with fat." The word, therefore, refers to the condition of a person in which he is soaked with wine.

The words, "wherein is excess," are to be construed with the entire clause, "Be not drunk with wine," not with the word "wine" alone, but with the becoming drunk with wine.

"Excess" is *asōtia*, from *sōzō*, "to save," and Alpha privative, the literal meaning being, "unsavingness"; that is, that which is *asōtia* has nothing of a saving quality about it, but rather, a destructive one. The word as it is generally used expresses the idea of an abandoned, debauched, profligate life. The words "profligacy, debauching," well describe its meaning. "Filled" is *plēroō*, "to fill up, to cause to abound, to furnish or supply liberally, to flood, to diffuse throughout." In Acts 6:15 we have Stephen, a man filled with faith and the Holy Spirit. Faith

filled Stephen in the sense that it controlled him. The Holy
Spirit filled Stephen in the sense that He controlled him. Therefore, the fullness of the Spirit has reference to His control over
the believer yielded to Him. The verb is in the present imperative; "Be constantly being filled with the Spirit." The interpretation is, "Be constantly, moment by moment, being controlled by the Spirit." Please consult the author's book, *Riches
in the Greek New Testament* for a detailed, practical treatment
of the fullness of the Holy Spirit.

"Speaking to yourselves" is *lalountes heautois,* literally,
"speaking with yourselves." But this translation is open to mis-
interpretation, namely, that of each Christian communing with
himself, which is not the idea. Saints are to speak to one
another. That is, in letting other saints know of their joy in
salvation, they are to do so in psalms and hymns and spiritual
songs. They are to find expression to the Spirit-filled life in
this way. As to the definitions of these terms, Expositors says:
"What the distinctions are, if any, between the three terms, has
been considerably disputed. *Psalms* are religious songs, especially those sung to a musical accompaniment, and *par excellence* an
O.T. psalm; *hymns* are properly speaking songs of praise; *songs,*
the most general term, are applicable to all kinds of songs,
secular or sacred, accompanied or unaccompanied. The three
words are brought together here with a view to rhetorical force,
and it is precarious, therefore, to build much upon supposed
differences between them."

Another way in which the Spirit-filled life is manifested, is in
the giving of thanks for all things. Regarding the all things,
Expositors says: "The 'for all things' is taken by many in its
widest possible extent, as including things evil as well as good.
The Epistle does not deal, however, particularly with the *sufferings* of the Christian, but with what he receives from God
and what his consequent duty is. It is most accordant therefore
with the context, to understand the 'all' as referring to all the
blessings of the Christian, the whole good that comes to him
from God."

Translation. *And stop being intoxicated with wine, in which (state of intoxication) there is profligacy. But be constantly filled (controlled) by the Spirit, speaking to one another in psalms and hymns and spiritual songs, singing and making melody in your hearts to the Lord, giving thanks always concerning all things in the name of our Lord Jesus Christ to God, even the Father.*

(5:21) In this verse Paul speaks of yet another way in which the Spirit-filled life should express itself. "Submitting" is *hupotassō*. The simple verb *tassō* was used in classical Greek in a military meaning, "to draw up in order of battle, to form, array, marshall" both troops or ships. It speaks of soldiers marshalled in military order under a commanding officer. Thus, it speaks of the subjection of one individual under or to another. The prefixed preposition *hupo* means "under." *Hupotassō* in classical Greek meant, "to subject, make subject." In N.T. Greek, it means, "to arrange under, to subordinate, put in subjection," in the middle voice as it is here, "to subject one's self to, to obey." Alford says: "As we are otherwise to be filled, otherwise to sing and rejoice, so also we are otherwise to behave — not blustering nor letting our voices rise in selfish vaunting, as such men do, — but subject to one another." Subjecting one's self to another is the opposite of self assertion, the opposite of an independent, autocratic spirit. It is the desire to get along with one another, being satisfied with less than one's due, a sweet reasonableness of attitude. The best texts have "Christ" instead of "God."

Translation. *Putting yourselves in subjection to one another in the fear of Christ.*

(5:22, 23) Expositors comments: "The great Christian law of mutual subjection or submissive consideration is now to be unfolded in its bearing on three particular relations which lie at the foundation of man's social life — those of husbands and wives, parents and children, masters and servants. The relation of husbands and wives, as the most fundamental, is taken up before the others, and the Christian duty of the wives is set forth first. The Greek has it, "The wives to their own husbands as to the Lord." The verb *hupotassō*, "submit, subject," is supplied from the preceding verse. "Your own" is *idios*, "one's own private, peculiar, unique possession." "As" is *hōs*, an adverb of comparison, and means, "even as, in the same manner as, like as." Expositors says: "That is, *to Christ;* not to the *husband* as lord and master. If the husband's supremacy had been in view, it would have been expressed by *tois kuriois* (your lords and masters). The *hōs* (as) denotes more than *similarly,* and more than 'just as they are submissive to Christ so should they be to their husbands.' The next sentence, and the whole statement of the relation between husband and wife in the following verse in terms of the relation between Christ and the Church, suggest that the point of the *hōs* (as) is that the wife is to regard the obedience she has to render to her husband as an obedience rendered to Christ, the Christian husband being head of the wife and representing to her Christ the Head of the whole Christian body."

Commenting on the words: "Because the husband is the head of the wife, as also Christ is the Head of the Church," Expositors says this: "Reason for a wifely subjection of the kind indicated. It is found in the relation of headship. In the marriage union the husband holds the same relation, namely, that of headship, as Christ holds to the Church, and the headship of the one represents the headship of the other." With regard to the words, "and He Himself is the Saviour of the body," the same authority says, "It is best taken as an *independent* clause, stating in a definite and emphatic way an important point in which Christ, who resembles the husband in respect to *headship,* at the same time *differs* from the husband. . . . The husband is head of the wife, and in that he is like Christ; but Christ is also that which the husband is not, namely, Saviour of that whereof He is Head."

Translation. *The wives, be putting yourselves in subjection to your own husbands as to the Lord, because the man is head of the wife as the Christ is Head of the Church, He Himself being the Saviour of the body.*

(5:24) "Therefore" is the A.V., translation of *alla*. Both Vincent and Expositors take exception to that rendering. The *alla* is the strongest adversative particle, *de,* a particle that opposes but continues and connects, being the milder one. *Alla* opposes and disannuls or discounts what has gone before. It should be rendered "but," or "nevertheless." Expositors shows its significance in this context as follows: "The twenty-fourth verse thus looks to the peculiarity mentioned as belonging to Christ's headship in distinction from the husband's, namely, the fact that He is not only the Head, but Saviour. And the idea becomes this — 'Christ indeed is Saviour of the body, and that the husband is not; nevertheless the question of *obedience* is not affected thereby; for all that, as the Church is subject to Christ so too are wives to be subject to their husbands.'" The words, "in everything" refer to everything in the marriage relation.

The verb "is subject" is *hupotassō,* which in the middle voice as it is here, means "to subject one's self to, to obey." This rendering lays upon the members of the Church in relation to Christ and upon wives in relation to their husbands, the duty of thus subjecting themselves to their respective heads and to render them obedience.

Translation. *Nevertheless, as the Church subjects itself to the Christ, in this manner also the wives should subject themselves to their husbands in all things.*

(5:25-27) The duty of the wives is to obey their husbands. The duty of the husband is to love his wife. The word for "love" here is *agapaō,* referring to the love that God is (I John 4:8), that God showed at Calvary (John 3:16), and the love that the Holy Spirit produces in the heart of the yielded believer (Gal. 5:22). This is a self-sacrificial love, a love that impels the one loving to give himself in self-sacrifice for the well-being of the one who is loved. The husband has three other kinds of love for his wife, a love of passion (*erōs*), a love of complacency and satisfaction (*stergō*), and a fondness or affection (*phileō*). All these are saturated with the *agapaō* love of the Spirit-filled husband, purified and made heavenly in character.

Expositors comments on the words, "that He might sanctify and cleanse it," as follows: "Statement of the great object with which Christ in His love for the Church gave Himself up to death for it. An object worthy of the self-sacrifice, described in definite terms and with a solemn significance — the sanctification and cleansing of the Church with a view to its final presentation in perfect holiness at the great day." "Sanctify" is *hagiazō*, "to set apart for a sacred use." The distinctive aspect of sanctification here is that of inward ethical purification as in I Thessalonians 5:23. The succeeding context points to this interpretation. "Cleanse" is a modal participle, showing how or in what manner the sanctification takes place. The translation so far reads: "In order that it He might sanctify, cleansing it." This cleansing is accomplished by "the washing of water by the word." "Washing" is *loutron*, "a bath." The words "of water" are genitive of description, describing the bath as one effected by water. "By the word" is *en hrēmati*, "in the sphere of the Word." That is, this inward ethical purification is accomplished by the Word of God having liberty in the heart of the Spirit-filled believer, displacing sin and substituting in its place, righteousness. The blood of Christ cleanses from actual sin, and thus cleanses the believer. The Word cleanses him in the sense above mentioned, water being a type of the Word of God.

The Greek of verse 27 begins as follows: "In order that He might Himself present to Himself the Church glorious." Expositors comments: "It is Christ Himself who is to present the Church, and it is to *Himself* He is to present it. He is at once the Agent and the End or Object of the presentation. . . . The idea, as the context suggests, is that of the Bridegroom *presenting* or *setting forth* the bride. The presentation in view, which is given here as the *final* object of Christ's surrendering of Himself to death, and (by use of the aorist) as a single definite act, cannot be anything done in the world that now is, but must be referred to the future consummation, the event of the Parousia (the Rapture)." The words, "not having spot or wrinkle," are an explanation on the negative side of what is meant in the word "glorious." The bride is to be without moral blemish.

"Holy" is *hagia*, "separate from evil"; "without blemish," *amōmos*, "faultless, unblamable," namely, free from faultiness, as a sacrificial animal without blemish.

Translation. *The husbands, be loving your wives in the manner in which Christ also loved the Church and gave Himself on behalf of it, in order that He might sanctify it, cleansing it by the bath of water in the sphere of the Word, in order that He might Himself present to Himself the Church glorious, not having spot nor wrinkle nor any of such things, but in order that it might be holy and unblamable.*

(5:28-30) Expositors' comment on verse 28 is as follows: "The idea, therefore, is that even as Christ loved the Church, so too ought husbands to love their wives, — as *their own bodies.* This is not to be reduced to 'like themselves': nor does *hōs* (as) here mean simply 'like,' as if all that is meant is that the husband's love for his wife is to be *similar* to his love for his own body. The *hōs* (as) has its qualitative force, 'as it were,' 'as being.' *Christ* and *husband* are each *head*, as Paul has already put it, and as the Church is the body in relation to the former, so is the wife in relation to the latter. The husband, the head, therefore, is to love the wife as being his body, even as Christ loved the Church as forming His body. The idea of husband and wife as being *one flesh* is probably also in view. *He that loveth his own wife loveth himself.* The relation of *head* and *body* means that the wife is part of the husband's *self.* To love his wife, therefore, in this character as being his body, is to love himself. It is a love consequently, not merely of *duty*, — but of *nature.*"

The same authority continues on verse 29. "The 'for' gives a reason for the preceding statement, looking to the *thought,* however, rather than to the *form* of the statement. The *thought* is the oneness of husband and wife, the position of the wife as part of the husband's self; and the connection is this; 'he should love her even as Christ loved the Church, for the wife, I say, is as the body in that natural relationship in which the husband is the head, so that in loving her he loves himself; and this is the reason in *nature* why he should love her, for according to this, to hate his wife is to hate his own flesh, which is contrary to nature and a thing never seen.' 'Flesh' here has its non-ethical sense, practically, *body.*"

In verse 30, the Greek order is, "Because members we are of His body." The word "members" has the emphatic position. Expositors says: "We are not something apart from Christ, nor do we occupy only an incidental relation to Him. We are veritable parts of that body of which He is Head, and this is the reason why He nourishes and cherishes the Church." The words, "of His flesh and of His bones" are a rejected reading by Nestle and also Westcott and Hort.

Translation. *In this manner ought also the husbands to love their wives as their own bodies. The one who loves his own wife loves himself, for no one ever yet hated his own flesh, but nourishes and cherishes it, even as the Christ, the Church, because members are we of His body.*

(5:31) "Leave" is *kataleipō,* "to leave behind, depart from." "Joined" is *proskollaō,* "to glue upon, to glue to, to join one's self to closely, cleave to, stick to." The compound verb denotes a most intimate union. "Shall be one flesh" does not include the preposition *eis* in the Greek text, which the A.V., does not translate. The full rendering is, "shall be unto one flesh." The Revision has "shall become one flesh."

Translation. *Because of this a man shall leave behind his father and his mother and shall be joined to his wife, and the two shall become one flesh.*

(5:32, 33) The word "great" is in the predicate, not the attributive position. It is, "This mystery is great." Vincent says; "The reference in *this mystery* is to the preceding statement of the conjugal relation of the Church with Christ, typified by the human marriage relation." The same authority translates, "In regard of Christ and the Church," and says: "Not calling your attention to the mere human relationship, but to the mysterious relation between Christ and His Church, of which that is a mere semblance."

Commenting on the words: "Let each one of you love his own wife as himself," Expositors says: "The 'each one' expresses still more emphatically the absoluteness and universality of the Christian duty of conjugal love — a duty from which no single husband is exempt. As in verse 28, the *hōs* (as) means not merely that each husband is to love his wife as he loves himself, but that he is to love her as *being* herself part and parcel of himself according to the divine idea of the marriage union."

The word "reverence" is *phobeō*, "to fear, to be afraid of, to reverence, to venerate, to treat with deference or reverential obedience." Expositors defines: "fear in the sense of *reverence*, spontaneous, obedient regard."

Translation. *This mystery is great. However, I am speaking with regard to Christ and the Church. Nevertheless also as for you, let each one in this manner be loving his own wife as himself, and the wife, let her be continually treating her husband with deference and reverential obedience.*

CHAPTER SIX

(6:1-3) "Obey" is *hupakouō,* the simple verb meaning "to hear," the prefixed preposition, "under," the compound verb meaning, "to hear under," that is, "to hear under" authority. It speaks of the one hearing as being under the authority of some one else. Thus, the verb comes to mean, "to hearken to a command, to obey, to be obedient to, submit to." The verb is in the present imperative, which construction commands habitual, constant obedience here. The phrase, "in the Lord" is to be construed with "obey." That is, as Expositors says; "It defines the quality of the obedience by defining the *sphere* within which it is to move — a Christian obedience fulfilled in communion with Christ." Vincent says: "The children being with their parents in the Lord, are to be influenced by religious duty as well as by natural affection." The word "right" is *dikaios,* "not in the sense of *befitting* merely, but in that of *righteous,* what is required by *law* — the law that is at once founded on the natural relation of children and parents and proclaimed in the divine commandment (v. 2)" (Expositors). "Honor" is *timaō,* "to estimate, fix the value." To honor someone therefore, is to evaluate that person accurately and honestly, and treat him with the deference, respect, reverence, kindness, courtesy, and obedience which his station in life or his character demands. Expositors says: "Obedience is the *duty;* honor is the disposition of which the obedience is born."

Translation. *The children, be always obedient to your parents in the Lord, for this is a righteous thing. Be always honoring your father and your mother, which is a commandment of such a nature as to be the first commandment with promise, in order that it may be well with you, and in order that you may be long-lived upon the earth.*

(6:4) "Provoke" is *parorgizō,* "to rouse to wrath, to provoke, exasperate, anger." Expositors says: "The parental duty is given first negatively, as avoidance of all calculated to *irritate* or *exasperate* the children — injustice, severity and the like, so as to make them indisposed to filial obedience and honor." "Bring up" is *ektrephō,* "to nourish up to maturity, to nurture, bring up, to rear up." The word is not confined to the nourishing of a child physically, but includes its bringing up or rearing in the various departments of its life.

"Nurture" is *paideia,* "the whole training and education of children which relates to the cultivation of mind and morals, and employs for this purpose, now commands and admonitions, now reproof and punishment" (Thayer). "Admonition" is *nouthesia,* "exhortation, admonition." Trench says of this word, "it is a training by word — by the word of encouragement, when that is sufficient, but also by that of remonstance, of reproof, of blame, where these may be required, as set over against the training by act and discipline which is *paideia.*"

Translation. *And the fathers, stop provoking your children to anger, but be rearing them in the discipline and admonition of the Lord.*

(6:5-8) "Servants" is *doulos,* "slaves." These were Christian slaves working for the most part for pagan masters. Vincent says, "In this appeal, Paul was addressing a numerous class. In many of the cities of Asia Minor, slaves outnumbered freemen." Expositors has a valuable note: "Many questions would inevitably arise with regard to the duties of masters and servants in a state of society in which slavery prevailed and had the sanction of ancient and undisputed use. Especially would this be the case when Christian slaves (of whom there were many) had a heathen master, and when the Christian master had heathen slaves. Hence the considerable place given in the N.T., to this relation and the application of Christian principles (I Cor. 7:21, 22; I Tim. 6:1, 2; Tit. 2:9, 10; and Philemon, in addition to Col. 3:22, 4:1, and I Pet. 2:18-25). Here, as elsewhere in the N. T., slavery is accepted as an existing institution, which is neither formally condemned nor formally approved. There is nothing to prompt revolutionary action, or to encourage repudiation of the position. Onesimus, the Christian convert, is sent back by Paul to his master, and the institution is left to be undermined and removed by the gradual operation of the great Christian principles of the equality of men in the sight of God, and a common Christian brotherhood, the spiritual freedom of the Christian man, and the Lordship of Christ to which every other lordship is subordinate."

The Greek order is, "Be constantly obedient to those who according to the flesh are your masters." The word "masters" here is *kurios,* while *despotēs* is used for "masters" in I Peter and the Pastoral Epistles. Expositors suggests that the phrase " 'according to the flesh' was used to distinguish these masters (*kurios*) who were masters of their slaves only so far as material and earthly consideration are concerned, while Christ is *Kurios* (Lord), Master in a spiritual relation as well." As one wise monarch once said, "My dominion over my subjects ends where that of God's begins."

As to the expression, "with fear and trembling," the same authority says: "The use of the same phrase with regard to Paul himself (I Cor. 2:3), the Corinthians (II Cor. 7:15), and Philippians (Phil. 2:12), is enough to show that nothing more is in view here than *solicitous zeal* in the discharge of duty, anxious care not to come short."

The words "in singleness of heart," qualify "be obedient," not "fear and trembling." "It states the spirit in which the obedience was to be rendered, — not in formality, pretence, or hypocrisy, but in inward reality and sincerity, and with an undivided heart" (Expositors). The same authority defines eyeservice as follows: "It is the service that is done only when one is under the master's eye — an obedience to save appearances and gain undeserved favor, which is not rendered when the master is absent as it is when his scrutiny is on us."

"Heart" is *psuchē,* "soul." Expositors says: "It belongs to the *character* (*hōs* as) of the bond-servant of Christ to do the will of God, the God and Father of Christ, in his condition in life, and to do that not grudgingly or formally, but with hearty readiness." In verse 7 the motive for service to a human master should be as to the Lord Jesus. In other words, the slave should serve the human master as if he were serving the Lord Jesus. The encouragement for doing this is found in the fact that whatever good the slave does for his human master, if done as to Christ, shall be rewarded (v. 8).

Translation. *The slaves, be constantly obedient to those who according to the flesh are your masters, with fear and trembling, in singleness of your heart as to the Christ, not in the way of eyeservice as menpleasers, but as Christ's bond-slaves, doing the will of God from the soul, with good will rendering a slave's service as to the Lord and not as to men, knowing that each one, whatever good he may do, this he will receive from the presence of the Lord, whether he is a slave or whether he is free.*

(6:9) "Masters" is *kurios*, the lords and masters of slaves. These slave-masters are Christians, for God has no exhortations to conduct for unsaved slave-masters. The words, "do the same things," do not mean that the masters are to render service to the slaves as the latter do to them, but that they are to treat them with the same Christian principles and consideration that the slaves show to the masters.

"Forbearing" is *aniēmi*, "giving up." "Threatening" has the definite article, referring to the well-known habit of masters threatening their slaves. The Greek text then follows: "knowing that also their Master and yours is in heaven." "Respect of persons" is *prosōpolempsia*, literally, "to receive face." Thayer defines: "the fault of one who when called on to requite or to give judgment has respect to the outward circumstances of men and not to their intrinsic merits, and so prefers, as the more worthy, one who is rich, high-born, or powerful, to another who is destitute of such gifts." The word "partiality" could translate it.

Translation. *And the masters, be practicing the same things toward them, giving up your threatening, knowing that also their*

Master and yours is in heaven, and there is not partiality with Him.

(6:10) "Be strong" is *endunamoō,* "to make strong, to endue with strength." The idea is, "to clothe one's self with strength as one puts on a garment." Here the verb is in the passive voice, "be continually strengthened." The qualifying phrase, "in the Lord," defines the strengthening as *Christian* strengthening, such as can take effect only in union with the Lord (Expositors). The rendering, "be strong," could encourage one to self-effort at being strong, whereas the translation "be strengthened," causes the saint to depend on the Lord for the supply of that strength.

"Power" is *kratos,* "relative or manifested power," and "might" is *ischuos,* "power as an enduement." The idea is, "in the active efficacy of the might that is inherent in Him."

Translation. *Finally, be constantly strengthened in the Lord and in the active efficacy of the might that is inherent in Him.*

(6:11) "Put on" is *enduō,* "to envelope in, to hide in, to clothe with." "Whole armor" is *panoplia,* made up of *pas,* "whole," and *hoplon,* "weapon"; literally "all the weapons." The word is from *panoplos,* "wholly armed, in full armor." It means "full armor, complete armor," shield, sword, lance, helmet, greaves, and breastplate. The word "panoply" is the English spelling of our word. In classical Greek, the word was used of the *full armor* of a *heavy-armed soldier.* Expositors says: " 'Of God' is the genitive of *origin* or *source,* the panoply which comes from God or is provided by Him. To put the emphasis on the words 'of God' is to miss the point and to suppose a contrast which there is nothing here to suggest, namely, with some *other* kind of panoply. The emphatic thing, as most exegetes notice, is the *panoplian,* the idea being that we need not only a divine equipment, but that equipment in its *completeness,* without the lack of any single part. The fact that, in order to meet our spiritual foe, we need to take to ourselves all that God provides for living and for overcoming, is expressed in a telling figure drawn from the world of soldiery. The figure of the Christian as a warrior with his *arms, wages, etc.*, occurs repeatedly in the Pauline writings. . . . No doubt the *Roman* soldier is particularly in view. Paul, the Roman citizen, would think of him, and it was the Roman military power that filled the eye when Paul labored and wrote."

"Wiles" is *methodeia*, "cunning arts, deceit, craft, trickery." The word comes from the verbal form *methodeuō*, "to follow up or investigate by method and settled plan, to follow craftily, frame devices, deceive." The word "strategem" will translate it adequately. The phrase "stand against" is a soldier's expression, used for standing one's ground, as against taking to flight.

Translation. *Clothe yourselves with the full armor of God to the end that you will be able to hold your ground against the strategems of the devil.*

(6:12) In the word "wrestle," (*palē*), Paul uses a Greek athletic term. Thayer defines as follows: "a contest between two in which each endeavors to throw the other, and which is decided when the victor is able to press and hold down his prostrate antagonist, namely, hold him down with his hand upon his neck." When we consider that the loser in a Greek wrestling contest had his eyes gouged out with resulting blindness for the rest of his days, we can form some conception of the Ephesian Greek's reaction to Paul's illustration. The Christian's wrestling against the powers of darkness is no less desperate and fateful. The literal Greek is, "Our wrestling is not against blood and flesh." The Greek reverses the order. The principalities and powers, are the *archē*, "first ones, preeminent ones, leaders," and the *exousia*, "authorities," the demons of Satan in the lower atmosphere who constitute his kingdom in the air.

The rulers of the darkness of this world, the *kosmokratōr*, "the world-rulers of this darkness," are Satan and his demons. They are also called "the spirit forces of perniciousness in the heavenly places." The heavenly places here are not those highest ones inhabited by the holy angels, but the lower heavens, the lower atmosphere surrounding this earth. One might be troubled at the change of figure from that of a Roman soldier to that of a

Greek wrestler, arguing that a soldier does not engage in a wrestling contest clad in full armor. But the difficulty disappears when one sees that the figure of a wrestling match speaks of a contest at close quarters, and an individual contest, between the Christian and his demon enemies.

Translation. *Because our wrestling is not against blood and flesh, but against the principalities, against the authorities, against the world-rulers of this darkness, against spirit-forces of perniciousness in the heavenly places.*

(6:13) "Wherefore" (*dia touto*), "on this account," because the fight is with such powers as the demons of Satan, "take unto you the whole armor of God." "Take unto you" is *analambanō*, "to take up" in order to use, "to take to one's self," thus, "take up" as one takes up armor to put it on. The verb is aorist imperative, which construction issues a command given with military snap and curtness, a command to be obeyed at once and once for all. Thus, the Christian is to take up and put on all the armor of God as a once-for-all act and keep that armor on during the entire course of his life, not relaxing the discipline necessary for the constant use of such protection. The historian, Gibbon, relates how the relaxation of discipline and the disuse of exercise rendered soldiers less willing and less able to support the fatigue of the service. They complained of the weight of their armor, and obtained permission to lay aside their cuirasses and helmets.

"Withstand" is *anthistēmi*, "to stand against, resist, oppose," here to stand against the onslaught of the demons. The definite article before "day," marks it out as a particular day, probably, as Expositors says, "the day of violent temptation and assault, whenever that may come to us during the present time." "Evil" is *ponēros*, "pernicious, evil in active opposition to the good." "Done" is *katergazomai*, "to perform, accomplish, achieve, to do that from which something results, to carry something to its ultimate conclusion."

Translation. *On this account, take to yourself at once and once for all, the complete armor of God in order that you may*

be able to resist in the day, the pernicious one, and having
achieved all things, to stand.

(6:14-17) "Having girt about" is *perizōnnuō*, "to gird
around, to fasten garments with a girdle or belt." It is in the
middle voice, not passive as A.V., since context is hortatory,
thus, "having girded about." The Christian must gird his loins
about with truth. That is his responsibility. Expositors says;
"First in the list of these articles of equipment is mentioned the
girdle. Appropriately so; for the soldier might be furnished with
every other part of his equipment, and yet, wanting the girdle,
would be neither fully accoutered nor securely armed. His belt
was no mere adornment of the soldier, but an essential part of
his equipment. Passing round the loins and by the end of the
breastplate (in later times supporting the sword), it was of especial use in keeping other parts in place, and in securing the
proper soldierly attitude and freedom of movement." As to the
reference to truth, the same authority says: "It is simplest and
most accordant with usage to take it so here (in the sense of
candour, sincerity, truthfulness). And this plain grace of *open-
ness,* truthfulness, reality, the mind that will practice no deceits
and attempt no disguises in our intercourse with God, is indeed
vital to Christian safety and essential to the due operation of all
the other qualities of character."

With regard to the breastplate, the same authority says: "As
the soldier covers his breast with the breastplate to make it secure
against the disabling wound, so the Christian is to endue himself with righteousness so as to make his heart and will proof
against the fatal thrust of his spiritual assailants." The righteousness here is not justifying righteousness given the believing
sinner when he first believes, but sanctifying righteousness, the
product of the Holy Spirit in the life of the yielded saint. It can
be defined as moral rectitude. The breastplate of righteousness
is therefore the breastplate which is righteousness or consists of
righteousness.

The Greek middle is used again in the exhortation, "and having shod your feet," the responsibility of the Christian soldier.

If the Christian soldier is to stand up against the attack of the demons, he must see to it that his feet are properly protected and equipped. The Roman soldier wore sandals which were bound by throngs over the instep and around the ankle, and the soles were thickly studded with nails. This would give him a firm footing in case of attack. The word "preparation" is *hetoimazō,* which was used in classical Greek in the sense of *establishment* or *firm foundation.* Thus, the Christian soldier should see to it that his feet are equipped with the sandals which will give him a firm footing, namely, the good news that speaks peace to a sinful heart, for the Lord Jesus made peace by the blood of His Cross, making a way for a holy God to reunite Himself with a believing sinner who in Adam had been separated from Him and His life. The Greek word "peace" is *eirēnē,* and means "that which has been bound together." Expositors says: "The preparedness, the mental alacrity with which we are inspired by the gospel with its message of peace with God, is to be to us the protection and equipment which the sandals that cover the feet are to the soldier. With this we shall be helped to face the foe with courage and with promptitude."

The "above all" of verse 16 is ambiguous. The thought in the original is, "in addition to all," that is, in addition to all the equipment just mentioned, the Christian should add that mentioned in verses 16 and 17. The word "shield" used here (*thureon*) designated the shield of the heavy infantry, a large, oblong one, four by two and one half feet, sometimes curved on the inner side. This shield which the Christian soldier uses is faith, a present faith in the Lord Jesus for victory over sin and the hosts of the devil. The fiery darts refer to arrows tipped with tow, pitch, or such material, set on fire before they were discharged. "The wicked" is *ho ponēros,* "the pernicious one," Satan, who is not content to perish in his own destruction, but seeks to drag everyone else down with him to the utter ruin that will be his in the future eternity. The fiery arrows represent the temptations with which he assails the saints.

These saints were saved in the sense that they were justified. The salvation spoken of here must therefore be salvation from the power of sin in this present life, salvation from the onslaughts of Satan. As to the expression, "the sword of the Spirit," Vincent says: "The word of God serves both for attack and to parry the thrusts of the enemy. Thus Christ used it in His temptation. It is the sword *of the Spirit* because the Spirit of God gives it and inspires it. The Spirit's aid is needed for its interpretation."

Translation. *Stand therefore, having girded your loins in the sphere of truth, and having clothed yourself with the breastplate of righteousness, and having sandalled your feet with a firm foundation of the glad tidings of peace; in addition to all these, taking to yourselves the shield of faith by means of which you will be able to quench all the fiery arrows of the pernicious one, and take the helmet of salvation, and the sword of the Spirit which is the Word of God.*

(6:18) "Always" is *en panti kairōi*, "on every occasion"; the Revision gives, "at all seasons," praying at all seasons with every *proseuchē* (prayer in general) and *deēseōs* (special supplication) in the sphere of the Spirit (that is, directed and empowered by the Spirit). Expositors says: "This great requirement of standing ready for the combat can be made good only when prayer, constant, earnest, spiritual prayer is added to the careful equipment with all the parts of the panoply." "Watching" is *agrupneō*, "to be sleepless, keep awake." It means "to be attentive, vigilent." It is the opposite of listlessness, expressing alertness. "Perseverance" is *proskartereō*, "to give constant attention to a thing, to give unremitting care to a thing."

Translation. *Through the instrumentality of every prayer and supplication for need, praying at all seasons by means of the Spirit, and maintaining a constant alertness in the same with every kind of unremitting care and supplication for all the saints.*

(6:19, 20) "Utterance" is *logos*, "a word." Paul asks that the Ephesian saints pray that God would give him a gift of utterance "in the opening of his mouth," that is, when he opens his mouth to speak. This utterance, this speech, Paul desires should be in boldness. "Boldness" is *parrēsia*, literally, "all speech." The word means "fearless, confident freedom in speaking."

Translation. *And on behalf of me, in order that there might be given me utterance in the opening of my mouth, in every fearless, confident freedom of speaking, to make known the mystery of the glad tidings, on behalf of which I am an ambassador in a chain, in order that in it I may speak with every fearless and confident freedom as it is necessary in the nature of the case for me to speak.*

(6:21-24) *But in order that you also might come to know my circumstances, what I am doing, all things to you Tychicus, the beloved brother and faithful ministering servant in the Lord, will make known, whom I sent to you for this same purpose, in order that you might come to know our circumstances and in order that he might comfort your hearts. Peace to the brethren and love with faith from God the Father and the Lord Jesus Christ. The grace be with all those who are loving our Lord Jesus Christ in sincerity.*

THE
EXPANDED TRANSLATION
OF
EPHESIANS

Read this through at a single sitting. In that way you will grasp the grand sweep of this wonderful letter. What you read will be that which the Ephesian saints read in all the richness of the Greek text.

THE EXPANDED TRANSLATION

OF

EPHESIANS

Translator's Note

The author has divided Paul's letters into paragraph divisions in order that the Bible student may be able to read them with more ease and facility. The great uncial manuscripts such as the Vaticanus and Sinaiticus (A.D. 350 and 375), consist of lines of Greek capital letters with no space between the letters or sentences, no punctuation, no accents or breathing marks. Manuscripts such as these were written on vellum, made from the skins of antelopes, specially prepared for this purpose. The Alexandrinus, another of the uncials, used the skins of 410 animals. The cost of hunting these animals and preparing the skins for manuscript purposes, made these early copies of the New Testament very expensive. One can readily see the reason for the crowding of the words and the lack of paragraph divisions to indicate the units of thought. For the same reason we can safely assume that the original manuscripts which left the hands of the inspired writers were written in the same form.

This necessity of crowding as much written material as possible into the least amount of space was a blessing in disguise, for it eliminated such a thing as chapter and verse divisions, which latter are a most convenient way of locating scripture portions, but which, on the other hand, militate against the proper method of scientific exegesis, and which if followed, often cut the trend of thought in two, and isolate things that should be construed together. This book provides the student with the opportunity of reading these letters as they should be read, and as they were read in the local church to which they were addressed.

The Expanded Translation:

Paul, an ambassador of Christ Jesus through the will of God, to the saints, the ones who are (in Ephesus), even believing ones in Christ Jesus. Grace to you and peace from God our Father and the Lord Jesus Christ.

May the God and Father of our Lord Jesus Christ be eulogized, the One who conferred benefactions upon us in the sphere of every spiritual blessing in the heavenly places in Christ, even as He selected us out for Himself in Him before the foundations of the universe were laid, to be holy ones and without blemish before His searching, penetrating gaze; in love having previously marked us out with the result that He placed us as adult sons through the intermediate agency of Jesus Christ for Himself according to that which seemed good in His heart's desire, resulting in praise of the glory of His grace which He freely bestowed upon us in the Beloved, in whom we are having our redemption through His blood, the putting away of our trespasses according to the wealth of His grace which He caused to superabound to us in the sphere of every wisdom and understanding, having made known to us the mystery of His will according to that which seemed good to Him, which good thing He purposed in Himself, with respect to an administration of the completion of the seasons, to bring back again to their original state the all things in the Christ, the things in the heavens and the things on the earth, in Him, in whom also we were made an inheritance, having been previously marked out according to the purpose of the One who operates the all things according to the counsel of His will, resulting in our being to the praise of His glory who had previously placed our hope in the Christ, in whom also, as for you, having heard the word of the truth, the good news of your salvation, in whom also having believed, you were sealed with the Spirit of the promise, the Holy (Spirit), who is the earnest of our inheritance guaranteeing the full payment of all to the redemption of the possession which is being preserved, with a view to the praise of His glory.

On account of this, I also, having heard of the faith in the Lord Jesus which is among you, and of your love to all the saints, do not cease giving thanks for you as I constantly make mention of you in my prayers, that the God and Father of our Lord Jesus Christ, the Father of the glory, might give to you a spirit of wisdom and revelation in the sphere of a full knowledge of Him, the eyes of your heart being in an enlightened state with a view to your knowing what is the hope of His calling, what is the wealth of the glory of His inheritance in the saints, and what is the superabounding greatness of His inherent power to us who are believing ones as measured by the operative energy of the manifested strength of His might, which (might) was operative in the Christ when He raised Him out from among the dead and seated Him at His right hand in the heavenly places, over above every government and authority and power and lordship and every name that is constantly being named not only in this age but also in the one about to come. And all things He put in subjection under His feet, and Him He gave as Head over all things to the Church, which is of such a nature as to be His body, the fulness of the One who constantly is filling the all things with all things.

And you being dead with reference to your trespasses and sins, He made alive; in the sphere of which (trespasses and sins) at one time you ordered your behavior as dominated by the age-spirit of this world system, as dominated by the leader of the authority of the lower atmosphere, (the leader also) of the spirit that is now operating in the sons of the impersuasableness, among whom also we all ordered our behavior in the sphere of the cravings of our flesh, continually practicing the desires of our flesh and of our thoughts, and were continually children of wrath by nature, as also the rest. But God, being wealthy in the sphere of mercy, because of His great love with which He loved us, and we being dead with respect to our trespasses, made us alive together with the Christ, by grace have

you been saved completely in past time, with the present result
that you are in a state of salvation which persists through present time, and raised us with Him and seated us with Him in the
heavenly places in Christ Jesus, in order that He might exhibit
for His own interest (glory) in the ages that will pile themselves upon one another in continuous succession, the surpassing
wealth of His grace in kindness to us in Christ Jesus. For by
the grace have you been saved in time past completely, through
faith, with the result that your salvation persists through present
time; and this (salvation) is not from you as a source. Of God
it is the gift; not from a source of works, in order that no one
might boast; for we are His handiwork, created in Christ Jesus
with a view to good works which God prepared beforehand in
order that within their sphere we may order our behavior.

On this account be remembering that at one time, you, the
Gentiles in the flesh, the ones habitually called uncircumcision by
that which is called circumcision in the flesh made by hand, that
you were at that time without Christ, alienated from the commonwealth of Israel and strangers from the covenants of the promise,
not having hope and without God in the world. But now in Christ
Jesus you who at one time were far off, have become near by the
blood of the Christ. For He Himself is our peace, the One who
made the both one, having broken down the middle wall of the
partition, the enmity, in His flesh having rendered inoperative
the law of the commandments in ordinances, in order that the
two He might create in Himself, resulting in one new man, making peace, and in order that He might reconcile the both in one
body to God through the Cross, having put to death the enmity by
it, and having come, He proclaimed glad tidings of peace to
you who were far off, and to you who were near, because through
Him we have our entree, the both of us, by one Spirit into the
presence of the Father.

Now then, no longer are you aliens and foreign sojourners,
but you are fellow-citizens of the saints and householders of
God, having been built up upon the foundation of the apostles
and prophets, there being a chief corner stone, Jesus Christ

Himself, in whom the whole building closely joined together, grows into a holy inner sanctuary in the Lord, in whom also you are being built together into a permanent dwelling place of God by the Spirit.

On this account I, Paul, the prisoner of the Messiah, Jesus, on behalf of you, the Gentiles, assuming that you heard of the administration of the grace of God which was given to me for you, that by revelation there was made known to me the mystery even as I wrote above in brief, in accordance with which you are able when you read to understand my insight into the mystery of the Christ which in other and different generations was not made known to the sons of men as now it has been revealed to His holy apostles and prophets by the Spirit, that the Gentiles are fellow-heirs, and belong jointly to the same body, and are fellow-partakers of His promise in the glad tidings, of which I became one who ministers according to the gift of the grace of God which (grace) was given to me according to the operative energy of His power.

To me, the one who is less than the least of all saints there was given this grace, to the Gentiles to proclaim the glad tidings of the wealth belonging to the Christ, and to bring to light what is the administration of the mystery which has been kept covered up from the beginning of the ages in the God who created the all things, in order that there might be made known now to the principalities and powers in the heavenly places, through the intermediate agency of the Church, the much-variegated wisdom of God, according to the eternal purpose which He carried into effect in the Christ, Jesus our Lord, in whom we are having our freedom of speech and entree in perfect confidence through faith in Him.

Wherefore, I am asking in my own interest, that you do not lose heart by reason of my tribulations on your behalf which are of such a nature as to be your glory. On this account I bow my knees to the Father from whom every family in heaven and on earth is named, that He would grant to you according to the wealth of His glory, with power to be strengthened through the

*Spirit into the inward man, that the Christ might finally settle
down and feel completely at home in your hearts through the
faith, in love having been firmly rooted and grounded in order
that you may be able to grasp with all the saints what is the
breadth and width and height and depth, and to know experientially the experiential-knowledge-surpassing love of the Christ
in order that you may be filled up to the measure of all the
fulness of God.*

*Now to the One who is able to do beyond all things, super-
abundantly beyond and over and above those things that we are
asking for ourselves and considering, in the measure of the power
which is operative in us, to Him be the glory in the Church and
in Christ Jesus into all the generations of the Age of the Ages.
Amen.*

*I beg of you, please, therefore, I, the prisoner in the Lord,
order your behavior in a manner worthy of the summons with
which you were called, with every lowliness and meekness, with
longsuffering, bearing with one another in love, doing your best
to safeguard the unanimity of the Spirit in the bond of peace.
One body and one Spirit, even as also you were called in one
hope of your calling, one Lord, one faith, one placing into, one
God and Father of all, the One above all and through all, and
in all.*

*But to each one of us there was given the grace in the measure
of the gift of the Christ. Wherefore He says, Having ascended
on high, He led away captive those taken captive, and gave gifts
to men. Now, the fact that He ascended, what is it except that
also He descended into the nether parts of the earth. The One
who descended, Himself is also the One who ascended above all
the heavens, in order that He might fill all things. And He
Himself gave some, on the one hand, as apostles, and on the
other hand, as prophets, and still again some as bringers of good
news, and finally, some as pastors who are also teachers, for
the equipping of the saints for ministering work, with a view to
the building up of the Body of Christ, until we all attain to the
unity of the faith and of the experiential, full, and precise knowl-*

*edge of the Son of God, to a mature man, to the measure of the
stature of the fulness of the Christ, in order that no longer we
may be immature ones, tossed to and fro and carried around in
circles by every wind of teaching in the cunning adroitness of
men, in craftiness which furthers the scheming deceitful art of
error, but speaking the truth in love, may grow up into Him in
all things, who is the Head, Christ, from whom all the body
constantly being joined closely together and constantly being
knit together through every joint of supply according to the
operative energy put forth to the capacity of each part, makes
for increased growth of the Body resulting in the building up
of itself in the sphere of love.*

*This, therefore, I am saying and solemnly declaring in the
Lord, that no longer are you to order your behavior as the
Gentiles order their behavior in the futility of their mind, being
those who have had their understanding darkened, who have
been alienated from the life of God through the ignorance which
is in them, through the hardening of their hearts, who, being
of such a nature as to have become callous, abandoned themselves
to wantonness, resulting in a performing of every uncleanness in
the sphere of greediness.*

*But as for you, not in this manner did you learn Christ, since
indeed, as is the case, you heard, and in Him were taught just
as truth is in Jesus, that you have put off once for all with reference to your former manner of life the old man which is being
corrupted according to the passionate desires of deceit; moreover
that you are being constantly renewed with reference to the
spirit of your mind; and that you have put on once for all the
new man which after God was created in righteousness and holiness of truth.*

*Wherefore, having put off the lie once for all, be speaking
truth each with his neighbor, because we are members belonging
to one another. Be constantly angry with a righteous indignation,
and stop sinning. Do not allow the sun to go down upon your
irritated, exasperated, embittered anger. And stop giving an
occasion for acting (opportunity) to the devil. The one who*

is stealing, let him no longer be stealing, but rather let him be
laboring, working with his own hands that which is good, in
order that he may be having wherewith to be sharing with the
one who is having need.   Every word that is rotten and unfit
for use, out of your mouth let it not be proceeding, but whatever is good, suitable for edification with respect to the need,
in order that it may impart grace to the hearers.   And stop
grieving the Spirit, the Holy Spirit of God, in whom you were
sealed with a view to the day of redemption.   All manner of
harshness and violent outbreaks of wrath and anger and brawling and slanderous speech, let it be put away from you together
with all manner of malice.   And be becoming kind to one another,
tenderhearted, forgiving each other even as and just as also God
in Christ forgave you.

Be becoming therefore imitators of God, as children beloved,
and be ordering your behavior within the sphere of love, even
as Christ also gave Himself up in our behalf and in our stead
as an offering and a sacrifice to God for an odor of a sweet smell.
But fornication and uncleanness, every kind of it, or covetousness,
let it not be even named among you, just as it is befitting to
saints; and obscenity and foolish talking or ribaldry, which things
have not been seemly or fitting, but rather giving of thanks, for
this you know absolutely and experientially, that every whoremonger or unclean person or covetous person who is an idolator,
does not have an inheritance in the kingdom of the Christ and
of God.   Let no one keep on deceiving you by means of empty
words, for because of these things there comes the wrath of God
upon the sons of the disobedience.

Stop therefore becoming joint-participants with them; for you
were at one time darkness, but now light in the Lord.   As children of light be habitually conducting yourselves; for the fruit
of this light is in the sphere of every beneficence and righteousness and truth, putting to the test and then approving what is
well-pleasing to the Lord.   And stop having fellowship with the
unfruitful works of this darkness, but rather be rebuking them

so as to bring out confession and conviction, for concerning the
things done in secret by them, it is shameful to be speaking.

But all the aforementioned things when they are reproved by
the light are made visibly plain, for everything that is being
made plain is light. Wherefore He says: Be waking up, the one
who is sleeping, and arise from the dead, and there shall shine
upon you, Christ. Be constantly taking heed therefore how accurately you are conducting yourselves, not as unwise ones but
as wise ones, buying up for yourselves the opportune time, because the days are pernicious. On this account stop becoming
those who are without reflection or intelligence, but be understanding what the will of the Lord is. And stop being intoxicated
with wine, in which (state of intoxication) there is profligacy.
But be constantly filled (controlled) by the Spirit, speaking to
one another in psalms and hymns and spiritual songs, singing
and making melody in your hearts to the Lord, giving thanks
always concerning all things in the name of our Lord Jesus Christ
to God, even the Father, putting yourselves in subjection to one
another in the fear of Christ.

The wives, be putting yourselves in subjection to your own
husbands as to the Lord, because the man is head of the wife
as the Christ is Head of the Church, He Himself being the
Saviour of the body. Nevertheless, as the Church subjects itself to the Christ, in this manner also the wives should subject
themselves to their husbands in all things. The husbands, be
loving your wives in the manner in which Christ also loved the
Church and gave Himself on behalf of it, in order that He might
sanctify it, cleansing it by the bath of water in the sphere of the
Word, in order that He might Himself present to Himself the
Church glorious, not having spot nor wrinkle nor any of such
things, but in order that it might be holy and unblamable. In
this manner ought also the husbands to love their wives as their
own bodies. The one who loves his own wife loves himself, for
no one ever yet hated his own flesh, but nourishes and cherishes
it, even as the Christ, the Church, because members are we of
His body. Because of this a man shall leave behind his father

*and his mother and shall be joined to his wife, and the two shall
become one flesh. This mystery is great. However, I am speaking with regard to Christ and the Church. Nevertheless also
as for you, let each one in this manner be loving his own wife as
himself, and the wife, let her be continually treating her husband
with deference and reverential obedience.*

*The children, be always obedient to your parents in the Lord,
for this is a righteous thing. Be always honoring your father
and your mother, which is a commandment of such a nature as
to be the first commandment with promise, in order that it may
be well with you, and in order that you may be long-lived upon
the earth. And the fathers, stop provoking your children to
anger, but be rearing them in the discipline and admonition of
the Lord. The slaves, be constantly obedient to those who according to the flesh are your masters, with fear and trembling,
in singleness of your heart as to the Christ, not in the way of
eyeservice as menpleasers, but as Christ's bond-slaves, doing the
will of God from the soul, with good will rendering a slave's
service as to the Lord and not as to men, knowing that each one,
whatever good he may do, this he will receive from the presence
of the Lord, whether he is a slave or whether he is free. And
the masters, be practicing the same things toward them, giving
up your threatening, knowing that also their Master and yours
is in heaven, and there is not partiality with Him.*

*Finally, be constantly strengthened in the Lord and in the
active efficacy of the might that is inherent in Him. Clothe yourselves with the full armor of God to the end that you will be able
to hold your ground against the strategems of the devil, because
our wrestling is not against blood and flesh, but against the
principalities, against the authorities, against the world-rulers of
this darkness, against spirit-forces of perniciousness in the
heavenly places. On this account, take to yourself at once and
once for all, the complete armor of God in order that you may
be able to resist in the day, the pernicious one, and having
achieved all things, to stand. Stand therefore, having girded your
loins in the sphere of truth, and having clothed yourself with*

*the breastplate of righteousness, and having sandalled your feet
with a firm foundation of the glad tidings of peace; in addition
to all these, taking to yourselves the shield of faith by means of
which you will be able to quench all the fiery arrows of the pernicious one, and take the helmet of salvation, and the sword of
the Spirit which is the Word of God; through the instrumentality
of every prayer and supplication for need, praying at all seasons
by means of the Spirit, and maintaining a constant alertness in
the same with every kind of unremitting care and supplication for
all the saints, and on behalf of me, in order that there might be
given me utterance in the opening of my mouth, in every fearless,
confident freedom of speaking, to make known the mystery of
the glad tidings, on behalf of which I am an ambassador in a
chain, in order that in it I may speak with every fearless and
confident freedom as it is necessary in the nature of the case for
me to speak.*

*But in order that you also might come to know my circum-
stances, what I am doing, all things to you, Tychicus, the beloved
brother and faithful ministering servant in the Lord, will make
known, whom I sent to you for this same purpose, in order that
you might come to know our circumstances and in order that he
might comfort your hearts. Peace to the brethren and love with
faith from God the Father and the Lord Jesus Christ. The
grace be with all those who are loving our Lord Jesus Christ in
sincerity.*

THE
COLOSSIAN
HERESY

THE COLOSSIAN HERESY

Bishop J. B. Lightfoot says of the Epistle to the Colossians, "The doctrine of the Person of Christ is here stated with greater precision and fulness than in any other of St. Paul's epistles." The reason for this is that the Colossian heresy in its attack upon the Person of the Lord Jesus, made it imperative that the great Apostle meet it with such precision and fulness in doctrine regarding His Person as would successfully cope with the false teachings of this system. In order to understand the full implications of the truth in Colossians, the student must first acquaint himself with this heresy.

Internal evidence in the letter indicates that the heresy with which Paul is dealing, contains two elements that are fused into one system. His mention of the observance of sabbaths and new moons, his distinction between meats and drinks, and his reference to circumcision, all point to an element of Judaism in this system. His reference to a self-imposed humility and service of angels, the hard treatment of the body, and a superior wisdom, indicates that he is dealing with a Gnostic element. The word "Gnostic" comes from the Greek *gnōsis* which means "knowledge." It is the name designating an intellectual oligarchy, a few who set themselves above all others as possessing a superior knowledge.

We will look at *Gnosticism.* This school of thought was concerned with two questions: *first,* How can the work of creation be explained? and, *second,* How are we to account for the existence of evil? These two questions posed the following problem, namely, How can one reconcile the creation of the world and the existence of evil with the conception of God as the absolute Being? In other words, How explain the fact of a holy God as Creator, and a universe in which there is sin? The

Gnostic argued as follows: If God had created the universe out
of nothing, and evolved it directly from Himself, then God being holy, could not have brought an evil universe into existence.
Otherwise, one is driven to the inescapable conclusion that God
created evil, which is impossible, since He is holy.

But the fact of a holy God and an evil universe still remained,
and the Gnostic must explain. He does so by putting forth the
theory of some antagonistic principle, independent of God, by
which His creative energy was thwarted and limited. This opposing principle of evil he thought of as the world of matter.
Thus, evil is seen by him to be residing in the material universe.
The Gnostic then asks the questions, How then is creation possible? How can the Infinite communicate with the finite, the
good with the evil? How can God act on matter? God, he says,
is perfect, absolute, incomprehensible.

The Gnostic answers his own question by saying that the
difficulty is solved by the theory that God must have limited
Himself in some way in the act of creation. There must have
been some evolution, some effluence from God. There was a
germination of God. This first germination evolved a second,
and so the process went on. The more numerous the emanations, the farther away from Deity they became, and as a result
the divine element in them became more feeble, until it became
so diffused that contact with matter was possible, and creation
took place. Thus, the gap between a holy creator God and
matter which, according to the Gnostic is evil, is bridged by these
emanations from God that are so far removed from a Deity who
is holy, that matter could be created which is inherently evil,
and this act of creation could not be attributed to a holy God.
In this way, the Gnostic brushes aside the intermediate agent
in creation, the Lord Jesus (John 1:3), and the fact that God
put a curse upon the perfect creation because of sin (Rom. 8:20).
Paul says in the latter text that the creation was made subject
to futility (vanity *mataios*). That is, God rendered it relatively
futile so far as glorifying Him was concerned.

From these philosophical speculations, two opposing codes of ethics emerged, a rigid asceticism and an unrestrained license. The problem confronting the Gnostic was as follows: Since matter is evil, how can one avoid its baneful influence and thus keep his higher nature unsullied?

The answer, according to one group, was a rigid asceticism. All contact with matter should be reduced to a minimum. Thus, the material part of man would be subdued and mortified. One should live on a spare diet and abstain from marriage. The edible flesh of animals was forbidden. The anointing of the body with olive oil, so necessary in hot climates, was prohibited.

But with others, such a negative course of procedure produced but slight and inadequate results. These argued that matter is everywhere. One cannot escape contact with it. Therefore, one should cultivate an entire indifference to the world of sense. One should not give matter any thought one way or the other, but just follow one's own impulses. How like the behavioristic psychology of today. This group argued that the ascetic principle gives a certain importance to matter, and thus he fails to assert his own independence to it. The true rule of life is to treat matter as foreign or alien to one, and as something towards which one has no duties or obligations, and which one can use or leave unused as one likes. This philosophy led to unbridled license.

Gnosticism as described above, had no connection with Christianity in itself. That which channeled it into the thinking of the professing Christian Church was a sect of Jews who were called Essenes. The Essene was a mystic, and a member of a brotherhood. The characteristic feature of Essenism was mystic speculation involving a rigid asceticism.

However, the Essene also included in his system, a rigorous observance of the Mosaic ritual. In his strict abstinence from work on the Sabbath, he far surpassed other Jews. He would not light a fire or move a vessel. He would not perform the most ordinary functions of life. His whole day was given over to religious exercises and the exposition of the Scriptures. After

God, the name of Moses was held in the highest reverence. The one who blasphemed the name of Moses, was punished by death.

But the Essenes went beyond the Mosaic legislation. Marriage to them was an abomination. To secure the continuance of the order, they adopted children. Some accepted marriage as necessary for the preservation of the race, but nevertheless regarded it as an evil. The Essenes drank no wine, nor did they eat animal food. They lived on bread and vegetables. They refused to anoint their bodies with olive oil, which in hot countries is almost necessary to life. They condemned in any form the natural cravings, and sought to disengage themselves from all conditions of physical life. In addition to these practices, the Essenes were sun-worshippers. At day-break they would address certain prayers to the sun as if entreating it to rise. They would bury all polluting substances so as not to insult the rays of the god.

The Essenes did not believe in the resurrection of the body, but confined themselves to a belief in the countinuance of the soul-life after death. This is, of course, in line with their belief that matter is evil. They maintained that the soul was confined in the body as a prisoner in jail, and that only after death, would it be free by reason of its escape from the body. They rejected the blood sacrifices of Judaism, and instead sent bloodless offerings to the Temple as gifts. They placed angels in the category of beings that should be worshipped. Like the Gnostics who prided themselves upon the exclusive possession of religious secrets, the Essenes had their secret doctrines which were the possession of an exclusive few, and these they refused to divulge except to initiates to their order.

These false doctrines and practices had crept in to the local church at Colossae. Paul's letter to this church was designed to combat them. One of these errors was an intellectual oligarchy in religion, namely, the teaching that a select few had a monopoly in a superior wisdom. The apostle meets this by contending for the *universality* of the gospel message. But Paul, in maintaining this doctrine, has changed his mode of attack. He is not here contending against a *national exclusiveness* in religion, which was true of Pharasaic Judaism, but against the *intellectual exclusiveness* in religion of the Essenes which was even more fatal to the claims of the gospel because more specious and insidious. Paul warns *every* man and teaches *every* man in *every* wisdom, that he may present *every* man perfect in Christ Jesus. The word "perfect" was the term applied by the Gnostics to members of the exclusive group which possessed the superior wisdom.

The Gnostics made much of wisdom (*sophia*), intelligence (*sunesis*), and knowledge (*epignōsis*). Paul takes up the language of the Gnostics and translates it to the higher spheres of Christian thought. Against the false wisdom of the Gnostics, the apostle sets the true wisdom of the gospel. The initiatory rites of these Gnostics in which certain were inducted into their order, were secret mysteries. Paul sets over against these the fact that all the treasures of wisdom and knowledge are hidden in that comprehensive mystery, the knowledge of God in Christ.

Paul had also to combat the Gnostic teaching of successive emanations from deity, the angelic mediators who were responsible for the act of creation, and for the headship of the spiritual creation, which took the place of the Lord Jesus as Creator of the universe and Head of the Church. The apostle meets these false doctrines by showing that "all things were created by Him," and "He is Head of the body, the Church."

As to the teaching of the Gnostic to the effect that the divine essence is distributed among the angelic emanations from deity, Paul declares that the *plērōma,* or plenitude of the divine essence is permanently at home in the Lord Jesus. For the totality of the divine essence, the Gnostics had this word *plērōma*, "fulness" or "plenitude." Paul says that Jesus Christ is not only the chief manifestation of the divine nature. *He exhausts the God-*

head. In Him resides the totality of the divine powers and attributes. From the necessities imposed upon Paul by the character of the Gnostic heresy, it is easy to see that as Bishop Lightfoot says: "The doctrine of the Person of Christ is here stated with greater precision and fulness than in any other of St. Paul's epistles."*

---

*The author acknowledges his indebtedness to Bishop Lightfoot for the above summary of his analysis of the Gnostic heresy.

THE
EXEGESIS
OF
COLOSSIANS

CHAPTER ONE

(1:1, 2) The only difference between Paul's opening words in Ephesians and those in this letter is the inclusion of Timothy as Paul's associate in the gospel at the time of the writing, and the fact that the words, "the Lord Jesus Christ," do not appear in the Nestle or the Westcott and Hort texts. For studies on the other words, please see notes on Ephesians 1:1, 2. Lightfoot, commenting on the words "faithful brethren in Christ," says: "This unusual addition is full of meaning. Some members of the Colossian church were shaken in their allegiance, even if they had not fallen from it. The Apostle therefore wishes to be understood that, when he speaks of the saints, he means the true and steadfast members of the brotherhood. In this way he obliquely hints at the defection. Thus, the words 'and faithful brethren' are a supplementary explanation of 'to the saints.' He does not directly exclude any, but he indirectly warns all. The epithet 'faithful' cannot mean simply 'believing'; for then it would add nothing which is not already contained in 'saints' and 'brethren.' Its passive sense, 'trustworthy, steadfast, unswerving' must be prominent here."

Translation. *Paul, an ambassador of Christ Jesus through the will of God, and Timothy our brother, to the saints in Colossae, even faithful brethren in Christ. Grace to you and peace from God our Father.*

(1:3-8) Lightfoot, Vincent, and Expositors concur in the opinion that "always" is to be construed with "give thanks" rather than "praying." The translation therefore reads, "giving thanks always to God the Father of our Lord Jesus Christ." The word "and" is not in the Greek text. The preposition "for" in "praying for you" is *peri*, "concerning." It was concerning the needs and the circumstances of the Colossian saints that

171

Paul was praying. The word "praying" is *proseuchomai* which speaks of prayer to God. It is never used of petitions to man. The prefixed preposition *pros* gives it the idea of definiteness and directness in prayer, with the consciousness on the part of the one praying that he is talking face to face with God.

Paul in verse four indicates what is the ground of his thanksgiving, namely, the Colossian's faith in the Lord Jesus and their love to all the saints. The preposition *eis* (to) is a preposition of motion. It is used in John 3:16, for instance, where the evangelist speaks of the initial act of faith which the sinner exercises in the Lord Jesus. It is literally, "believes into Him." The preposition used here (1:4) is *en,* a preposition of rest. Having placed our faith in the Lord Jesus as our Saviour, it now rests in Him. Lightfoot says that the preposition here "denotes the sphere in which their faith moves, rather than the object to which it is directed." The particular love which the Colossian saints had for all the saints was that *agapē* love which is produced in the heart of the yielded saint by the Holy Spirit, a love which impels one to sacrifice one's self for the object or person loved. The preposition "to" is not *pros,* "to, towards," but *eis,* "into," showing that the Colossian's love reached into the very hearts of the other saints.

The A.V., connects "We give thanks" with "for the hope," but Expositors, Vincent, and Lightfoot demur, saying that it is to be construed with the words, "your faith, etc.," saying that the words "for the hope" are too far removed from "We give thanks" to be taken with the latter words. Vincent says, "Faith works by love, and the ground of their love is found in the hope set before them. The motive is subordinate, but legitimate. 'The hope laid up in heaven is not the deepest reason or motive for faith and love, but both are made more vivid when it is strong. It is not the light at which their lamps are lit, but it is the odorous oil which feeds their flame' (Maclaren)." As to "hope," Vincent says; "In the N.T., the word signifies both the sentiment of hope and the thing hoped for. Here the latter. Lightfoot observes that the sentiment oscillates between the subjective feeling and the objective realization.   The translation reads; "having heard of your faith in Christ Jesus and the love which you are having to all the saints on account of the hope." That is, this hope of reward has been an incentive to the Colossians in their faith in the Lord Jesus and their love to the saints, encouraging both and causing both to make progress and grow more intense.   The preposition "for" is *dia*, which is a preposition of intermediate agency.   This shows clearly that the hope is an active thing, working in the saints, energizing that faith and love to a greater intensity.

Paul speaks of this hope "which is laid up for you in heaven." "Laid up" is the perfect participle of *apokeimai*, made up of *keimai*, "to lie," as in the sentence, "The book lies on the table," speaking of its position, and *apo*, "off, away from."   Thus, the compound verb means "to be laid away, to be reserved, put to one side," metaphorically, "to be reserved for one, awaiting him," used with the dative of the person involved.   The perfect participle gives, "the hope which has been laid away in times past with the present result that it is reserved for and awaiting you."   Lightfoot translates, "which is stored up."   Vincent quotes Bishop Wilson, "Deposited, reserved, put by in store out of reach of all enemies and sorrows."   This hope is laid up in heaven, all of which means that the saints will enjoy it in the future life.   There are treasures in heaven earned by the saints while on earth (Matt. 6:20), our citizenship is in heaven (Phil. 3:20), and we have an inheritance reserved for us in heaven (I Pet. 1:4).

Concerning the words, "whereof ye heard before in the word of the gospel," Lightfoot says: "seems intended to contrast their earlier with their later lessons — the true gospel of Epaphras with the false gospel of their recent teachers."   Epaphras was the saint who brought the gospel to Colossae, having heard it from the great apostle himself.

In verse 6, Paul further defines the gospel so as to identify it and differentiate it from the false message of the Gnostics.   He says, "which is come unto you."   The Greek idea is, "which is

being alongside you." Lightfoot translates, "which reached you."
The idea is that the gospel has snuggled close up to the Colossian
saints and they have taken it into their hearts. But not only
does that identify it from the Gnostic message, but the gospel
Paul gave them is making progress all over the world in that
it is constantly bearing fruit and increasing even as it has been
doing among the Colossians from the day in which they heard it
and came to know the grace of God in the sphere of truth. The
words, "in all the world," are "hyperbolical, possibly with a suggestion of the universal character of the gospel as contrasted with
the local and special character of false gospels" (Vincent). The
participles "bearing fruit" and "increasing" are in the middle
voice. Lightfoot comments; "The middle denotes the inherent
energy. The gospel is essentially a reproductive organism, a
plant whose 'seed is in itself' . . . . The gospel is not like those
plants which exhaust themselves bearing fruit and wither away
The external growth keeps pace with the reproductive energy.
While 'bearing fruit' describes the inner working, 'increasing'
gives the outward extension of the gospel." The expression,
"the grace of God in truth," means "the grace of God in its
genuine simplicity, without adulteration" (Lightfoot). But
Paul identifies the true gospel again by saying that it was the
message which they heard from Epaphras whom he calls "the
beloved" and "his fellow-bondslave," also the minister (*diakonos*
servant) to the Colossians; the one who ministered the Word of
God to them, the one who declared to Paul the Colossians' love
in the sphere of the Spirit. The word "love" here is again,
agapē, that supernatural love which God is and which God the
Holy Spirit produces in the heart of the yielded saint.

Translation. *I am giving thanks to God the Father of our
Lord Jesus Christ, concerning you constantly offering petitions,
having heard of your faith in Christ Jesus and of the love which
you constantly have to all the saints through the agency of the
hope laid aside for you in heaven, concerning which you heard
before in the word of the truth of the glad tidings which are with
you, even as also they are in all the world constantly bearing*

fruit and increasing, just as they are also among you from the day when you heard them and came to know experientially the grace of God in the sphere of truth, even as you learned from Epaphras, the beloved, our fellow-bondslave, who is faithful on your behalf as a servant of Christ, who also declared to us your love in the sphere of the Spirit.

(1:9, 10) "For this cause" is *dia touto*, "on this account, because of this," namely, the good report from Colossae as given in verses 4-8, the motive that prompted Paul to pray for these saints. "Also" indicates that they had been praying for him. "Pray" is *proseuchomai*, a general word for prayer, meaning "to offer petitions." "Desire" is *aiteō*, a specific word for prayer which signifies to ask for something to be given, not done, giving prominence to the thing asked for rather than the person. The word "desire," used in the sense of *ask,* is found in Shakespeare and Spenser, which accounts for the A.V., rendering.

"Knowledge" is *epignōsis*. The word is an advance upon *gnōsis* (knowledge) in that it denotes a larger and more thorough knowledge. It is a knowledge which grasps and penetrates into an object. It was a favorite word of the Gnostics who used it to designate the superior knowledge which they claimed as their exclusive possession. Paul prays that all the saints might become possessors of this knowledge, indicating that it was open for all to appropriate, not a secret mystery into which only a favored few could be initiated. If the Gnostics had their superior knowledge, so did the Christian Church. The former was speculative and false, the latter, positive and true. Paul prays that they not only might have it but that they might be filled with it. His petition is that the Colossian saints might be filled with a thorough knowledge of God's will. As to God's will, Expositors says, "This does not mean God's counsel of redemption, nor 'the whole counsel of God as made known to us in Christ' (Findlay), but, as the context indicates (v. 10), the moral aspect of God's will, 'His will for the conduct of our lives' (Meyer)."

This thorough, perfect knowledge of God's will should be in the sphere of "all wisdom and spiritual understanding." Again, Paul uses two Gnostic words, *sophia* (wisdom) and *sunesis* (understanding). Expositors in defining these words, says: "*sophia* is general, *sunesis*, special. *Sophia* embraces the whole range of mental faculties; *sunesis* is the special faculty of intelligence or insight which discriminates between the false and the true, and grasps the relations in which things stand to each other. The addition of *pneumatikos,* (spiritual) shows that both are to proceed from the inspiration of the Holy Spirit. They thus stand in opposition to fleshly wisdom (II Cor. 1:12), and especially, it would seem, though Haupt denies this, to the false wisdom by which the Colossians were in danger of being ensnared." The word "all," qualifying "knowledge" and "understanding," is better, "every kind of." This is another thrust on the part of Paul against the religious exclusiveness of the Gnostics.

Paul prays that the Colossian saints might be filled with the knowledge of God's will in the sphere of every kind of thorough wisdom and intelligence in order that they "might walk worthy of the Lord." "Walk" is *peripateō,* "to order one's behavior, to conduct one's self." "Worthy" is *axiōs.* When this word is used with the genitive case as it is here, it means, "having the weight of (weighing as much as) another thing." It means, "of like value, worth as much." The saints are to see to it that their manner of life, their conduct, weighs as much as the character of their Lord. That is, He is to be their example in life, and the copy must be like the example. Peter says: "Christ also suffered on your behalf, leaving behind for you a model to imitate, in order that by close application you might follow in His footprints" (I Pet. 2:21). Expositors says: "This lofty wisdom and insight is not an end in itself. It must issue in right practice. Doctrines and ethics are for Paul inseparable. Right conduct must be founded on right thinking, but right thinking must also lead to right conduct." The words "unto all pleasing" are *eis pasan areskian,* "with a view to every pleasing." Lightfoot explains, "so as to please God in all ways."

One of the activities of the saint in the sphere of a behavior which is worthy of the Lord, is fruitbearing. This fruitbearing and increasing is to be, not *in* the knowledge of God, since the latter is the motivating energy which produces the former, but *by means of* the knowledge of God. It is the instrumental case here, not the locative. Lightfoot and Expositors concur in this. Vincent gives this as the reading of the best texts.

Translation. *Because of this, we also, from the day we heard, do not cease on behalf of you offering our petitions and presenting our definite requests, that you might be filled with the advanced and perfect knowledge of His will in the sphere of every kind of wisdom and intelligence which is spiritual, so that you may order your behavior worthily of the Lord with a view to pleasing Him in everything, in every work which is good, constantly bearing fruit and increasing by means of the thorough and perfect knowledge of God.*

(1:11, 12)   In the expression "strengthened with all might," the verb is *dunamoō,* the noun, *dunamis.* The reader will observe that both words have the same stem, which means that intrinsically they have the same meaning. *Dunamis,* the noun, has the following meanings, "strength, ability, power, inherent power, power residing in a thing by virtue of its nature, power which a person or thing exerts and puts forth." The verb *dunamai* means "to be able, to have power." Thus, it is easy to see that these words speak of inherent power which gives one the ability to do something. *Dunamoō,* which is used here, means "to make strong, to strengthen." One could translate, "by every enabling power being constantly strengthened." The word "power" is *kratos,* "relative and manifested power." The Greek has it, "according to the manifested power of His glory." Lightfoot says: "The glory here, as frequently, stands for the majesty or the power or the goodness of God, as *manifested* to men. The *doxa* (glory), the bright light over the mercy-seat (Rom. 9:4), was a symbol of such manifestations. God's revelation of Himself to us, however this revelation may be made, is the one source of all our highest strength." Commenting on the words "according to" (*kata*), Expositors says: "The equipment with power is proportioned not simply to the recipient's need, but to the divine supply." This being strengthened by God results in "all patience and longsuffering with joyfulness." "Patience" is *hupomonē*, "longsuffering," *makrothumia*. Trench's note on these words is valuable: "*Makrothumia* will be found to express patience in respect of persons, *hupomonē*, in respect of things. The man *makrothumei*, who having to do with injurious persons, does not suffer himself easily to be provoked by them, or to blaze up in anger (II Tim. 4:2). The man *hupomonē*, who under a great siege of trials, bears up, and does not lose heart or courage (Rom. 5:3; II Cor. 1:6)." In another place, commenting on the word *makrothumia*, the same authority defines it as "a long holding out of the mind before it gives room to action or passion — generally to passion. 'Forbearing one another in love' (Eph. 4:2) beautifully expounds the meaning which attaches to the word. Anger usually, but not universally is the passion thus held aloof . . . Still, it is not necessarily anger which is excluded or set at a distance, for when the historian of the Maccabees describes how the Romans had won the world 'by their policy and their patience,' *makrothumia* expresses there that Roman persistency which would never make peace under defeat." Commenting upon *hupomonē*, Trench says; "It does not mark merely *endurance*, or even *patience*, but the perseverence, the *brave* patience with which the Christian contends against the various hindrances, persecutions, and temptations that befall him in his conflict with the inward and outward world." In brief, *makrothumia* is patience exhibited under ill-treatment by persons, *hupomonē*, patience shown under trials, difficulties, hardships.

This patience and longsuffering is to be accompanied with joyfulness. Expositors says; "It (joyfulness) forms a very necessary addition, for the peculiar danger of the exercise of those qualities is that it tends to produce a certain gloominess or sourness of disposition. The remedy is that the Christian should be so filled with joy that he is able to meet all his trials with a buoyant sense of mastery."

The Father to whom constant thanksgiving should be expressed is He who "hath made us meet to be partakers of the inheritance of the saints in light." "Made meet" is *hikanoō,* "to make sufficient, render fit, qualify." The standing of the believer in Christ is here in view, not his Christian character. The Father qualified believers to partake of the inheritance of the saints by placing them in Christ, in whom they enjoy a standing which makes them the objects of God's grace.

"Partakers of the inheritance" is *tēn merida tou klērou,* "the portion of the lot." The word *klēroō* means "to cast lots, to determine by lot." *Klēros* means "an object used in casting lots." The lot of the saints, namely, that which is determined upon the saints is future blessedness, not only in the future life, but also here on earth. "The path of the just is as the shining light, that shineth more and more unto the perfect day" (Prov. 4:18).

The words "in light" qualify "inheritance" not "saints." Expositors, Vincent, Alford, and Lightfoot concur on this. "The light is the region in which the inheritance of the saints, and consequently our share in it, is situated" (Alford). Vincent says: "The inheritance which is in light. This need not be limited to future glory. The children of God walk in light on earth. See I John 1:7, 2:10."

Translation. *By every enabling power being constantly strengthened in proportion to the manifested power of His glory resulting in every patience and forbearance with joy, constantly giving thanks to the Father who qualified you for the portion of the lot of the saints in the light.*

(1:13) "Delivered" is *ruomai,* "to draw to one's self, to rescue, to deliver." Lightfoot says; *"rescued, delivered us* by His strong arm, as a mighty conqueror." "Power" is *exousia.* Lightfoot defines and describes this word as follows: "Here, arbitrary power, tyranny. The word *exousia* properly signifies liberty of action, and thus, like the corresponding English word *license,* involves secondary ideas, of which either may be so prominent as to eclipse the other; (1) authority, *delegated* power (Luke 22:2), or (2) tyranny, lawlessness, *unrestrained* or arbitrary power . . . This latter idea of a capricious unruly rule is prominent here. The expression 'the power of darkness' occurs also in Luke 22:53, where again the idea of disorder is involved. The transference from darkness to light is here represented as a transference from an arbitrary tyranny, an *exousia,* to a well-ordered sovereignty, a kingdom." The phrase refers to the tyrannical rule of Satan and his demons over the unsaved.

"Translated" is *methistēmi,* "to transpose, transfer, remove from one place to another," thus, speaks of a change of situation or place. Lightfoot translates, "removed," and says, "the image of *methistēmi* is supplied by the wholesale transportation of peoples, of which the history of oriental monarchies supplied so many examples."

The Greek has it, "unto the kingdom of the Son of His love." Vincent says; "The Son who is the object of His love, and to whom, therefore, the kingdom is given. See Psalm 2:7, 8; Heb. 1:3-9. It is true that love is the essence of the Son as of the Father; also, that the Son's mission is the revelation of the Father's love; but, as Meyer correctly says, 'the language refers to the exalted Christ who rules.'" Lightfoot, commenting on the word "Son" says, "Not of inferior angels, as the false teachers would have it (2:18), but of His own Son. The same contrast between a dispensation of angels and a dispensation of the Son underlies the words here, which is explicitly brought out in Hebrews 1:1-8."

Translation. *Who delivered us out of the tyrannical rule of the darkness and transferred us into the kingdom of the Son of His love.*

(1:14) "Redemption" is *apolutrōsis,* "a releasing effected by payment of ransom, liberation procured by the payment of ransom." Paul continues the image of an enslaved people. He defines this liberation on payment of ransom as a forgiveness. The

word is *aphesis,* "release as from bondage or imprisonment."
This word in turn comes from *aphiēmi,* "to send from one's self,
to send away, to bid go away or depart." It speaks of the act of
God at Calvary, paying the penalty of human sin, thus satisfying
the just demands of His holy law, putting away sin, bidding it
go away. This was symbolized in the O.T., by the goat, laden
with the sins of Israel, being led away into the wilderness and
lost. Israel never saw that goat again, and thus never saw its
sins again.

Vincent says, "Lightfoot's suggestion is very interesting that
this precise definition may convey an allusion to the perversion
of the term *apolutrōsis* by the Gnostics of a later age, and which
was possibly foreshadowed in the teaching of the Colossian
heretics. The Gnostic used it to signify the result of initiation
into certain mysteries. . . . The idea of a redemption of the
world, and (in a perverted form) of the person and work of
Christ as having part in it, distinctively marked the Gnostic
schools. That from which the world was redeemed, however,
was not sin in the proper sense of the term, but something inherent in the constitution of the world itself, and therefore due
to its Creator."

Translation. *In whom we are having our liberation, procured
by the payment of ransom, the putting away of our sins.*

(1:15) We now come to a very important section of Colossians, and one in which Paul comes to grips with the Gnostic
teaching. Lightfoot says, "In the passage which follows, Paul
defines the Person of Christ, claiming for Him the absolute
supremacy, (1) in relation to the *universe,* the *natural* creation
(vv. 15-17); (2) in relation to the *Church,* the new *moral*
creation (v. 18); and he then combines the two, 'in order that
in all things, He might have the preeminence,' explaining this
twofold sovereignty by the absolute indwelling of the *plērōma*
(fullness) in Christ, and showing how, as a consequence, the
reconciliation and harmony of all things must be effected in Him
(vv. 19, 20). As the idea of the Logos (Word) underlies the
whole passage, though the term does not appear, a few words

explanatory of this term will be necessary by way of preface. The word *logos* then, denoting both 'reason' and 'speech,' was a philosophical term adopted by Alexandrian Judaism before Paul wrote, to express the *manifestation* of the unseen God, the Absolute Being, in the creation and government of the world. It includes all modes by which God makes Himself known to man. As His *reason,* it denoted His purpose or design; as His *speech,* it implied His revelation. . . . Christian teachers, when they adopted this term, exalted and fixed its meaning by attaching to it two precise and definite ideas: (1) The Word is a divine Person (John 1:1), and (2) The Word became flesh (John 1:14)."

Now, for an exposition of the phrase, "Who is the image of the invisible God." Lightfoot says; "The Person of Christ is described *first* in relation more especially to Deity, and *secondly,* in relation more especially to created things. The fundamental conception of the *Logos* involves the idea of mediation between God and creation. A perverted view respecting the nature of the mediation between the two lay at the root of the heretical teaching at Colossae, and required to be met by the true doctrine of Christ as the Eternal Logos."

"Image" is *eikōn.* The word means "a likeness," and this idea involves two other ideas. One is that of *representation.* Lightfoot says; "In this respect it is allied to *charaktēr,* 'a mark or figure burned or stamped on, an impression, a precise reproduction in every respect,' and differs from *homoiōma,* 'a likeness.' In *homoiōma* the resemblance may be accidental, as one egg is like another, but *eikōn* implies an archetype of which it is a copy. The *eikōn* might be the result of direct imitation like the head of a sovereign on a coin, or it might be due to natural causes like the parental features in the child, but in any case, it was derived from its prototype." The Lord Jesus is therefore the image of God in the sense that as the Son to the Father He is derived by eternal generation in a birth that never took place because it always was. Our Lord said, "He that hath seen Me hath seen the Father" (John 14:9). That is, the Son is the exact reproduction of the Father, a derived image. The other idea involved in the word "representation" is that of manifestation, the manifestation of the hidden. The Logos is the revelation of the Unseen Father, whether pre-incarnate or incarnate. Lightfoot says that the idea of the invisible God "must not be confined to the apprehension of the bodily senses, but will include the cognizance of the inward eye also."

The word "firstborn" is *prōtotokos*. The Greek word implied two things, *priority* to all creation and *sovereignty* over all creation. In the first meaning we see the absolute pre-existence of the Logos. Since our Lord existed before all created things, He must be uncreated. Since He is uncreated, He is eternal. Since He is eternal, He is God. Since He is God, He cannot be one of the emanations from deity of which the Gnostic speaks, even though He proceeds from God the Father as the Son. In the second meaning we see that He is the natural ruler, the acknowledged head of God's household. Thus again, He cannot be one of the emanations from deity in whom the divine essence is present but diffused. *He is Lord of creation.*

Translation. *Who is a derived reproduction and manifestation of the Deity, the invisible One, the One who has priority to and sovereignty over all creation.*

(1:16) "For" is *hoti*, "because." Lightfoot says; "We have in this sentence the justification of the title given the Son in the preceding clause, 'the firstborn of every creature.' It must therefore be taken to explain the sense in which this title is used. Thus connected, it shows that the *prōtotokos* (firstborn) is not included in 'every creature'; for the expression used is not 'the other things of a like nature' or, 'the rest of the things,' but 'the all things were created' — words which are absolute and comprehensive, and will admit of no exception."

"By Him" is *en autōi*, here, not instrumental but locative; "in Him" were all things created. Vincent says: *"In* is not *instrumental* but *local;* not denying the instrumentality, but putting the fact of creation with reference to its sphere and center. *In Him,* within the sphere of His personality, resides the Creative will and the creative energy, and in that sphere the creative act takes place. Thus creation is dependent on Him." "All things" is *ta panta,*" the all things." Vincent says; "The article gives the collective sense — *the* all, the whole universe of things. Without the article it would be *all things severally.*" "Were created" is *ektisthē,* the aorist verb, which speaks of a definite historical event.

The qualifying phrases, "that are in heaven," and "that are in earth," Lightfoot says, present "a classification by locality, as the words visible and invisible, speak of a classification by essences. Heaven and earth together comprehend all space; and all things whether material or immaterial are conceived for the purposes of the classification as having their abode in space."

The words, "thrones, dominions, principalities, and powers" refer to both holy and fallen angels, to demons and man. Vincent says; "The passage is aimed at the angel-worship of the Colossians; showing that while they have been discussing the various grades of angels which fill the space between God and men, and depending on them as media of communion with God, they have degraded Christ who is above them all, and is the sole mediator."

"By Him" is *dia autou,* "through His intermediate agency." "For Him" is *eis auton,* "unto Him." Vincent says; "All things came to pass within the sphere of His personality and as dependent upon it . . . All things, as they had their beginning in Him, tend *to* Him as their consummation, to depend on and serve Him. . . . The false teachers maintained that the universe proceeded from God indirectly, through a succession of emanations. Christ, at best, was only one of these. As such, the universe could not find its consummation in Him." Lightfoot says; "As all creation passed out from Him, so does it all converge again towards Him." The first use of the word "created" in this verse is aorist, and the second, perfect in tense, the latter showing the abiding result.

Translation. *Because in Him were created the all things in the heavens and upon the earth, the visible things and the invisible ones, whether they are thrones or lordships or principalities*

*or authorities. The all things through Him as intermediate agent
and with a view to Him stand created.*

(1:17)   The personal pronoun in the Greek text is used for
emphasis. It is, "And He Himself is before all things." Lightfoot says; "The *autos* (Himself) is as necessary for the completeness of the meaning, as the *estin* (is). The one emphasizes the
personality, as the other declares the *pre-existence.*" The verb
of being emphasizes our Lord's absolute existence as well.
"Before all things" is "before all things" in time.

The word "consist" is *sunistēmi,* and is used here in the perfect
tense. Lightfoot translates; "hold together, cohere." He says;
"He is the principle of cohesion in the universe. He impresses
upon creation that unity and solidarity which makes it a *cosmos*
(an ordered system) instead of a *chaos* (an unformed mass).
Thus (to take one instance) the action of gravitation, which
keeps in their places things fixed and regulates the motions of
things moving, is an expression of His mind."

Translation. *And He Himself is before all things, and the all
things in Him hold together.*

(1:18)   Again, the personal pronoun is used for emphasis.
"He Himself is the Head of His body, the Church." Lightfoot
says; "The Creator of the world is also Head of the Church.
There is no blind ignorance, no imperfect sympathy, no latent
conflict, in the relation of the demiurgic power to the gospel
dispensation, as the heretical teachers were disposed consciously
or unconsciously to assume, but an absolute unity of origin." As
to our Lord as the Head of His body, the Church, Lightfoot says;
"*the head,* the inspiring, ruling, guiding, combining, sustaining
power, the mainspring of its activity, the center of its unity, and
the seat of its life."

He is the "beginning." The word is *archē,* "the origin, the
beginning," this in relation to the Church. The word *archē* here
involves *priority in time;* our Lord was the first-fruits from
among the dead; and *originating power;* He was also the source
of life (Lightfoot).

In the words, "the firstborn of the dead," Paul shows how Christ is the beginning of the new spiritual life in the Church, by His resurrection. "He comes forth from among the dead as the first-born issues from the womb. Compare Acts 2:4, 'having loosed *the pains* of death' where the Greek is *ōdinas,* 'birth-throes' " (Vincent).

"Might have the preeminence" is *genētai prōteuōn, "might become being first; Prōteuō to be first* only here in the N.T. *Genētai* (become) states a new relation into which Christ *came* in the course of time: *estin* (is) (the firstborn of all creation) states a relation of Christ's *absolute being.* He *became* head of the Church through His incarnation and passion, as He *is* head of the universe in virtue of His absolute and eternal being" (Vincent).

Translation. *And He Himself is the Head of His body, the Church, who is the originator, firstborn out from among the dead, in order that He might become in all things Himself the One who is preeminent.*

(1:19) The words, "the Father," are in italics in the A.V., which means that they are not in the Greek text and are supplied by the translators. The word "pleased" is *eudokeō,* "to think it good, to be well pleased." The word studies suggest "God." The article occurs before "fulness." Thus we have, "because in Him God was well pleased that all the fulness should dwell." The word "fulness" is *plērōma.* Vincent says: "The word must be taken in its passive sense — *that with which a thing is filled,* not *that which fills. The fulness* denotes *the sum-total of the divine powers and attributes.* In Christ dwelt all the fulness of God as deity." Lightfoot says; *"to plērōma, the plenitude,* a recognized technical term in theology, denoting the totality of the divine powers and attributes." Vincent continues: "There must also be taken into account the selection of this word *fulness* with reference to the false teaching in the Colossian church, the errors which afterward were developed more distinctly in the Gnostic schools. *Plērōma* (fulness) was used by the Gnostic teachers in a technical sense, to express the sum-total of the divine powers and attributes. 'From the *plērōma* they supposed that all those agencies issued through which God has at any time exerted His power in creation, or manifested His will through revelation. These mediatorial beings would retain more or less of its influence, according as they claimed direct parentage from it, or traced their descent through successive evolutions. But in all cases this *plērōma* was distributed, diluted, transformed, and darkened by foreign admixture. They were only partial and blurred images, often deceptive caricatures of their original, broken lights of the great Central Light' (Lightfoot). Christ may have been ranked with these inferior images of the divine by the Colossian teachers. Hence the significance of the assertion that the totality of the divine dwells in Him" (Vincent).

The word "dwell" is *katoikeō*, "to be at home permanently" in a certain place. The Greek word for a "home" is *oikos*, "to live at home," *oikeō*. The prefixed preposition *kata*, the local meaning of which is "down," adds permanency to the idea in the verb. The Greeks had a word, *paroikeō*, used of transient sojourning. But *katoikeō*, used here, speaks of the fact that all the divine fulness is at home permanently in the Lord Jesus, *at home in the sense that this divine fulness was not something added to His Being that was not natural to Him, but that it was part of His essential Being as part of His very constitution, and that permanently.*

Translation. *Because in Him God was well pleased that all the fulness be permanently at home.*

(1:20) Commenting on this verse, Lightfoot says; "The false teachers aimed at effecting a partial reconciliation between God and man through the interposition of angelic mediators. The apostle speaks of an absolute and complete reconciliation of universal nature to God, effected through the mediation of the Incarnate Word. Their mediators were ineffective, because they were neither human nor divine. It was necessary that in Him all the plenitude of the Godhead should dwell. It was necessary also that He should be born into the world and should suffer for man."

Both the Nestle and the Westcott and Hort texts put "reconcile" before "having made peace." The translation is as follows: "Because in Him God was well pleased that all the fulness be permanently at home, and (God was well pleased) through Him to reconcile all things to Himself, having made peace through the blood of His Cross." The fulness of the Godhead that resides permanently in Christ constituted Him equal to the task of reconciliation, and His act of making peace effected that reconciliation, His Blood being that which satisfied the just demands of the broken law. The Greek word "to make peace" (*eirō*) means "to bind together." Our Lord by His death on the Cross bound together again a holy God and sinful man who placed his faith in the Saviour. Likewise, the curse placed upon the material universe because of sin, will one day be removed through that same precious Blood.

Reconciliation in the case of God and man is twofold. A holy God is reconciled in that justice has been satisfied at the Cross, and sinful man is reconciled in that, in the case of the believing sinner, his attitude of enmity towards God is changed to one of friendship. The verb "reconcile" is *apokatalassō*. Vincent says that "the compounded preposition *apo* gives the force of *back,* hinting at restoration to a primal unity." Lightfoot says; "The whole universe of things, material as well as spiritual, shall be restored to harmony with God." We must be careful here to remember that when Paul wrote "the all things" he did not include the lost in eternity. Any portion of Scripture must be considered in the light of what the rest of Scripture teaches.

Translation. *And (God was well pleased) to reconcile the all things to Himself, having concluded peace through the blood of His Cross, through Him, whether the things upon the earth or the things in the heavens.*

(1:21, 22) "Alienated" is *apallatrioō,* "to alienate, to estrange." Here it is in the form of a perfect participle, passive in voice. The Colossians had been in their unsaved state, estranged from God, and permanently so. "Enemies" is *echtros,* "hostile," and in an active sense. "By wicked works" is *en tois ergois tois ponēr-*

ois, "in the sphere of works which were pernicious." Vincent says;
"*In your evil works.* In the performance of the sphere in which,
outwardly, their alienation had exhibited itself." As to the
qualifying phrase "in the body of His flesh," Expositors says;
"The most satisfactory view is that Paul has in mind the false
spiritualism which thought reconciliation could be accomplished
by spiritual beings only, and hence attached little or no value
to the work of Christ in a body composed of flesh. In opposition to this, Paul emphasizes the fact that it was just by the
putting to death of this body composed of flesh that reconciliation was effected, and thereby excludes from the work the angels
who had no body of flesh."

"To present" is *paristēmi,* "to place beside or near, to present,
to proffer." In Romans 12:2 it is used of presenting our bodies
as a sacrifice. "Holy" is *hagios.* The fundamental idea in this
word is separation to God and from worldly defilement. "Unblamable" is *amōmos,* "without blemish," like an O.T. animal
sacrifice free from defects, without blemish. "Unreprovable" is
anegklētos, "not only free from the blemish but from the charge
of it" (Vincent). "Sight" is *katenōpion,* made up of *kata,*
"down," *en,* "in," and *ōp,* "to look," thus "to look down in,"
speaking of a searching, penetrating gaze.

Translation. *And you who were at one time those who were
in a settled state of alienation, and hostile with respect to your
intents in the sphere of your works which were pernicious, yet
now He reconciled in the body of His flesh through His death,
in order that He might present you holy and without blemish
and unchargeable in His searching and penetrating gaze.*

(1:23) The word "if" here is not *ean,* an unfulfilled, hypothetical condition used with the subjunctive mode, presenting the
possibility of a future realization, but *ei* with the indicative,
having here the idea of "assuming that you continue in the
faith." That is, continuance in the gospel as it was preached
by Paul would show that the person was saved and thus would
be presented holy, without blemish, and unchargeable before
God. That is, Paul was here addressing truly born-again Colos-

sians, not unsaved professors of Christianity who would follow
the Colossian heresy. Heretics would not so be presented, only
true believers. It is not the *retention* of salvation that is in the
apostle's mind, but the *possession* of it that would be shown by
their continuance in the gospel. Expositors says; "This is
directed against the false teacher's assurance that the gospel
they had heard needed to be supplemented if they wished to attain salvation."

"Continue" is *menō,* "to persist in, adhere to, stay at or with,
abide by." The faith here is not the Christian system of doctrine, but their faith as exercised in the gospel message. As to
the words, "grounded and settled," Lightfoot translates, "built
on a foundation and so firm." Bengel says: "The former is
metaphorical, the latter more literal. The one implies greater
respect to the foundation by which the believers are supported;
but *settled* suggests inward strength which believers themselves
possess." Expositors says; " 'Grounded' refers to the firm
foundation, 'settled,' to the stability of the building." "Grounded"
is the perfect participle of *themelioō,* "to lay a foundation." The
perfect tense speaks of an action completed in past time having
present results. Those Colossians who were saved, had been
placed on the foundation, the Lord Jesus, with the result that
they were grounded on Him. That is a once-for-all act on the
part of God, having permanent results. That is what happens
to a sinner who puts his faith in the Lord Jesus. In the case
of those Colossians who professed to be recipients of this work
of God, and who followed the Colossian heresy, this would only
go to prove that their profession did not accord with the facts,
namely, that they were never placed on that foundation, the
Lord Jesus.

Translation. *Assuming indeed, that you are adhering to your
faith, having been placed upon a foundation with the present
result that you are on that foundation, firmly established, and
that you are not continually being shifted away from your hope
held out by the gospel which you heard, that gospel which was*

*proclaimed in all creation which is under heaven, of which I,
Paul, became one who ministers.*

(1:24)   The relative pronoun "who" is omitted by the Nestle
and the Westcott and Hort texts. "Now" is *nun,* and Vincent
says: "*Now* is temporal: in the midst of my imprisonment and
sufferings, after having become a minister of the gospel, and
having preached it." Lightfoot says; "The underlying *nun*
(now) seems to be this: 'If ever I have been disposed to repine
at my lot, if ever I have felt my cross almost too heavy to bear,
yet *now,* — now, when I contemplate the lavish wealth of God's
mercy — now when I see all the glory of bearing a part in this
magnificent work — my sorrow is turned into joy." Commenting on the words, "now I rejoice," the same authority has this
to say; "A sudden outburst of thanksgiving, that he, who is less
than the least, who was not worthy to be called an apostle, should
be allowed to share and even supplement the sufferings of Christ."
As to the phrase, "in my sufferings," Vincent says; "not as our
idiom, *rejoice in,* as rejoice in the Lord, but *in the midst of*:
while enduring. It is not over my sufferings, but in the sphere
of my sufferings. Paul was surrounded with sufferings in his
prison in Rome, but he was rejoicing in the midst of them."

"Fill up" is *antanapleroō,* "to fill up in turn." The prefixed
preposition *anti* "signifies that the supply comes *from an opposite
quarter* to the deficiency" (Lightfoot). Thus, the translation
reads: "I fill up on my part." "The afflictions of Christ" here
do not refer to His expiatory sufferings on the Cross, but to His
sufferings endured in His humiliation prior to that event, sufferings for righteousness' sake, sufferings incurred through ex-
hausting service, heart-sufferings due to the opposition of sinners,
sufferings which were the result of persecution; and for two
reasons, *first,* because the atonement was a finished work, and
second, because the word for "sufferings" here, *thlipsis,* is never
used of the vicarious sufferings of the Lord Jesus. These sufferings incurred during His earthly ministry, were necessarily
curtailed by reason of His limited life on earth, and needed to
be continued in His servants if the work of preaching the Word

was to be carried on. Thus, all the saints down the ages are partakers of these sufferings when they are faithful to the obligation they have of preaching the Word. The word "church" is *ekklēsia*, from *ekkaleō*, "to call out of." The word was used in classical Greek of a gathering of citizens called out from their homes into some public place. It was used among the Greeks of an assembly of the people convened at the public place of council for the purpose of deliberation. In the Christian sense, it is used of an assembly of Christians gathered for worship, and then of the entire Mystical Body of Christ, as it is here.

Translation. *I now am rejoicing in my sufferings on your behalf, and on my part am filling up the things lacking of the afflictions of Christ in my flesh for the sake of His Body, which is the Church.*

(1:25) "Whereof" refers back to "Church." Paul was made a minister (*diakonos,* a servant). "Dispensation" is *oikonomian,* made up of *oikos,* "house," and *nomos,* "law," namely, the law of the household, the method of administrating the household. It speaks of a house-steward, one to whom is given the responsibility of administering the laws regulating the proper conduct of affairs in the household. Here the meaning is that of stewardship. Paul was given the responsibility of preaching the Word of God and seeing to it that it was guided rightly in its initial impact upon the Roman Empire. Commenting on the word "fulfil," Lightfoot says; "to preach fully, to give its complete development to" the Word. Vincent says; "Fully discharge my office, so that the divine intent shall be fully carried out in the preaching of the gospel to the Gentiles no less than to the Jews."

Translation. *Of which I became a servant according to the stewardship of God which was given to me for you, to fulfil the Word of God.*

(1:26) Lightfoot says concerning the word "mystery": "This is not the only term borrowed from the ancient mysteries which Paul employs to describe the teaching of the gospel. . . . There is this difference, however; that, whereas the heathen mysteries were strictly confined to a narrow circle, the Christian mysteries are fully communicated to all. There is therefore an intentional paradox in the employment of the image by Paul. Thus, the idea of *secrecy* or *reserve* disappears when *mustērion* (mystery) is adopted into the Christian vocabulary by Paul, and the word signifies simply a truth which was once hidden but now is revealed, a truth which without special revelation would have been unknown. Of the nature of the truth itself the word says nothing. . . But the one special mystery which absorbs Paul's thoughts in the Epistles to the Colossians and Ephesians is the free admission of the Gentiles on equal terms to the privileges of the covenant. See also Ephesians 3:1-6 for the same mystery."

Commenting on the words, "From ages and from generations," Vincent says; "The unit and the factors: the *aeon* or age being made up of *generations*. . . The preposition *apo* (from), differs from *pro* (before). as marking the point *from* which concealment could properly begin. *Before* the beginning of the ages of the world, the counsel of God was ordained, but not *concealed,* because there were no human beings from whom to conceal it. The concealment began *from* the beginning of the world, with the entrance of subjects to whom it could be a fact."

Translation. *The mystery which has been kept hidden from the ages and from the generations, but now was made known to His saints.*

(1:27) "Would" is *thelō,* "to desire." Thus the translation reads, "to whom God desired to make known." Lightfoot says; "It was God's grace, it was no merit of their own." As to the words, "the riches of the glory of this mystery," Vincent says; "The mystery of the admission of the Gentiles to the gospel covenant, now revealed through Paul's preaching, was divinely rich and glorious. . . . The richness exhibited itself in the free dispensation of the gospel to the Gentile as well as the Jew. It was not limited by national lines."

The wealth of the glory of this mystery among the Gentiles is Christ. Lightfoot explains; "i.e., 'as exhibited among the Gentiles.' It was just here that this 'mystery,' this dispensation of grace, achieved its greatest triumphs and displayed its transcendant glory. . . . Here too was its *wealth;* for it overflowed all barriers of caste or race. Judaism was 'beggarly' (Gal. 4:9) in comparison, since its treasures sufficed only for a few."

As to the words, "the hope of the glory," Vincent says; "The Gentiles, in receiving the manifestation of Christ, did not realize all its glory. The full glory of the inheritance was *a hope,* to be realized when Christ should appear. . . . *Glory* refers to *the glory of the mystery;* hence *the* glory consummated at Christ's coming — the glory which shall be revealed."

Translation. *To whom God desired to make known what is the wealth of the glory of this mystery among the Gentiles, which is Christ in you, the hope of the glory.*

(1:28) "Whom" goes back to Christ. Paul preached, not a system of doctrine so much as a Person, the Lord Jesus. His statements regarding that Person and what He did on the Cross, constituted the doctrine he preached. "Preached" is *kataggelō,* "to announce." "Warning" is *noutheteō,* "to admonish, exhort, warn." "Teaching" is *didaskō,* "to instruct." Lightfoot says; "The two words present complementary aspects of the preacher's duty, and are related the one to the other, as *repentance* to faith, *warning* to repent, *instructing* in the faith."

Commenting on the repetition of the word "every," Lightfoot says; "three times repeated for the sake of emphasizing the universality of the gospel. This great truth for which Paul gave his life, was now again endangered by the doctrine of an intellectual exclusiveness taught by the Gnosticizers at Colossae, as before it had been endangered by the doctrine of a ceremonial exclusiveness taught by the Judaizers in Galatia." "In all wisdom" is more properly "in every wisdom," that is, "in every kind of wisdom." Lightfoot says; "The Gnostic spoke of the blind faith for the many, of the higher *Gnōsis* (knowledge) for the few. Paul declares that the fullest wisdom is offered to all alike. The character of the teaching is as free from restriction, as are the qualifications of the recipient."

The word "perfect" is *teleios* which when used of a believer as it is here, means "mature," spiritually mature and complete. Vincent says that "there may be in this word, a hint of its use in the ancient mysteries to designate the fully instructed as distinguished from the novices." Lightfoot says; "The language of the heathen mysteries is transferred by Paul to the Christian dispensation, that he may the more effectively contrast the things signified. The true gospel also has its mysteries, its *hierophants* (priests), its initiation; but these are open to all alike. In Christ, every believer is *teleios, fully initiated,* for he has been admitted as an *eye-witness* of its most profound, most awful secrets."

Translation. *Whom we are constantly announcing, admonishing every man and instructing every man in every wisdom in that we may present every man fully mature in Christ Jesus.*

(1:29) "Labor" is *kopiaō,* "to grow weary, exhausted, to labor with wearisome effort, to labor to the point of exhaustion." Lightfoot says; "This word is used especially of the labor undergone by the athlete in his training, and therefore fitly introduces the metaphor of *agōnizomai* (to contend in athletic games)" (striving). "Working" is *energeia,* "working, efficiency, used only of superhuman power, whether of God or the devil." It is power in exercise. Our word "energy" is derived from this word. "Mightily" is *dunamis,* "power" in the sense of natural, inherent ability. Expositors says; "The struggle is carried on in proportion, not to his natural powers, but to the mightily working energy of Christ within him."

Translation. *To which end also I am constantly laboring to the point of exhaustion, engaging in a contest according to His efficient power in exercise which is working in me in power.*

CHAPTER TWO

(2:1)   The better translation is, "For I desire you to know." There is no optative of wishing here, just the plain indicative mode.   Paul is imparting some information.   "Conflict" is *agōn,* continuing the metaphor of 1:29 in the word "striving," *agōnizomai.*   The noun refers to the arena of the contest to which *agōnizomai* in the preceding verse has reference.   The conflict could be either outward or inward, fightings without or fears within.   Here it is the inward struggle, the wrestling in prayer for the Colossian saints (Lightfoot).

Translation. *For I desire you to know how great a conflict I am having in your behalf and in behalf of those in Laodicea, and as many as have not seen my face in the flesh.*

(2:2, 3)   "Comforted" is *parakaleō,* "encouraged, confirmed." The word "comfort" had these meanings when the A.V., was translated.   In the words "being knit together," Expositors says; "there may be a reference to the divisive tendencies of the false teaching."   The translation reads so far: "In order that your hearts may be established, having been knit together in love and resulting in all the wealth of the full assurance of the understanding, resulting in a full knowledge of the mystery of God, Christ, in whom are all the treasures of the wisdom and of knowledge, hidden ones."   The words, "of the Father," are not in the best manuscripts. The word "Christ" is in the same case as "mystery," placing it in apposition with it.   The mystery is Christ.   The word "hid" is plural in number and an adjective describing "treasures."   They are hidden treasures.   The words, "to the acknowledgment of," are *eis epignōsin,* "resulting in a full knowledge."   Expositors comments: "The force of this passage then is this: all, and not merely some of the treasures of wisdom and knowledge are contained in Christ; therefore the search for them outside of Him is doomed to failure. But not only are they in Christ, but they are contained in a hidden way. Therefore they do not lie on the surface, but must be sought for earnestly, as men seek for hidden treasure. They are not matters of external observances, such as the false teachers enjoined, but to be apprehended by deep and serious meditation."

Translation. *In order that your hearts may be established, having been knit together in the sphere of love and resulting in all the wealth of the full assurance of the understanding, resulting in a full knowledge of the mystery of God, Christ, in whom are all the treasures of the wisdom and knowledge, hidden ones.*

(2:4) Commenting on the words, "And this I say," Lightfoot quotes Paul as saying in effect, "I say all this to you, lest you should be led astray by those false teachers who speak of another knowledge, of other mysteries." "Beguile" is *paralogizomai*, literally, "to reason alongside," thus, "to reckon wrong, to deceive by false reasoning, delude, to lead astray by false reasoning." "Enticing words" is *pithanlogia*, from *peithō*, "to persuade," and *logos*, "word," thus, "persuasive words, speech adapted to persuade, discourse in which probable arguments are adduced"; in a bad sense, "persuasiveness of speech, specious discourse leading others into error."

Translation. *This I am saying in order that no one may be leading you astray by false reasoning with specious discourse.*

(2:5) The phrase "in the spirit" refers to Paul's human spirit. "It is the common antithesis of the flesh and the spirit, or body and spirit" (Lightfoot). The words, "rejoicing and beholding," the same authority says, "must not be regarded as a logical inversion. The contemplation of their orderly array, though it might have been the first cause, was afterwards the consequence of the apostle's rejoicing. He looked because it gave him satisfaction to look." "Order" is *taxis*, a military term speaking of an orderly array of soldiers. Paul wrote this from his prison in Rome where he had constant contact with soldiers. "Steadfastness" is *stereōma*, another military word, a noun form coming from the verb *stereoō*, "to make solid." First Maccabees has the verb; "he solidified the battle, massed his lines." "Faith is represented as a host solidly drawn up: your *solid front, close phalanx*" (Vincent). Expositors says; "It is clear that the Church as a whole remained true to the doctrine it had been taught."

Translation. *For, as is the case, I am in fact absent in my flesh, yet I am with you in my spirit, rejoicing and beholding your orderly array and the solid front of your faith in Christ.*

(2:6, 7) 'As" is *hōs,* "In the same manner as, like as." "Received" is *paralambanō,* "to take to, to join to one's self." The simple verb *lambanō* means "to appropriate," the prefixed preposition *para,* "beside," thus, "to take to one's side," thus "to personally appropriate to one's self." Expositors says; *"paralambanō* is practically equivalent to *manthanō* 'to receive by instruction,' rather than received into the heart." That is, Paul is speaking of the doctrines regarding the Person and Work of the Lord Jesus, rather than of Him personally, for the former were involved in the Colossian heresy. The exhortation therefore is that in the same manner as the Colossian saints received the instruction regarding Christ as to His Person and Work, they should also order their behavior. They are to keep to the doctrines pertaining to Him in which they were first instructed by Paul. Regarding the words, "Christ Jesus the Lord," Vincent says; *"The* Christ, specially defined by the following words, thus emphasizing the personal Christ rather than the gospel, because the true doctrine of Christ's Person was perverted by the Colossian teachers. *The Christ, even, Jesus, the Lord."*

"Rooted" is a perfect participle in the Greek text expressing an abiding result, "having been rooted with the present result that you are firmly anchored." "Built up" is a present participle, speaking of continuous action, "being constantly built up." Vincent says; "Note the changing metaphor from the solidity of military array to *walking, rooting* of a *tree,* and then to *building."* "In Him" is *en autōi.* "Rather than upon Him, as might have been expected. In this and in the Ephesian epistle, Christ is represented as the sphere within which the building goes on.

Compare Ephesians 2:20. The whole upbuilding of the Church proceeds within the compass of Christ's personality, life, and power" (Vincent).

"Stablished" is *bebaioō*, "to make firm, establish." A present participle, emphasizing continuous action, it refers to a process going on, "constantly being established." "In the faith" is *tēi pistei*, which Lightfoot says is dative of the instrument, and which in modern grammar is called the instrumental case. He translates, "by your faith," making "faith" the instrument by which they were being established. Alford and Expositors demur, and take this as a dative of reference, Alford saying that there is no question of instrumental of means in this passage. Thus, the translation would be, "constantly being established with reference to your faith." "Abounding" is *perisseuō*, "to be in abundance." This phrase qualifying "faith" seems conclusive for the latter interpretation. That is, as their faith was constantly being established, they would have it in abundance. "Therein" is *en autōi*, which Nestle omits and Westcott and Hort bracket. It appeared in some manuscripts. Thanksgiving is the sphere in which the abundance is manifested.

Translation. *In the same manner, therefore, as you received the Christ, Jesus, the Lord, in Him be constantly ordering your behavior, having been rooted, with the present result that you are firmly anchored, and constantly being built up in Him and constantly being established with reference to your faith even as you were instructed, abounding in it in the sphere of thanksgiving.*

(2:8) "Beware" is *blepete*, "Be constantly looking out, keep a watchful eye ever open." Lightfoot says; "The form of the sentence is a measure of the imminence of the peril." Expositors says; "The future indicative after *mē* (not) implies a more serious estimate of the danger than the subjunctive." The Greek is, "Be ever on your guard lest there shall be anyone who spoils you." "Spoil" is *sulagōgeō*, "to carry off booty, to carry off as a captive and slave." Expositors translates, "lead you away as prey." Vincent says: "The A.V., is ambiguous, and might be taken to mean *corrupt* or *damage* you."

"Philosophy" is *philosophia.* Vincent says; "It had originally a good meaning, *the love of wisdom,* but is used by Paul in the sense of *vain speculation,* and with special reference to its being the name by which the false teachers at Colossae designated not only their speculative system, but also their practical system, so that it covered their ascetic practices no less than their mysticism. Bishop Lightfoot remarks upon the fact that *philosophy,* by which the Greeks expressed the highest effort of the intellect, and *virtue (aretē),* their expression for the highest moral excellence, are each used but once by Paul, showing 'that the gospel had deposed the terms as inadequate to the higher standard, whether of knowledge or practice, which it had introduced.' "

The definite article appears before "philosophy." It is "his philosophy." "And" is *kai,* and should here be rendered "even," making the words "vain deceit," explanatory of "philosophy." Paul's warning is not against all philosophy, only against that which is vain deceit, as that of Colossian heretics. "Vain" is *kenos,* "empty, devoid of truth, futile, fruitless, without effect." It is used of things that will not succeed, that are to no purpose, that are in vain. "Tradition" is *paradosis,* "that which is handed down" from generation to generation. The phrase describes "philosophy" and "vain deceit." Vincent says; "The term is especially appropriate to the Judaeo-Gnostic teachings in Colossae, which depended for their authority, not on ancient writings, but on tradition. The later mystical theology or metaphysic of the Jews was called Kabbala, literally meaning *reception* or *received doctrines, tradition.*"

"Rudiments" is *stoicheia,* "rudimentary teachings," such as "ceremonialism, meats, drinks, washings, Essenic asceticism, pagan symbolic mysteries and initiatory rites — all belonged to a rudimentary moral stage" (Vincent). "World" is *kosmos.* Lightfoot defines; "belonging to the sphere of material and external things."

Expositors says of the phrase, "not after Christ"; "Christ means the Person of Christ, not teaching about Christ . . . The false teachers put these angels in the place of Christ."

Translation. *Be ever on your guard lest there shall be someone who leads you astray through his vain speculation, even futile deceit, which is according to the tradition of men, according to the rudimentary teachings of the world, and not according to Christ.*

(2:9) Commenting on the contents of this verse, Lightfoot says; "The apostle justifies the foregoing charge that the doctrine was not according to Christ: 'In Christ dwells the whole *plērōma* (fulness, plenitude), the entire fulness of the Godhead, whereas they represent it to you as dispersed among several spiritual agencies. Christ is the fountain-head of all spiritual life, whereas they teach you to seek it in communion with inferior creatures.' "

"Dwelleth" is *katoikei. Oikeō* means "to be at home." *Kata,* prefixed, means "down," thus showing permanence. The compound verb was used of the permanent residents of a town as compared with the transient community. The verb is in the present tense, showing durative action. The translation reads: "Because in Him there is continuously and permanently at home all the fulness of the Godhead in bodily fashion."

Vincent says; "The indwelling of the divine fulness in Him is characteristic of Him as Christ, from all ages and to all ages. Hence the fulness of the Godhead dwelt in Him before His incarnation, when He was 'in the form of God' (Phil. 2:6). The Word in the beginning was with God and was God (John 1:1). It dwelt in Him *during* His incarnation. It was the Word that became flesh and dwelt among us, full of grace and truth, and His glory which was *beheld* was the glory as of the Only-begotten of the Father (John 1:14; compare I John 1:1-3). The fulness of the Godhead dwells *in His glorified humanity* in heaven. The fulness of the Godhead dwells in Him *in a bodily way, clothed with a body.* This means that it dwells in Him as one having a human body. This could not be true of His pre-incarnate state, when He was 'in the form of God,' for the human body was *taken out* by Him in the fulness of time, when He *became* in the likeness of men (Phil. 2:7), when the Word *became* flesh. The fulness of the Godhead dwelt in His person from His birth to His ascension. He carried His human body with Him into heaven, and in His glorified body now and ever dwells the fulness of the Godhead." Meyer says; "What a contrast to the human tradition and the rudiments of the world." Vincent adds; "What a contrast to the spiritual agencies conceived as intermediate between God and men, in each of which the divine fulness was abridged and the divine glory shaded, in proportion to the remoteness from God in successive emanation." "All the fulness" is *pan to plērōma,* which Lightfoot defines as "the totality of the divine powers and attributes."

As to the word "Godhead," it is found three times in the A.V., of the New Testament, Acts 17:29, Romans 1:20, and in this verse. The one word "Godhead" is the translation of two Greek words which have a real distinction between them, a distinction that grounds itself on their different derivations. In Romans 1:20 we have the word *theiotēs.* In this word, Trench says that "Paul is declaring how much of God may be known from the revelation of Himself which He has made in nature, from those vestiges of Himself which men may everywhere trace in the world around them. Yet it is not the personal God whom any man may learn to know by these aids: He can be known only by the revelation of Himself in His Son; but only His divine attributes, His majesty and glory. . . . And it is not to be doubted that St. Paul uses this vaguer, more abstract, and less personal word, just because he would affirm that men may know God's power and majesty, His *theia dunamis* (divine power) (II Pet. 1:3), from His works; but would not imply that they may know Himself from these, or from anything short of the revelation of His eternal Word. Motives not dissimilar induce him to use *to theion* rather than *ho theos* in addressing the Athenians on Mars' Hill (Acts 17:29)."

In Romans 1:20, Paul states that the invisible things of God, here, His eternal power and His *theiotēs,* His divinity, namely, the fact that He is a Being having divine attributes, are clearly seen by man through the created universe. Man, reasoning upon the basis of the law of cause and effect, namely, that every effect demands an adequate cause, comes to the conclusion that the universe as an effect demands an adequate cause, and that adequate cause must be a Being having divine attributes. It was as the creator of the universe that fallen man knew God (v. 21). Perhaps the word "Godhead" is the best one-word translation of *theiotēs* in Romans 1:20. But the term must be explained as above for a proper exegesis of this passage. The same is true of Acts 17:29. When Paul speaks of all men as the offspring of God, he uses the word *theos* for "God," the word that implies deity as Paul knows God. But when he speaks of the Greeks' conception of God or of what they as pagans might conceive God to be, he uses *theiotēs,* for the Greeks could, apart from the revelation of God in Christ, only know Him as a Being of divine attributes.

In Colossians 2:9, *theotēs* is used. Here Trench says, "Paul is declaring that in the Son there dwells all the fulness of absolute Godhead; they were no mere rays of divine glory which gilded Him, lighting up His Person for a season and with splendor not His own; but He was, and is, absolute and perfect God; and the apostle uses *theotēs* to express this essential and personal Godhead of the Son." Here the word "divinity" will not do, only the word "deity." It is well in these days of apostasy, to speak of the *deity* of the Lord Jesus, not using the word "divinity" when we are referring to the fact that He is Very God. Modernism believes in His divinity, but in a way different from the scriptural conception of the term. Modernism has the pantheistic conception of the deity permeating all things and every man. Thus divinty, it says, is resident in every human being. It was resident in Christ as in all men. The difference between the divinity of Christ and that of all other men, it says, is one of degree, not of kind. Paul never speaks of the divinity of Christ, only of His deity. Our Lord has divine attributes since He is deity, but that is quite another matter from the Modernistic conception.

Translation. *Because in Him there is continuously and permanently at home all the fulness of the Godhead in bodily fashion.*

(2:10) "Are complete" is *plēroō,* the verbal form of our word *plērōma.* It is a participle in the perfect tense. Literally it is, "And you are in Him, having been filled full, with the present result that you are in a state of fulness." Paul says in Ephesians 3:19, "In order that you may be filled with all the fulness of God." Vincent says; "Not, *ye are made full in Him,* but *ye are in Him, made full.* In Him dwells the fulness; being in Him, ye are filled." Lightfoot says; "*Being fulfilled* with a direct reference to the preceding *plērōma;* 'your fulness comes from His fulness; His *plērōma* (fulness) is transfused into you by virtue of your incorporation in Him.' . . . Hence also the Church, as ideally regarded, is called the *plērōma* (fulness) of Christ because all His graces and energies are communicated to her." We must be careful to note that the fulness of God communicated to the saints does not consist of the divine essence which is alone possessed by Deity, but of such qualities as holiness, righteousness, and the like, as in Ephesians 3:19. Expositors says; "What Paul means is that in Christ they find the satisfaction of every spiritual want. It therefore follows of itself that they do not need the angelic powers. That Christ is the Head of every principality and power is a further reason why they should not seek to them. All they need they have in Christ."

Translation. *And you are in Him, having been completely filled full, with the present result that you are in a state of fulness, in Him who is the Head of every principality and authority.*

(2:11) Lightfoot has a valuable note. "The previous verses have dealt with the theological tenets of the false teachers. The apostle now turns to their practical errors. 'You do not need the circumcision of the flesh; for you have received the circumcision of the heart. The distinguishing features of this higher circumcision are threefold: (1) It is not external but inward, not made with hands, but wrought by the Spirit. (2) It divests not of a part only of the flesh, but of the whole body of carnal affections. (3) It is the circumcision not of Moses nor of the patriarchs, but of Christ.' Thus, it is distinguished, as regards *first* its character, *second,* its extent, and *third,* its author."

Vincent has an excellent word study on the words ·"putting off." "The verb *ekduomai* means *to strip off from one's self,* as clothes or armor: *ek, out of,* having the force of *getting out of* one's garments. By the addition to the verb of *apo, from,* there is added to the idea of getting *out* of one's clothes, that of getting *away* from them; so that the word is a strong expression for *wholly putting away from one's self. In* the putting off, is, *in the act or process of.* Not *by.*"

The expression, "the body of the sins of the flesh," needs careful study. The words "of the sins," are not in the best texts, so that the expression is "the body of the flesh." Lightfoot, Expositors, Alford, and Vincent concur in the teaching that the body here is the physical body, and the flesh is indwelling sin. The body that was put off when the Colossian saints were saved was the physical body as dominated by the totally depraved nature. This body, while still the possession of the believer, was put off in the sense that it was rendered inoperative so far as the constant control of the evil nature was concerned. Paul states the same truth in Romans 6:6 when he says: "Knowing this, that our old self was crucified with Him in order that the body possessed by sin might be rendered inoperative, so that henceforth we are not yielding an habitual slave's obedience to sin." The power of the sinful nature was broken, and it was deprived of its control over the body.

This was accomplished "by the circumcision of Christ." Vincent defines: "The spiritual circumcision effected through Christ. *In,* as above. The fleshly circumcision removed only a portion of the body. In spiritual circumcision, through Christ, the whole corrupt, carnal nature is put away like a garment which is taken off and laid aside." We must be careful to note here that the evil nature is not eradicated. That remains in the believer until death (I John 1:8). Its power is broken, and it has no more power over the believer than he allows it to have. It is the physical body as dominated by the evil nature that is put away in favor of a physical body now dominated by the divine nature.

Translation. *In whom you were circumcised by a circumcision not effected by hand, in the putting off and away from yourselves the body of the flesh in the circumcision of Christ.*

(2:12) To understand this verse we must go back to Romans 6:3, 4, where Paul says: "Do you not know that so many of us as were placed in Jesus Christ, were introduced into His death? Therefore we were buried with Him by this aforementioned introduction into His death in order that just as Christ was raised up from among the dead by the glory of the Father, even so we also may be able to order our behavior in the energy of a new life imparted." The believing sinner's identification with Christ in His death, broke the power of indwelling sin. His identification with Him in His resurrection, resulted in the impartation of the divine nature. The baptism (placing, introduction into) is that effected by the Holy Spirit. The baptism in our Colossian passage is the same. Thus, "risen with Him" does not refer to our future physical resurrection, but to that spiritual resurrection from a sinful state into divine life. This was in answer to our faith in the operation of God who raised Christ from the dead. It is only fair to the reader to say that the authorities the author is consulting, all see water baptism in this passage. The words, "the placing into," give the sense in which the Greek reader of the first century would understand this text.

Translation. *Having been entombed with Him in the placing into, in which placing into also you were raised with Him through your faith in the effectual working energy of the God who raised Him out from among the dead.*

(2:13) "You" refers to Gentiles, as in the parallel passages in Ephesians 1:13, 2:1, 11, 13, 17, 22, 3:2, 4:17. The Colossian church was composed mainly of Gentiles. "Sins" is *paraptōma*, "a fall beside, a lapse or deviation from the truth and uprightness, a trespass." The word is dative of reference. They were dead with reference to their trespasses. That is, the death spoken of was spiritual death, a death involving wrong doing. They were physically alive while walking around in a state of spiritual death, devoid of the life of God and activated by a totally depraved nature.

They were also dead with reference to the uncircumcision of their flesh. Lightfoot says: "The *paraptōma* (trespasses) are the actual definite transgressions, while the *akrobustia tēs sarkas* (uncircumcision of the flesh) is the impure carnal disposition which prompts them. . . . The external fact is mentioned, not for its own sake, but for its symbolical meaning. The outward uncircumcision of the Gentiles is a type of their unchastened carnal mind. In other words, though the literal meaning is not excluded, the spiritual reference is most prominent."

Paul is still talking about the fact that when God saves a person, He breaks the power of the indwelling sinful nature. He speaks of that in Romans 6:3, 4, and here in Colossians 2:11, in the words, "in putting off the body of the flesh." The Colossians in their unsaved state, were possessed by the sinful nature, the power of which is not cut off until salvation. Thus, their flesh was uncircumcised.

"Quickened together" is *sunzōpoieō*, "to make alive together with" some one else. This occurred when our Lord was raised from the dead. All believers at that time in the mind and purpose of God were identified with Him in His resurrection, and potentially given divine life, which latter was actually received by them when they placed their faith in Him as Saviour.

Translation. *And you being dead with reference to your trespasses and the uncircumcision of your flesh, He gave life together with Him, having in grace forgiven you all your trespasses.*

(2:14) "Blotting out" is *exaleiphō*, "to wipe off, wipe away, to obliterate, erase." "Handwriting" is *cheirographon*, "an autograph, a note of hand, a bond." This bond consisted of ordinances. This bond was against us, both Jew and Gentile. Vincent says: "As Paul declares this bond to be against us, including both Jews and Gentiles, the reference, while primarily to the Mosaic law, is to be taken in a wider sense, as including the moral law of God in general, which applied to the Gentiles as much as to the Jews. See Romans 3:19. The law is frequently conceived by Paul with this wider reference, as a principle which has its chief representative in the Mosaic law, but the applications of which are much wider. This law is conceived here as a *bond,* a *bill of debt,* standing against those who have not received Christ. As the form of error at Colossae was largely Judaic, insisting on the Jewish ceremonial law, the phrase is probably colored by this fact."

Paul says that this bond was not only against us, but contrary to us. Vincent says: "He has just said *which was against us;* which stood to our debt, binding us legally. This phrase enlarges on that idea, emphasizing the hostile character of the bond, as a hindrance. Compare Romans 4:15, 5:20, I Corinthians 15:56; Galatians 3:23. 'Law is against us, because it comes like a taskmaster, bidding us do, but neither putting the inclination into our hearts nor the power in our hands. And law is against us, because the revelation of unfulfilled duty is the accusation of the defaulter, and a revelation to him of his guilt. And law is against us, because it comes with threatenings and foretastes of penalty and pain. Thus, as standard, accuser, and avenger it is against us' (Maclaren)."

"Took out of the way" is in the Greek, literally, "took out of the midst." Our Lord nailed it to the Cross. Again Vincent is helpful: "The law with its decrees was abolished in Christ's death, as if crucified with Him. It was no longer *in the midst,* in the foreground, as a debtor's obligation is perpetually before him, embarrassing his whole life."

Translation. *Having obliterated the bond consisting of ordinances, the one against us, which was directly opposed to us, and it He removed out of the midst with the result that it is no longer there, having nailed it to the Cross.*

(2:15) The principalities and authorities here are the same as in Ephesians 6:12, the demons of Satan in the atmosphere of this earth. Our Lord, after His death on the Cross, needed to present Himself at the heavenly Mercy Seat in His bloodless body glorified, as the great High Priest, thus completing the atonement, fulfilling the O.T. type when the High Priest on the Day of Atonement killed the sacrifice at the Brazen Altar and then carried the blood into the Holy of Holies, sprinkling it on the Mercy Seat, thus completing in type the atonement for sin. In order to do this, our Lord had to pass through the kingdoms of Satan in the air. The demons offered opposition. He, stripping them off and away from Himself (*apekduomai* spoiled A.V.), displayed them boldly (*deigmatizō,* "to make an example of," "made a shew of" A.V.), leading them in triumph in it. These are the captives taken by our Lord in His ascension as He left the tomb (Eph. 4:8).

Translation. *Having stripped off and away from Himself the principalities and authorities, He boldly made an example of them, leading them in triumph in it.*

(2:16, 17) After informing His readers that the bond consisting of ordinances was obliterated, Paul tells them that they should not go back to their former obedience to it. "Judge" is *krinō,* "take you to task, sit in judgment." "Meat" is *brōsis,* "the act of eating," and "drink" is *posis,* "the act of drinking." Expositors comments: *"brōsei kai posei;* 'eating and drinking,' not food and drink, for which Paul would have used *brōma* and *poma.* The question is not altogether between lawful and unlawful food, but between eating and drinking or abstinence. Asceticism rather than ritual cleanness is in his mind. The Law is not ascetic in its character, its prohibitions of meats rests on the view that they are unclean, and drinks are forbidden, save in exceptional cases, and then not for ascetic reasons. But these injunctions stand along with ordinances of the Law itself, partly, because they may have been regarded as extensions of its principles, partly, we may suppose, because, like the Law, they were attributed to the angels by the false teachers." Vincent says:

"The Mosaic law contained very few provisions concerning drinks. See Leviticus 10:9, 11:34, 36; Numbers 6:3. Hence it is probable that the false teachers had extended the prohibitions as to the use of wine to all Christians. The Essenes abjured both wine and animal food."

"In respect" is *en merei,* "in the division or category." Lightfoot translates, "in the matter of." "Holy day" is *heortēs,* "a festival or feast day." It is not a holiday, but a holy day, a sacred day. As to the new moon, Vincent says: "The festival of the new moon is placed beside the Sabbath (Isaiah 1:13, Ezekiel 46:1). The day was celebrated by blowing of trumpets, special sacrifice, feasting, and religious instruction. Labor was suspended, and no national or private feasts were permitted to take place. The authorities were at great pains to fix accurately the commencement of the month denoted by the appearance of the new moon. Messengers were placed at commanding heights to watch the sky, and as soon as the new moon appeared, they hastened to communicate it to the synod, being allowed even to travel on the Sabbath for this purpose. The witnesses were assembled and examined, and when the judges were satisfied, the president pronounced the words *it is sanctified,* and the day was declared *new moon."* The Sabbath here is the weekly festival of the Sabbath. As to the words, "shadow of things to come," Vincent says: "Shadow, not sketch or *outline,* as is shown by *body* following. The Mosaic ritual system was to the great verities of the gospel what the shadow is to the man, a mere general type or resemblance. The *substance* belongs to the Christian economy. It is derived from Christ, and can be realized only through union with Him." The word "body" here means "substance, reality," as opposed to the shadow.

Translation. *Stop therefore allowing anyone to be sitting in judgment upon you in eating or drinking or in the matter of a feast-day or a new-moon, or a Sabbath-day, which things are a shadow of those things about to come. But the body belongs to Christ.*

(2:18, 19) "Beguile of reward" is *katabrabeuō*. The word is made up of *kata*, "against," and *brabeuō*, "to act as a judge or umpire." The compound word means, "to decide against, to declare unworthy of the prize." The use of this word follows the idea of the previous verse where the act of sitting in judgment is spoken of. Vincent says: "The attitude of the false teachers would involve their sitting in judgment as to the future reward of those who refused their doctrine of angelic mediation. Paul speaks from the standpoint of their *claim*." We could go a step farther and say that these false teachers would actually deprive those Christians who would be led astray by them, of their reward at the Judgment Seat of Christ by reason of the fact that their Christian experience would be affected, and in a bad way.

"Voluntary" is *thelō*, "taking delight in, devoting himself to, delighting in." Vincent says: "It falls in, in the regular participial series, with the other declarations as to the vain conceit of the teachers; signifying not their *purpose* or their wish to deprive the Christians of their reward, but their vain enthusiasm for their false doctrine, and their conceited self-complacency which prompted them to sit as judges. The worship of angels involved a show of humility, an affectation of superior reverence for God, as shown in the reluctance to attempt to approach God otherwise than indirectly: in its assumption that humanity, debased by the contact with matter, must reach after God through successive grades of intermediate beings."

As to the word "humility," *tapeinophrosunē*, in this setting, Lightfoot says: "Humility is a vice with heathen moralists, but a virtue with Christian apostles. In this passage, which, with verse 23, forms the sole exception to the general language of the apostles, the divergence is rather apparent than real. The disparagement is in the accompaniments and not in the word itself. Humility, when it becomes self-conscious, ceases to have any value; and self-consciousness at least, if not affection, is implied by *thelō* (voluntary A.V.). Moreover, the character of the humility in this case is further defined as a worshipping of angels, which was altogether a perversion of the truth."

Regarding the worship of angels, Lightfoot says: "This word *thrēskeia* (worship) is closely connected with the preceding by the bond of union of the same preposition. There was an officious parade of humility in selecting these lower beings as intercessors, rather than appealing directly to the throne of grace. The word refers properly to the external rites of religion, and so gets to signify an over-scrupulous devotion to external forms."

"Intruding" is *embateuō,* "to enter, investigate, search into, scrutinize minutely." The word "not" is not in the best texts. These false teachers scrutinized minutely the things which they imagined or professed to have seen in a vision. "Vainly" is *eikē,* "in vain, without success or effort." "Puffed up" is *phusioō,* "to inflate, blow up, to be puffed up, bear one's self loftily, be proud." The translation reads, "being futilely puffed up." "Fleshly mind" is rather "by the mind of the flesh." Vincent says: "The intellectual faculty in its moral aspects as determined by the fleshly, sinful nature. . . . The teachers boasted that they were guided by the higher *reason.* Paul describes their higher reason as *carnal."*

The word "Head" here refers to our Lord as Head of His Body, the Church. Lightfoot says: "*the Head* regarded as a title, so that a person is at once suggested, and the relative which follows is masculine." The English reader should understand that the Greek word for "head," *kephalē,* is feminine, and that a relative pronoun agrees with its antecedent in gender. The pronoun here is masculine and refers back to "Head." This violates grammar and for the purpose of showing the personality of the Head. Lightfoot again says: "The supplication and worship of angels is a substitution of inferior members for the Head, which is the only source of spiritual life and energy." Expositors says: "Paul proceeds to point out that so far from securing spiritual growth of a higher order, the false teaching, by loosening the hold on Christ, prevented any growth at all,

since it obstructed or severed the very channel of spiritual life."
The same authority translates, "and not holding fast the head."

As to the words, "joints and bands," Vincent says: "The
word (joints) means primarily *touching,* and is used in classical
Greek of the touch upon harpstrings, or the grip of a wrestler,
not quite the same as *joints* in the sense of the *parts in contact,*
but *the relations* between the adjacent parts. The *actual connection* is expressed by *bands or ligaments.*" Lightfoot says:
"When applied to the human body, they would be 'joints,' provided that we use the word accurately of the relations between
contiguous limbs, and not loosely of the parts of the limbs themselves in the neighborhood of the contact."

As to the words, "knit together," Lightfoot says: "The dis-
coveries of modern physiology have invested the apostle's language with far greater distinctness and force than it can have
worn to his own contemporaries. Any exposition of the nervous
system more especially reads like a commentary on his image
of the relations between the body and the head. At every turn
we meet with some fresh illustration which kindles it with a
flood of light. The volition communicated from the brain to the
limbs, the sensations of the extremities telegraphed back to the
brain, the absolute sympathy between the head and the members,
the instantaneous paralysis ensuing on the interruption of con-
tinuity, all these add to the completeness and life of the image."
How this truth should give us pause as to the delicate and close
relations which we should maintain in unbroken fellowship with
our Lord. *Think of the instant paralysis of our spiritual life and
service that obtains when sin enters our experience.*

As to the words, "having nourishment ministered," Lightfoot
says: "The two functions performed by the joints and bands,
are *first,* the supply of nutriment, and *second,* the compacting of
the frame (knit together). In other words, they are the communication of life and energy, and the preservation of unity and
order. The source of all is Christ Himself, the Head; but the
channels of communication are the different members of His
body, in their relation one to another. . . . By the two-fold means

of contact and attachment, nutriment has been diffused and structural unity has been attained, but these are not the ultimate result; they are only intermediate processes; the end is growth."

Concerning the words, "of God," Lightfoot has this valuable note: "i.e., which partakes of God, which belongs to God, which has its abode in God. Thus the finite is truly united with the Infinite; the end which the false teachers strove in vain to compass is attained; the gospel vindicates itself as the true theanthropism (union of the human being with God), after which the human heart is yearning and the human intellect is feeling."

Translation. *Let no one as a judge declare you unworthy of a reward, taking delight in a self-imposed humility and a worship of the angels, scrutinizing minutely the things he has seen, being futilely puffed up by the mind of the flesh, and not holding fast the Head out from whom all the body, through the instrumentality of the joints and ligaments, being constantly supplied with nourishment and being constantly compacted together, increases with the increase wrought by God.*

(2:20-23) "If ye be dead" is *ei apethanete,* the conditional particle of a fulfilled condition, and the aorist indicative verb which speaks of a past action. It is, "in view of the fact that you died with Christ," or, "if, as is the case, you died with Christ." Death means separation. The Colossian believers died with Christ at the Cross (Romans 6:2-4), and thus were separated from all such things as are mentioned in verses 20-23. Expositors says: "The apostle, recalling them to the time of their conversion, points out how inconsistent with a death to the elemental spirits any submission to ordinances belonging to their sphere would be. The death of the believer with Christ is a death to his old relations, to sin, law, guilt, the world. It is a death which Christ has Himself undergone (Romans 6:10). Here it is specially their death to the angels who had ruled their old life, and under whose charge the Law and its ceremonies especially stood. They had died with Christ to legalism, how absurd then for ordinances to be imposed upon them." "Wherefore" is not in the best texts.

"Rudiments" is *stoicheia,* "elementary teachings and practices." "World" has its ethical sense, "the sum-total of human life in the ordered world, considered apart from, alienated from, and hostile to God, and of the earthly things which seduce from God."

"Are ye subject to ordinances" is *dogmatizō,* "subject yourselves to ordinances." The verb is better taken as passive.

"Touch" is *haptomai,* "to fasten one's self to, to cling to." The idea is more than that of inadvertently touching. It refers to a conscious effort to touch. "Handle" is *thigganō,* "to handle in a superficial or transitory way." Lightfoot says: "These prohibitions relate to defilement contrasted in diverse ways by contact with impure objects. Some were doubtless reenactments of the Mosaic law, while others would be exaggerations or additions of a rigorous asceticism, such as we find among the Essene prototypes of these Colossian heretics, e.g. the avoidance of oil, of wine, or of flesh-meat, the shunning of contact with a stranger or a religious inferior, and the like." "Which" refers to the meats and the drinks.

The words, "are to perish," are *estin eis phthoran, "are for corruption;* destined for *(eis). Corruption,* in the physical sense of *decomposition"* (Vincent). "With the using" is *tēi apochrēsei,* "rather, *using up, consumption.* Their very using destroys them" (Vincent).

The phrase, "after the commandments and doctrines of men," describes the rudiments of verse 20. "Commandment" is *entalma,* "a precept," and "doctrines" is *didaskalia,* "teachings, doctrinal instructions."

"Which things" is *hatina.* "The relative and indefinite pronoun classifies, putting these precepts and teachings, and all that are like them in one category: *a class of things* which" (Vincent).

These "have a show of wisdom." "Show" is *logon,* "a plausible reason, a show of reason," hence, a reputation for wisdom. "Will worship" is *ethelothrēskeia,* "voluntary, arbitrary worship, a worship which one devises and prescribes for himself, contrary to the contents and nature of the faith which ought to

be directed to Christ" (Thayer). Lightfoot defines, "in vol-
unteered, self-imposed, officious, supererogatory *service,* one or
both of these two ideas, (1) excessive readiness, officious zeal,
(2) affectation, unreality, are involved in this and similar com-
pounds." The word "humility" is here disparaged by its connection (Lightfoot). Vincent says: "voluntary and affected."

"Neglecting of the body" is *apheidiāi sōmatos,* "hard treatment
of the body." The word *apheidia* is from *pheidomai,* "to spare,"
and Alpha privative, the compound word meaning, "unsparing
treatment or severity." The word "honor" is *timē.* Vincent
defines: "*of any value.*" "The real value of these practices contrasted with their popular estimation. *Price* or *value* is the
original meaning of *timē,* and its use in this sense is frequent in
classical Greek." Commenting on the words, "to the satisfying
of the flesh," the same authority says: "*To* means *as a remedy
against.* Plēsmonēn (satisfying) denotes *repletion, surfeiting.*
Paul says that these ascetic observances, while they appeal to
men as indications of superior wisdom and piety, have no value
as remedies against sensual indulgence." Lightfoot translates:
"not of any value to remedy indulgence of the flesh."

Translation. *In view of the fact that you died with Christ
from the rudimentary things of the world, why, as living in the
world, are you subjecting yourselves to ordinances: Do not begin
to touch, neither begin to taste, nor begin to handle, which things
all are destined for corruption in their consumption; (ordinances)
which are according to the precepts and teachings of men? Which
things as a class have a reputation for wisdom in a voluntary
worship and an affected humility and an unsparing and severe
treatment of the body, not of any value as a remedy against the
indulgence of the flesh.*

CHAPTER THREE

(3:1) "If ye be risen" is subjunctive and presents a hypothetical case. The Greek text has *ei,* the particle of a fulfilled condition, followed by the indicative mode. It is, "In view of the fact, therefore, that you were raised with Christ." Paul bases his exhortation to seek those things which are above, not on an unfulfilled hypothetical case, but upon a fulfilled condition. The people to whom he was writing, were saved. They had been identified with Christ in His resurrection (Romans 6:2-4). His was a physical resurrection out from among the dead, theirs, a spiritual resurrection out from among the spiritually dead and from a state of spiritual death into that of spiritual life. This was potential at the time Christ died, and actual for them when they placed their faith in Him as Saviour.

The Greek text follows: "The things above be constantly seeking." The word "things" is in the emphatic position, contrasting the above things with those earthly things which the heretics were seeking after. The word "above" is *anō*. *Kata* means "down," *anō*, "above, a higher place." The reference is to heavenly things. The word is defined as to the location to which it refers by the words, "where Christ sitteth on the right hand of God." That is a place, heaven itself, where a glorified Man, Himself God the Son, is seated, His work of salvation finished.

Translation. *In view of the fact, therefore, that you were raised with Christ, the things above be constantly seeking, where Christ is, on the right hand of God, seated.*

(3:2-4) "Set your affection" is *phroneō*, "to direct one's mind to a thing." Lightfoot says: "The same expression repeated for emphasis; 'You must not only *seek* heaven; you must also *think* heaven' . . . Here the apostle points the antithesis to controvert a Gnostic asceticism: in the Philippian letter he uses the same contrast to denounce an Epicurean sensualism. Both alike are guilty of the same fundamental error; both alike concentrate their thoughts on material, mundane things." Vincent translates, *"be minded, think."* The Revision gives, *"set your mind."* Vincent says: *"Seek* marks *the practical striving; set your mind, the inward impulse and disposition.* Both must be directed at things above." Expositors says: "'The things on the earth' are not in themselves sinful, but become so if sought and thought on in preference to the things above."

"Ye are dead" is *apethanete,* an aorist indicative, referring to a past fact. The translation should be, "Ye died," that is, so far as your spiritual being is concerned, you died to, that is, were separated from the former life and everything of an evil nature that pertained to it.

The word "life" is *zōē,* here, the resurrection life which the saint enjoys. It is the eternal life given him as the motivating energy and directive agent of the new kind of life he lives, together with that life lived out. It is hidden with Christ in the sense that as Vincent says; "Your new spiritual life is no longer in the sphere of the earthly and sensual, but is with the life of the risen Christ, who is unseen with God." Expositors says: *"In God* asserts Christ's own union with God, and emphasizes our union with God in Him."

"Appear" is *phaneroō,* "to make manifest or visible," in the passive voice, "to become manifest or visible." The reference is to the second Advent when our Lord shall come from heaven with all His glorified saints in glory. Commenting on the words, "our life," Lightfoot says: "It is not enough to have said that the life is shared *with* Christ. The apostle declares that the life *is* Christ." Expositors comments: "This life is not always to remain hidden, it will be manifested at the second coming, and that not merely in union with Christ, for it is Christ Himself who is our Life. This is not to be toned down to mean that Christ is the possessor and giver of eternal life. Paul means quite literally what he says, that Christ is Himself the essence of the

Christian life. . . . His manifestation therefore includes that of those who are one with Him. And this can only be a manifestation in glory." Lightfoot says: "The veil which now shrouds your higher life from others, will then be withdrawn. The world which now persecutes, despises, ignores now, will then be blinded with the dazzling glory of the revelation."

Translation. *The things above be constantly setting your mind upon, not the things on the earth; for you died, and your life has been hidden with Christ in God. When Christ shall be made visible, our life, then also you with Him shall be made visible in glory.*

(3:5-7) Lightfoot has a valuable note: "The false doctrine of the Gnostics had failed to check sensual indulgence (2:23). The true doctrine of the apostle has power to kill the whole carnal man. The substitution of a comprehensive principle for special precepts — of the heavenly life in Christ for a code of minute ordinances — at length attains the end after which the Gnostic teachers have striven, and striven in vain." "Mortify" is *nekroō*, "to put to death, to deprive of power, to destroy the strength of." "Mortify" is obsolete English. Erasmus wrote, "Christ was mortified and killed." Lightfoot says: "Carry out this principle of *death* (2:20, 3:3), and kill everything that is mundane and carnal in your being."

"Members" refer to the "physical members so far as they are employed in the service of sin" (Vincent). Paul has the same thought in mind in Romans 6:6, when he says: "Knowing this, that our old self was crucified with Him in order that the body possessed by sin might be rendered inoperative (in that respect), that henceforth we are not yielding an habitual slave's obedience to sin." God in salvation has broken the power of the evil nature over the believer's physical body. Now, the believer is charged with the responsibility of maintaining in his experience that state of liberation, and, as the behests of the evil nature come before him, he is to put them to death, that is, refuse to obey them. The words "which are upon the earth," describe these members as organs of the earthly, sensuous life. The words "fornication, inordinate affection," etc., are in apposition to "members," and denote the manner in which the members exert themselves in a sinful way (Vincent). "Fornication" is *porneia*, "illicit sexual intercourse in general." "Uncleanness" is *akatharsia*, "uncleanness in a moral sense, the impurity of lustful, luxurious, profligate living." "Inordinate affection" is *pathos*, "depraved passion." "Evil concupiscence" is *epithumia kakē*, "evil, wicked cravings." "Covetousness" is *pleonexia*, "greedy desire to have more, avarice." "Idolatry" is *eidolatreia*, "the worship of false gods," used here of the worship of Mammon.

The words, "the children of disobedience," are not in the best texts. "In the which" (*en hois*) refers to the things of verse 6. The Colossian saints at one time ordered their behaviour, conducted themselves (walked *peripateō*) in the sphere of these evil things. That is, their entire lives were circumscribed by these sins. Not a ray of light from God, not a single good thing in the sight of God penetrated that circle. That is total depravity.

Translation. *By a once-for-all act put to death your members, the ones upon the earth; fornication, impurity, depraved passions, wicked cravings, and avarice which is of such a nature as to be idolatry; because of which things there comes the wrath of God; in the sphere of which things also you ordered your behaviour at one time when you lived in them.*

(3:8) "But now" says in effect, "Now that you have passed from that life of sinful conduct, see that you strip yourselves of these vices" (Expositors). "Anger" is *orgē*, "an abiding, settled, and habitual anger that includes in its scope the purpose of revenge." "Wrath" is *thumos*, "the boiling agitation of the feelings, a sudden violent anger." "Malice" is *kakia*, "malignity, ill-will, desire to injure, wickedness, depravity." "Blasphemy" is *blasphēmia*, "slander, detraction, speech injurious to another's good name." "Filthy communication" is *aischrologia*, "foul speaking, low and obscene speech."

Translation. *But now put away once for all also all these things; an habitual, revengeful anger, violent fits of anger, malignity, slander, obscene speech out of your mouth.*

(3:9-11) "Lie" is present imperative in a prohibition, forbidding the continuance of an action already going on. It is, "Stop lying to one another." These Colossian saints had carried over into the new life, the sin of lying. They should stop lying because they had put off the old man with his practices, that person they were before they were saved, and had put on the new man, that person they were now in Christ Jesus, this new person being constantly renewed with respect to a complete and perfect knowledge which is according to the image of the One who created him. Lightfoot says: "*Which is ever being renewed unto perfect knowledge,* the true knowledge in Christ, as opposed to the false knowledge of the heretical teachers." Regarding the reference to "the image of Him that created him," the same authority offers this explanation: "This reference however does not imply an identity of the creation here mentioned with the creation of Genesis, but only an analogy between the two. The spiritual man in each believer's heart, like the primal man in the beginning of the world, was created after God's image. The new creation in this respect resembles the first creation. The pronoun 'him' cannot refer to anything else than the new man, the regenerate man . . . The new birth was a recreation in God's image; the subsequent life must be a deepening of this image thus stamped upon the man." This putting off of the old man and this putting on of the new man took place at the moment the Colossian sinner put his faith in Christ.

"Where" is *hopou,* "in which state," namely, in the renewed state. "There is" is *eni* from *eneimi.* The verb as used here signifies not only the fact but the impossibility. Lightfoot says: "Not only does the distinction not exist, but it *cannot* exist. It is a mundane distinction, and therefore has disappeared." Expositors translates, "where there cannot be."

Vincent comments on this verse as follows: "National, ritual, intellectual, and social diversities are specified. The reference is probably shaped by the conditions of the Colossian Church, where the form of error was partly Judaistic and ceremonial, insisting on circumcision; where the pretence of superior knowledge affected contempt for the rude barbarian, and where the distinction of master and slave had place as elsewhere."

Lightfoot says: "To the Jew the whole world was divided into Jews and Greeks, the privileged and unprivileged portions of mankind, religious prerogative being taken as a line of demarcation. To the Greek and Roman it was similarly divided into Greeks and Barbarians, again the privileged and unprivileged portion of the human race, civilization and culture being now the criterion of distinction. Thus from one point of view the Greek is contrasted disadvantageously with the Jew, while from the other he is contrasted disadvantageously with the Barbarian. Both distinctions are equally antagonistic to the spirit of the gospel. The apostle declares both alike null and void in Christ. The two-fold character of the Colossian heresy enables him to strike at these two opposite forms of error with one blow. The word 'Barbarian' properly denoted one who spoke an inarticulate, stammering, unintelligible language." The Scythians were the lowest type of barbarian. Bengel describes them as "more barbarous than the barbarians."

"Bond" is *doulos,* "a slave." "Free" is *eleutheros,* "free born, one who is not a slave." Lightfoot translates: *"Christ is all things and in all things.* Christ has dispossessed and obliterated all distinctions of religious prerogative and intellectual preeminence and social caste; Christ has substituted Himself for all these; Christ occupies the whole sphere of human life and permeates all its developments."

Translation. *Stop lying to one another, having stripped off and away from yourselves and for your own advantage, the old man with his wicked doings, and having clothed yourselves with the new man who is constantly being renewed, with a resulting full and perfect knowledge which is according to the image of the One who created him; in which state there cannot be Greek or Jew, circumcision or uncircumcision, Barbarian, Scythian, slave, or free man, but Christ is all things and in all things.*

(3:12, 13) "Put on" is *endunō*, "to envelope in, clothe with." Thayer, commenting on the use of this verb in 3:10 (put on the new man), defines it as follows: "to become so possessed of the mind of Christ as in thought, feeling, and action to resemble Him and, as it were, reproduce the life He lived." The verb in 3:12 is imperative in mode. This is a command to be obeyed. It is aorist in tense, which means that the command must be obeyed at once. Commenting on "therefore," Lightfoot says: "as men to whom Christ has become all in all. The incidental mention of Christ as superseding all other relations, gives occasion to this argumentative 'therefore.'"

"The elect of God" is *eklektoi tou theou.* The adjective *eklektoi* is from the verb *eklegō*, "to select out from a number." It refers to God's choice of certain from among mankind who were as saved individuals, to be channels through which others might learn the way of salvation, this choice having been made before the universe was created. "As" is *hōs*, "like as, even as, in the same manner as." The word is an adverb of comparison. It does not merely identify. The idea is, "Put on therefore in the same manner as the elect of God." That is, see that your manner of life is fitting, seemly, in accordance with that kind of life the elect of God should live.

"Holy" is *hagios*, from *hagizō*, "to set apart for God." The elect are those set apart for God. The word speaks of their standing in grace as separated ones, to live a separated life. The same adjective is translated "saints" in 1:2. "Beloved" is *agapaō*, a perfect participle. This is the Greek word for God's love, the love shown at Calvary, a love that denies self for the benefit of the object loved. The perfect tense is used to show the far reaching and the abiding character of that love. The saints are those who have been loved by God with the present result that they are the objects of His love.

"Bowels" is *splagchnon.* Thayer says that "in the Greek poets the bowels were regarded as the seat of the more violent passions, such as anger and love; but by the Hebrews as the seat of the tenderer affections, especially kindness, benevolence, compassion, hence, our *heart*, tender mercies, affections." "Mercies" is *oiktirmos*, "compassion, pity, mercy." Thayer translates, "a heart of compassion." "Kindness" is *chrēstotēs*, "benignity, kindness." The word speaks of a gentle, gracious disposition. "Humbleness of mind," is *tapeinophrosunē*, "the having a humble opinion of one's self, a deep sense of one's (moral) littleness, modesty, lowliness of mind." "Meekness" is *praotēs*, "an inwrought grace of the soul, that temper of spirit in which we accept God's dealings with us as good, and therefore without disputing or resisting. It is the humble heart which is also the meek; and which, as such, does not fight against God, and more or less struggle and contend with Him. This meekness, however, being first of all a meekness before God, is also such in the face of men, even of evil men, out of a sense that these, with the insults and injuries which they may inflict, are permitted and employed by God for the chastening and purifying of His elect" (Trench). "Longsuffering," *makrothumia*, speaks of "the man, who, having to do with injurious persons, does not suffer himself easily to be provoked by them, or to blaze up in anger." The word expresses patience under the ill-treatment of others.

"Forbearing" is *anechō*, "to bear with, endure." "Forgiving" is *charizomai*, "to show one's self gracious, kind, benevolent, to grant forgiveness." The Greek word "grace" is *charis*, and has the same form as this word. "Quarrel" is *momphē*, "cause of blame, matter of complaint." "Even as" is *kathōs*, "according as, just as, in proportion as, in the degree that." We are to forgive others because God forgave us, and in the degree that He forgave, that is, a full forgiveness.

Translation. *Put on therefore, as chosen-out ones of God, saints, beloved ones, a heart of compassion, kindness, humility, longsuffering, bearing with one another and forgiving one another, if any one has a matter of complaint against anyone. Even as and in the degree that the Lord forgave you, in the same manner also you forgive.*

(3:14) "Above" is *epi*, which latter could better be translated here, "upon." That is, Paul is carrying on the figure of putting on as a garment all the qualities spoken of in verses 12 and 13, and he exhorts the Colossian saints to put on over these, love as the binding factor, which will hold them together and make them usable. "Charity" is *agapē*, God's love produced in the heart of the yielded believer. Vincent says: "Love embraces and knits together all the virtues." Lightfoot says: "Love is the outer garment which holds the others in their places." Expositors says: "These virtues are manifestations of love, but may be conceivably exhibited where love is absent." All of which goes to say that when these virtues are practiced without the accompaniment of divine love, they are as sounding brass and a tinkling cymbal.

This love, Paul says, is the "bond of perfectness." Lightfoot defines: "*the bond of perfection,* i.e., the power which unites and holds together all those graces and virtues which together make up perfection." "Bond" is *sundesmos*, "that which binds together." Thayer comments on this expression: "that in which all the virtues are so bound together that perfection is the result, and not one of them is wanting to that perfection." "Perfection" is *teleiotēs*. The word *teleios* means "completeness, full growth, maturity, in good working order." All these describe the Christian in whose life the virtues of verses 12-14 are present as the result of the fulness of the Spirit. Vincent says that *teleiotēs* "is a collective idea, *a result of combination,* to which *bond* is appropriate." He quotes Plato: "But two things cannot be held together without a third; they must have some bond of union. And the fairest bond is that which most completely fuses and is fused into the things which are bound." How true that last sentence is. How completely divine love is fused with the other virtues as it binds them together into one harmonious whole and makes them usable.

Translation. *And upon all these, put on divine love which is a binding factor of completeness.*

(3:15) It is the peace of Christ here. Best texts read "Christ," not "God." It is the peace, tranquility of heart, which He left as a legacy to His disciples (John 14:27). "Rule" is *brabeuō,* an athletic term, "be umpire." Lightfoot says: "Wherever there is a conflict of motives or impulses or reasons, the peace of Christ must step in and decide which is to prevail." Vincent comments: "Literally, *be umpire.* The previous reference to occasions for meekness, long-suffering, forbearance, forgiveness, etc., indicates a conflict of passions and motives in the heart. Christ is the one who adjusts all these, so that the metaphorical sense is appropriate."

Into the enjoyment of this peace the saints are called by the effectual call of God into salvation. This calling into a participation in and enjoyment of peace was in one body. That is, as members of the One Body of Christ, the saints are to enjoy peace. This peace not only refers to individual tranquility of heart, but extends to peace among the members of the Body in their relations to one another. Alford says: "Oneness of body being the sphere and element in which that peace of Christ was to be carried on and realized." Expositors says: "Disunion in the body is incompatible with the peace of the individual members."

Translation. *And the peace of Christ, let it be acting as umpire in your hearts, into which also you were called in one body. And be constantly thankful ones.*

(3:16, 17) "The word of Christ" is the word spoken by Christ. This expression is not limited to His utterances while on earth in His humiliation, but refers to the entire body of truth as given through the N.T. writers. "Dwell in" is *enoikeō.* The word *oikos* means "a home." *Oikeō* means "to live in a home." The exhortation is to the effect that the Christian is to so yield himself to the Word that there is a certain at-homeness of the Word in his being. The Word should be able to feel at home in his heart. The saint should give it unrestricted liberty in his life. "Richly" is *plousiōs,* "abundantly." Not only must the saint be yielded to the Word, but he must have a good knowledge of it. The Holy Spirit uses the Word of God that we know as He talks to us and guides our lives. He can efficiently talk to us to the extent to which we know the Word. That is the language He uses.

The words, "in wisdom," are to be understood with that which follows, since "dwell in" is sufficiently qualified by "richly." Thus, the saints are in all wisdom to teach and admonish one another. The participles "teaching" and "admonishing" are imperative in force. They exhort. "Admonishing" is *noutheteō*, "to warn, exhort, admonish." The word contains the ideas of encouragement, reproof, blame, as well.

This teaching and admonition was to be in the form of psalms, hymns, and spiritual songs. Vincent is authority for the statement that in the early Christian Church, it was not unusual to employ verse or rhythm for theological teaching or statement. That would explain Paul's exhortation embracing this form of pedagogy, a system which we do not use today in any formal presentation of theological or doctrinal teaching, although in congregational singing, we do still follow the custom. Lightfoot defines these as follows: "While the leading idea of *psalmos* (psalms) is a musical accompaniment and that of *humnos* (hymns), praise to God, *ōide* (spiritual songs) is the general word for a song, whether accompanied or unaccompanied, whether of praise or on any other subject. Thus it was quite possible for the same song to be at once a psalm, hymn, and a spiritual song. In the text, the reference to psalms, we may suppose, is specially, though not exclusively (I Cor. 14:26), to the Psalms of David, which would early form part of the religious worship of the Christian brotherhood. On the other hand, hymns would more appropriately designate those hymns of praise which were composed by the Christians themselves on distinctly Christian themes, being either set forms of words or spontaneous effusions of the moment. The third word, spiritual songs, gathers up the other two, and extends the precept to all forms of song, with the limitation however, that they must be spiritual."

The saints are to sing with grace in their hearts to the Lord. The article occurs before "grace," marking it out as a particular grace, the grace of God supplied by the Holy Spirit to the yielded saint, the grace for daily living, that divine energy produced in the heart by the Holy Spirit. The word "grace," *charis,* also means "thanksgiving," which element should be included in our singing. This singing should be as to God, (the word "Lord" is not in the better manuscripts). That is, our singing should have for its purpose the glory of God, not the display of one's voice or musical technique.

Translation. *The word of Christ, let it be at home in you in abundance; with wisdom teaching and admonishing each other by means of psalms, hymns, spiritual songs, with the grace singing in your hearts to God. And all, whatever you do in the sphere of word or deed, do all in the name of the Lord Jesus, constantly giving thanks to God the Father through Him.*

(3:18-22) Paul now turns from general exhortations to those addressed to particular individuals, wives, husbands, children, fathers, servants.

In verse 18, the expression, "as is fit in the Lord," needs some exposition. "Fit" is *anēkō.* The word is used of actions that are due someone. Lightfoot says: "The idea of propriety is the link which connects the primary meaning of such words as *anēkein, prosēkein, kathēkein,* 'aiming at or pertaining to,' with their ultimate meaning of moral obligation." The verb is in the imperfect tense which speaks of an action going on in past time. Vincent says: "The imperfect tense, *was fitting,* or *became fitting,* points to the time of their entrance upon the Christian life. Not necessarily presupposing that the duty remained unperformed. Lightfoot illustrates by *ought,* the past tense of *owed,* and says: 'the past tense perhaps implies an *essential* a *priori* obligation." The term *a priori* refers to that which is known by reasoning from what is self-evident and therefore known without any appeal to the particular facts of experience. What Lightfoot says is that the use of the past tense here points to the fact that the wife's submission to her husband is an obligation that is a self-evident one which is arrived at from reasoning regarding the proper relation of the wife to the husband. The words, "in the Lord," are to be construed with the word "fitting." This obligation on the part of the wife is fitting in the Lord in the sense that she is as to her position in salvation, in Christ, and a person in such a position has the moral obligation to obey the scriptures when they admonish the wife to be in subjection to her husband.

The husbands are exhorted to love their wives. The word here is not *phileō,* a non-ethical fondness or affection. They all did that. That was the type of love which was exercised when they fell in love with them. It is *agapē,* the love that was shown at Calvary, the love produced in the heart of the yielded saint by the Holy Spirit, the love that will cause the husband to sacrifice himself and his own wishes in the interest of the well-being of the wife. "Be bitter" is *pikrainō,* "to embitter, exasperate, irritate." Lightfoot translates, "show no bitterness, behave not harshly."

"Well pleasing" is *euareston,* "commendable, well pleasing." The expression, "unto the Lord," should read "in the Lord," the preposition *en* appearing in the best texts. Lightfoot says "implies 'as judged by a Christian standard,' 'as judged by those who are members of Christ's body.'" "Provoke" is *erethizō,* "provoke, irritate." Lightfoot says: "Irritation is the first consequence of being too exacting with children, and irritation leads to moroseness." "Discouraged" is *athumeō,* "to be disheartened, dispirited, broken in spirit, lose heart." "Servants" is *doulos,* "slaves." These were Christian slaves working for the most part in the service of pagan masters. Expositors comments: "The case of slaves is treated at greater length than that of the other family relations, probably on account of Onesimus. But Paul was much possessed with the need for keeping Christianity free from the suspicion it naturally created of undermining the constitution of society. So while *doulos* (a slave), *eleutheros* (a free man) is a distinction which has vanished for Christianity, in the interests of Christianity as a spiritual power, social free-

dom had to be cheerfully foregone till the new religion was able
to assert its principle with success. An instructive parallel is
the exhortation to submission to constituted authority in Romans
13. In Paul's time, slaves probably made up the larger part of
the population of the empire."

The expression, "according to the flesh," describes the masters
as contrasted to the Lord who was the Master of these slaves
with reference to their spiritual lives. "Eyeservice" is *ophthal-
modouleia*, "service performed under the master's eye, service
which is most zealous when the eye of the master or overseer
is upon them." Expositors, commenting on "menpleasers," says:
"It is the Christian's first duty to please the Lord, and this he
can do only by conscientious performance of his tasks quite
apart from the recognition he receives from men. If the principle of his conduct is the pleasing of men, he will neglect his
duty where this motive cannot operate." The words, "in singleness of heart," are contrasted to the idea of the double-dealing
of eyeservice (Expositors). Lightfoot explains; "with *undivided* service." As to fearing the Lord ("Lord," not "God" in
best texts), they are to do that as fearing "*the* one Lord and
Master, as contrasted with the masters according to the flesh"
(Lightfoot).

Translation. *Wives, be constantly subjecting yourselves to
your husbands as you ought to do in the Lord. Husbands, be
loving your wives with a divine love which impels you to deny
yourselves for their benefit, and stop being bitter and harsh to
them. Children, be obeying your parents in all things, for this
is commendable in the Lord. Fathers, stop irritating your children, lest they become disheartened. Slaves, be constantly obedient in all things to your human masters, not with eyeservice as
menpleasers, but with an undivided heart, fearing the Lord.*

(3:23-25) It is, "Whatsoever ye do (*poieō*), do (*ergazomai*)
it." The English reader will observe that the two occurrences
of the word "do" are translated from two different words in the
Greek text. The first (*poieō*) refers to the mere doing of something. The second is an advance upon the first word. *Ergazomai*

means, "to labor, do work." It is opposed to inactivity or idleness. Lightfoot translates. "do it diligently." Expositors says: "Not only must the slave's work be done in the fear of the Lord, but done as if it were actually for the Lord that he was doing it, and not for a mere human master. And this principle is to govern every detail of his varied service. Their service, Paul would say, is not to be rendered at all to their human master, but exclusively to Christ. However their earthly master may reward their service, there is a Master who will give them a just recompense; although they cannot receive an earthly, He will give them a heavenly inheritance."

"Heartily" is literally, "out from the soul." "Reward" is *antapodoma,* "that which is paid back, a requital." Lightfoot translates, "the just recompense." "Of the inheritance" is genitive of apposition. Translate 'which consists in the inheritance' " (Lightfoot). The same authority translates the words, *tōi Kuriōi Christōi douleuete,* you serve (as your Master) *the* (great) *Master, Christ.* The word *kurios* (Lord), also means "master."

Vincent comments on the words, "He that doeth wrong," as follows: "The reference is primarily to the slave; but the following clause extends it to the master. If the slave do wrong, he shall be punished; but the master who does wrong will not be excused; for there is no respect of persons. Tychicus, who carried this letter to Colossae, carried at the same time the letter to Philemon, and escorted Onesimus to his master."

Lightfoot comments: "The recent fault of Onesimus would make the apostle doubly anxious to emphasize the duties of the slave towards the master, lest in his love for the offender, he should seem to condone the offence. But on the other hand, it is the apostle's business to show that justice has a double edge. There must be a *reciprocity* between the master and the slave. The philosophers of Greece taught, and the laws of Rome assumed, that the slave was a chattel. But a chattel could have no rights. It would be absurd to talk of treating a chattel with justice. St. Paul places the relations of the master and the slave in a wholly different light. Justice and equity are the expression of the divine Mind, and with God there is no respect of persons. With Him the claims of the slave are as real as the claims of the master."

"Receive," *komizō*, in the middle voice here, means "to recover, to get back, to be recompensed." "Respect of persons" is *prosōpolempsia*, made up of *lambanō* "to receive," and *prosōpon*, "face," thus, "receiving of face," thus, "judging upon the basis of outward appearance," thus, "showing partiality."

Translation. *Whatever you do, from your soul do it diligently as to the Lord and not to men, knowing that from the Lord you will receive back the just recompense which consists of the inheritance. The Master, Christ, you are serving. For the one who is doing wrong, will get back that which he did which is wrong. And there is no showing of partiality.*

CHAPTER FOUR

(4:1) This verse really belongs to the material in the closing words of the previous chapter. It contains a final word to masters of slaves. "Give" is *parechō*, "to exhibit or offer on one's own part, to render or afford from one's own resources or by one's own power." The idea is, "render on your own part." "Equal" is *isotēs*, "equity, fairness, what is equitable." Vincent says: "Literally, *the equality*. Not equality of condition, but the brotherly equality growing out of the Christian relation, in which there is neither bond nor free." Expositors says: "The master should regulate his treatment of his slave, not by caprice, but by equity." It should be kept in mind that these masters were Christians.

Translation. *Masters, that which is just and equitable, be rendering on your part to your slaves, knowing that also you have a Master in heaven.*

(4:2-4) "Continue" is *proskartereō*, "to give constant attention to a thing, to give unremitting care to a thing, to persevere, to wait continually upon, to be in constant readiness for." "Watch" is *grēgoreō*, "to give strict attention to, to be active, to take heed lest through remissness and indolence some destructive calamity suddenly overtake one." Lightfoot says: "Long continuance in prayer is apt to produce listlessness. Hence the additional charge that the heart must be *awake*, if the prayer is to have any value."

"Withal" is *hama*, "at the same time." The "us" refers to Paul and his associates in the ministry of the Word, and in particular to Timothy (1:1) and Epaphras (4:3, 4). "A door of utterance" is *thuran tou logou*, "a door of the Word." Lightfoot interprets, "*a door* of admission *for the Word*, i.e., an opportunity of preaching the gospel." "To speak" is *laleō*. It is an infinitive of the consequence, "so as to speak" (Lightfoot). The mystery here is that spoken of in Ephesians 3:6, to the effect that the Gentiles are to be one body with the Jew in the mystical body of Christ, the Church. "I am in bonds" is *dedemai,* the perfect tense of *deō,* "to bind." The translation reads, "I have been bound with the present result that I am in a bound condition." Paul was a closely guarded prisoner of the Roman empire, handcuffed to a Roman soldier twenty-four hours a day. The words, "that I may make it manifest," go back to, "praying for us." Paul's imprisonment curtailed his activities in the preaching of the gospel.

Translation. *Be giving constant attention to prayer, constantly active in it with thanksgiving, praying at the same time also concerning us, that God would open for us a door for the Word, to speak the mystery of Christ, because of which (mystery) also I have been bound, in order that I may make it plain as it is necessary in the nature of the case for me to speak.*

(4:5) "Walk" is *peripateō,* "to order one's behavior." "Them that are without" is *tous exō,* "those outside," namely, those without the pale of the Church, the unbelievers. Expositors says: "They must be wise in their relations with them so as not to give them an unfavorable impression of the gospel." "Redeeming" is *exagorazō,* "to buy up the opportunity for one's self," that is, to make a wise and sacred use of every opportunity for doing good, so that zeal and well-doing are, as it were, the purchase-money by which we make the time our own" (Thayer). Expositors quotes Ramsay, "making your market fully from the occasion," and goes on to say, "They are to seize the fitting opportunity when it occurs, to do good to 'those without,' and thus promote the spread of the gospel." "Time" is *kairos,* "a strategic point of time."

Translation. *In wisdom be ordering your behavior towards those on the outside, buying up for yourselves the strategic, opportune time.*

(4:6) "Speech" is *logos,* "a word." "With grace" is *en chariti.* Expositors says: "probably gracious; 'pleasant' is the meaning; by the sweetness and courtesy of their conversation they are to impress favorably the heathen." As to the expression, "seasoned with salt," Lightfoot says: "Salt has a twofold purpose; (1) It gives flavor to the discourse and recommends it to the palate. This is the primary idea of the metaphor here, as the word 'seasoned' seems to show; (2) It preserves from corruption and renders wholesome. It may be inferred that this secondary application of the metaphor was present to the apostle's mind here, because of the parallel epistle (Eph. 4:29), 'Let no corrupt communication proceed out of your mouth.'" Lightfoot quotes Plutarch, "The many call *salt charitas, graces,* because, mingled with most things, it makes them agreeable and pleasant to taste." Expositors says: "They must strive to cultivate the gift of pleasant and wise conversation, so that they may be able to speak appropriately to each individual (with his peculiar needs) with whom they come in contact."

Translation. *Your word, let it always be with graciousness, with salt thoroughly seasoned, to the end that you may know how it is necessary in the nature of the case to answer every one.*

(4:7-9) Lightfoot says: "Tychicus was charged by Paul at the same time with a more extended mission. He was entrusted with copies of the circular letter, which he was enjoined to deliver in the principal churches of proconsular Asia. This mission would bring him to Laodicea, which was one of these great centers of Christianity, and, as Colossae was only a few miles distant, the apostle would naturally engage him to pay a visit to the Colossians."

"All my state" is *ta kat eme panta,* "all that relates to me" (Lightfoot). "Brother" is *adelphos,* a brother Christian. "Minister" is *diakonos,* "servant," to Paul in the ministry of the Word. Fellow-servant is *sundoulos.* Vincent says: "By this term he designates Tychicus as, in common with himself, a servant of Jesus Christ." The word *doulos* was used of a slave. Here one could translate, "fellow-bondslave."

"I have sent" is the epistolary aorist, in which the writer puts himself at the standpoint of the reader when he receives the

letter, and looks at the writing of the letter which is a present
event with him, as a past event. Paul sent this letter with
Tychicus. "Your estate" is literally, "the things concerning you."
"Comfort" is *parakaleō*, "to encourage," here by his tidings and
exhortations. Regarding Onesimus, Lightfoot writes, "The man
whom the Colossians had only known hitherto, if they knew him
at all, is thus commended to them as no more slave but a brother,
no more dishonest and faithless but trustworthy, no more an object of contempt but of love."

Translation. *All that relates to me, Tychicus will make
known to you, the beloved brother and faithful minister and my
fellow-bondslave in the Lord, whom I sent to you for this same
purpose, in order that you may come to know the things concerning me and in order that he may encourage your hearts;
with Onesimus the faithful and beloved brother, who is one of
you. All things to you they will make known, the things here.*

(4:10, 11) As to the significance of the term "fellow-prisoner" as applied to Aristarchus, authorities disagree. Lightfoot
says: "The most probable solution would be, that his relations
with St. Paul in Rome excited suspicion and led to a temporary
confinement. Another possible hypothesis is that he voluntarily
shared the apostle's captivity by living with him." "Saluteth"
is *aspazomai*, "to greet, wish well." Marcus is John Mark, the
writer of the Gospel. "Sister's son" is *anepsios,* "a cousin."
Expositors says: "Paul may have feared that Mark's defection
from him, which led to the sharp quarrel between him and
Barnabas, might prejudice the Colossians against him. The
mention of his relationship to Barnabas was probably intended
as a recommendation to their kindness. He seems to have been
unknown to the Colossians."

The name "Jesus" is the transliteration of the Greek *Iēsous*,
which in turn is the transliteration of the Hebrew name from
which we get "Joshua" or "Jehoshua." In Hebrews 4:8, the
name *Iēsous* refers in its context, not to the Jesus of the first
century, but to the Joshua of the conquest of Canaan. The
case is the same here. This man was probably known by the

name "Joshua." "Justus," Lightfoot says, is "a common name or surname of Jews and proselytes, denoting obedience and devotion to the law." Aristarchus and Joshua here are described as of the circumcision. They were converts from Judaism. The word "only" marks these two men out as the only Jewish Christians in Rome who were fellow-workers of Paul. Lightfoot says that this description must not be closely pressed, as if absolutely no Jewish Christians besides had remained friendly; they will only imply that among the more prominent members of the body, the apostle can only name these three as steadfast in their allegiance. "Comfort" is *parēgoria*, "comfort, solace, relief, alleviation, consolation, encouragement." They were a medicine for Paul. The word "paregoric" comes from this Greek word.

Translation. *There greets you Aristarchus, my fellow-prisoner, and Mark, the cousin of Barnabas, concerning whom you received commandments; if he comes to you, receive him; and Joshua, the one called Justus, who are of the circumcision. These are my only fellow-workers with respect to the kingdom of God who are of such a character as to have become a solace to me.*

(4:12, 13) The name "Epaphras" is the shortened form of Epaphroditus. He was not the man of that same name who was associated with Paul in the Philippian letter. Lightfoot suggests that he was the one who brought the gospel to Colossae. He was a native of that city as is seen by the phrase, "who is of you." "Servant" is *doulos*, "a slave." Lightfoot says: "This title, which the apostle uses several times of himself, is not found elsewhere conferred on any other individual, except once on Timothy (Phil. 1:1), and probably points to exceptional services on the part of Epaphras."

"Laboring fervently" is *agōnizomai*, "to contend in the gymnastic games, to contend with adversaries," figuratively, "to contend, struggle with difficulties and dangers antagonistic to the gospel." Lightfoot translates, "wrestling," Vincent, "striving." "Stand" is *stathēte*, "to stand fast." "Perfect" is *teleios*, "complete, spiritually mature, full-grown." The word does not mean "sinless." "Complete" is the perfect participle of *plērophoreō,* "to bear or bring to the full, to carry through to the end, to make full, to pursuade, fully convince." Lightfoot translates, "fully persuaded." Vincent quotes the Revision, "fully assured."

The phrase "in all the will of God" is *en panti thelēmati tou theou,* "in everything willed by God." "Zeal" is from *zēlon* which does not appear in the best texts, *ponon,* "toil," being found. Lightfoot says: *"much toil,* both inward and outward, though from the connection, the former notion seems to predominate." Expositors says: "The anxiety of Epaphras for these churches was probably due to his connection with them either as founder or teacher."

Translation. *There greets you Epaphras, the one who is one of your number, a bondslave of Christ Jesus, always wrestling on your behalf in his prayers, to the effect that you may stand fast, spiritually mature ones, and those who have been brought to the place of full assurance in everything willed by God; for I bear witness to him that he has much toil on your behalf and on behalf of those in Laodicea, and those in Hierapolis.*

(4:14)   The Greek text has, "Luke, the physician, the beloved one." The word "physician" is *iatros,* the verbal form of which is *iaomai,* "to heal, cure." This is Luke, the evangelist, and the writer of the Gospel that bears his name. He was a Greek, a Gentile, as is shown by his Greek name, and the fact that Paul does not include him with those of the circumcision of verse 11. He shows a knowledge of medical terms in the Gospel he wrote. The practice of medicine was highly developed among the Greeks, Greek doctors being in attendance at the royal courts in the Roman empire. Luke was the personal physician of Paul. The words, "the beloved one," breathe with Paul's gratitude for his services. My illustrious Greek professor at Northwestern University, the late John A. Scott, writes in the closing words of his book, *Luke, Greek Physician and Historian,* "Without Luke's help as a physician, as a companion and friend, Paul could never have carried his heavy load in the Christian ministry, and without Luke's pen, the same grave that covered Paul's body would also have covered his name. In my mind, the most important event in the history of time took place on that day when a poor, sick, discouraged Jew went into the office of Luke, the Greek physician; with the single exception of that Friday afternoon when Jesus hung from the cross on Calvary."

As to the bare mention of Demas, Lightfoot says: "While Luke is described with a special tenderness as the Physician, the beloved one, Demas alone is dismissed with a bare mention and without any epithet of commendation." Alford says: "The absence of any honorable or endearing mention here may be owing to the commencement of this apostasy, or some unfavorable indication in his character." This is the Demas who let Paul down during Paul's second Roman imprisonment (II Tim. 4:10). The word "forsaken" in the latter scripture is *egkataleipō*, "to let one down."

Translation. *There greets you Luke, the physician, the beloved one, and Demas.*

(4:15) The words, "the church which is in his house," are explained as follows: "There is no clear example of a separate building set apart for Christian worship within the limits of the Roman empire before the third century, though apartments in private houses might be specially devoted to this purpose" (Lightfoot). An assembly of the saints met in the home of Nymphas for worship. The Nestle text has the personal pronoun in the feminine gender, indicating that Nymphas was a woman.

Translation. *Greet the brethren in Laodicea, and Nymphas, and the assembly in her home.*

(4:16) As to the letter from Laodicea, Expositors says: "clearly a letter sent by Paul to Laodicea, which the Colossians are instructed to procure and read. It may be a lost letter, or it may be our so-called Epistle to the Ephesians, to which Marcion refers as the Epistle to the Laodiceans, and which was probably a circular letter."

Translation. *And when this letter is read in your presence, see to it that also it is read in the assembly of Laodicea, and the letter from Laodicea, see to it that you also read it.*

(4:17)   As to the ministry committed to Archippus, Lightfoot says: "From the stress which is laid upon it, the *diakonia* (ministry) here would seem to refer, as in the case of Timothy . . . , to some higher function than the diaconate properly so called." "Fulfil" is *plēroō*, "to discharge fully."

Translation. *And say to Archippus; Look to the ministry which you received in the Lord, that you discharge it fully.*

(4:18)   Paul wrote the salutation or greeting (1:1, 2) with his own hand. The rest of the letter was written by a secretary at the dictation of Paul. The reason for the latter practice is found in the fact that the great apostle suffered from an oriental eye disease called ophthalmia, which induced almost total blindness, and which caused a repulsive appearance. This he contracted on his first missionary journey as he was going through the lowlands of Pamphylia where this disease was prevalent. He had his heart set on Athens, going by way of Pisidian Antioch, but God took this means of leading Paul to evangelize the Galatian cities, for it was evidently not His will at the time for him to go to Athens. Paul writes to the Galatians that he had brought the gospel to them because he was prevented by illness from going on, and reminds them that they at that time were willing to dig out their own eyes and give them to him, the inference being clear that he needed a new pair of eyes (Gal. 4:13-15). In the same letter (6:11) he writes, "You see with what large letters I wrote to you in my own hand." The Galatian heresy was a delicate problem for Paul to handle, and he wrote the entire letter to the Galatians in inch-high Greek capital letters in order that in his semi-blindness he could see what he was doing. In the case of his other letters, he dictated them to a secretary. In Romans 16:22 we have, "I, Tertius, who wrote this epistle, salute you in the Lord." The reason why Paul was careful to put his signature on every letter in his own handwriting, is found in the fact that someone had written a letter to the Thessalonian church and had forged Paul's name to it (II Thess. 2:2, "letter as from us," and 3:17, "The salutation of Paul with my own hand, which is the token in every epistle"). A pathetic note is struck in the words, "Remember my bonds." Expositors says: "As he writes, his chain, fastened on his left hand, would impress itself on his notice. Hence the touching request, 'Remember my bonds,' which may bear the special sense, 'remember in your prayers.'" Alford says: "These words extend further than to mere pecuniary support, or even mere prayers: they were ever to keep before them the fact that one who so deeply cared for them, and loved them, and to whom their perils of false doctrine occasioned such anxiety, was a prisoner in chains: and that remembrance was to work and produce its various fruits — of prayer for him, of affectionate remembrance of his wants, of deep regard for his words."

Translation. *The greeting by my hand, the hand of Paul. Be remembering my bonds. The grace be with you.*

THE
EXPANDED TRANSLATION
OF
COLOSSIANS

Read this through at a single sitting. In that
way you will grasp the contents of this letter
as a complete and unified whole. What you
read will be that which the Colossian saints
read in all the richness of the original.

THE EXPANDED TRANSLATION
O F
COLOSSIANS

Paul, an ambassador of Christ Jesus through the will of God, and Timothy our brother, to the saints in Colossae, even faithful brethren in Christ. Grace to you and peace from God our Father.

I am giving thanks to God the Father of our Lord Jesus Christ, concerning you constantly offering petitions, having heard of your faith in Christ Jesus and of the love which you constantly have to all the saints through the agency of the hope laid aside for you in heaven, concerning which you heard before in the word of the truth of the glad tidings which are with you, even as also they are in all the world constantly bearing fruit and increasing, just as they are also among you from the day when you heard them and came to know experientially the grace of God in the sphere of truth, even as you learned from Epaphras, the beloved, our fellow-bondslave, who is faithful on your behalf as a servant of Christ, who also declared to us your love in the sphere of the Spirit.

Because of this, we also, from the day we heard, do not cease on behalf of you offering our petitions and presenting our definite requests, that you might be filled with the advanced and perfect knowledge of His will in the sphere of every kind of wisdom and intelligence which is spiritual, so that you may order your behavior worthily of the Lord with a view to pleasing Him in everything, in every work which is good, constantly bearing fruit and increasing by means of the thorough and perfect knowledge of God, by every enabling power being constantly strengthened *in proportion to the manifested power of His glory resulting in every patience and forbearance with joy, constantly giving thanks to the Father who qualified you for the portion of the lot of the saints in the light; who delivered us out of the tyrannical rule of the darkness and transferred us into the kingdom of the Son of His love, in whom we are having our liberation procured by the payment of ransom, the putting away of our sins; who is a derived reproduction and manifestation of the Deity, the invisible One, the One who has priority to and sovereignty over all creation, because in Him were created the all things in the heavens and upon the earth, the visible things and the invisible ones, whether they are thrones or lordships or principalities or authorities. The all things through Him as intermediate agent and with a view to Him stand created.*

And He Himself is before all things, and the all things in Him hold together. And He Himself is the Head of His body, the Church, who is the originator, firstborn out from among the dead, in order that He might become in all things Himself the One who is preeminent, because in Him God was well pleased that all the fulness be permanently at home. And (God was well pleased) to reconcile the all things to Himself, having concluded peace through the blood of His Cross, through Him, whether the things upon the earth or the things in the heavens.

And you who were at one time those who were in a settled state of alienation, and hostile with respect to your intents in the sphere of your works which were pernicious, yet now He reconciled in the body of His flesh through His death, in order that He might present you holy and without blemish and unchargeable in His searching and penetrating gaze; assuming indeed, that you are adhering to your faith, having been placed upon a foundation with the present result that you are on that foundation, firmly established, and that you are not continually being shifted away from your hope held out by the gospel which you heard, that gospel which was proclaimed in all creation which is under heaven, of which, I, Paul, became one who ministers. I now am rejoicing in my sufferings on your behalf, and on my part am filling up the things lacking of the afflictions of Christ in my flesh for the sake of His Body, which is the Church, of which I became a servant according to the stewardship of God which was given to me for you, to fulfil the Word of God, the mystery which has been kept hidden from the ages and from the generations, but now was made known to His saints, to whom God desired to make known what is the wealth of the glory of this mystery among the Gentiles, which is Christ in you, the hope of the glory, whom we are constantly announcing, admonishing every man and instructing every man in every wisdom in order that we may present every man fully mature in Christ Jesus, to which end also I am constantly laboring to the point of exhaustion, engaging in a contest according to His efficient power in exercise which is working in me in power.

For I desire you to know how great a conflict I am having in your behalf and in behalf of those in Laodicea, and as many as have not seen my face in the flesh, in order that your hearts may be established, having been knit together in the sphere of love and resulting in all the wealth of the full assurance of the understanding, resulting in a full knowledge of the mystery of God, Christ, in whom are all the treasures of the wisdom and knowledge, hidden ones.

This I am saying in order that no one may be leading you astray by false reasoning with specious discourse. For, as is the case, I am in fact absent in my flesh, yet I am with you in my spirit, rejoicing and beholding your orderly array and the solid front of your faith in Christ. In the same manner, therefore, as you received the Christ, Jesus, the Lord, in Him be constantly ordering your behavior, having been rooted, with the present result that you are firmly anchored, and constantly being built up in Him and constantly being established with reference to your faith even as you were instructed, abounding in it in the sphere of thanksgiving. Be ever on your guard lest there shall be someone who leads you astray through his vain speculation, even futile deceit, which is according to the tradition of men, according to the rudimentary teachings of the world, and not according to Christ, because in Him there is continuously and permanently at home all the fulness of the Godhead in bodily fashion. And you are in Him, having been completely filled full, with the present result that you are in a state of fulness, in Him who is the Head of every principality and authority, in whom you were circumcised by a circumcision not effected by hand, in the putting off and away from yourselves the body of the flesh in the circumcision of Christ, having been entombed with Him in the placing into, in which placing into also you were raised with Him through your faith in the effectual working energy of the God who raised Him out from among the dead.

And you being dead with reference to your trespasses and the uncircumcision of your flesh, He gave life together with Him, having in grace forgiven you all your trespasses, having obliterated the bond consisting of ordinances, the one against us, which was directly opposed to us, and it He removed out of the midst with the result that it is no longer there, having nailed it to the Cross; having stripped off and away from Himself the principalities and authorities, He boldly made an example of them, leading them in triumph in it. Stop therefore allowing anyone to be sitting in judgment upon you in eating or drinking or in the matter of a feast-day or a new-moon, or a Sabbath-day, which things are a shadow of those things about to come. But the body belongs to Christ.

Let no one as a judge declare you unworthy of a reward, taking delight in a self-imposed humility and a worship of the angels, scrutinizing minutely the things he has seen, being futilely puffed up by the mind of the flesh, and not holding fast the Head out from whom all the body, through the instrumentality of the joints and ligaments, being constantly supplied with nourishment and being constantly compacted together, increases with the increase wrought by God.

In view of the fact that you died with Christ from the rudimentary things of the world, why, as living in the world, are you subjecting yourselves to ordinances: Do not begin to touch, neither begin to taste, nor begin to handle, which things all are destined for corruption in their consumption; (ordinances) which are according to the precepts and teachings of men? which things as a class have a reputation for wisdom in a voluntary worship and an affected humility and an unsparing and severe treatment of the body, not of any value as a remedy against the indulgence of the flesh.

In view of the fact, therefore, that you were raised with Christ, the things above be constantly seeking, where Christ is, on the right hand of God, seated. The things above be constantly setting your mind upon, not the things on the earth; for you died, and your life has been hidden with Christ in God. When Christ shall be made visible, our life, then also you with Him shall be made visible in glory.

By a once-for-all act put to death your members, the ones upon the earth; fornication, impurity, depraved passions, wicked cravings, and avarice which is of such a nature as to be idolatry; because of which things there comes the wrath of God; in the sphere of which things also you ordered your behaviour at one time when you lived in them. But now put away once for all also all these things; an habitual, revengeful anger, violent fits of anger, malignity, slander, obscene speech out of your mouth. Stop lying to one another, having stripped off and away from yourselves and for your own advantage, the old man with his wicked doings, and having clothed yourselves with the new man who is constantly being renewed, with a resulting full and perfect knowledge which is according to the image of the One who created him; in which state there cannot be Greek or Jew, circumcision or uncircumcision, Barbarian, Scythian, slave, or free man, but Christ is all things and in all things.

Put on therefore, as chosen-out ones of God, saints, beloved ones, a heart of compassion, kindness, humility, longsuffering, bearing with one another and forgiving one another, if any one has a matter of complaint against anyone. Even as and in the degree that the Lord forgave you, in the same manner also you forgive. And upon all these, put on divine love which is a binding factor of completeness. And the peace of Christ, let it be

*acting as umpire in your hearts, into which also you were called
in one body. And be constantly thankful ones. The word of
Christ, let it be at home in you in abundance; with wisdom
teaching and admonishing each other by means of psalms, hymns,
spiritual songs, with the grace singing in your hearts to God.
And all, whatever you do in the sphere of word or deed, do all
in the name of the Lord Jesus, constantly giving thanks to God
the Father through Him.*

*Wives, be constantly subjecting yourselves to your husbands
as you ought to do in the Lord. Husbands, be loving your wives
with a divine love which impels you to deny yourselves for their
benefit, and stop being bitter and harsh to them. Children, be
obeying your parents in all things, for this is commendable in
the Lord. Fathers, stop irritating your children, lest they become
disheartened. Slaves, be constantly obedient in all things to
your human masters, not with eyeservice as men-pleasers, but
with an undivided heart, fearing the Lord.*

*Whatever you do, from your soul do it diligently as to the
Lord and not to men, knowing that from the Lord you will receive back the just recompense which consists of the inheritance.
The Master, Christ, you are serving. For the one who is doing
wrong, will get back that which he did which is wrong. And
there is no showing of partiality. Masters, that which is just
and equitable, be rendering on your part to your slaves, knowing
that also you have a Master in heaven.*

*Be giving constant attention to prayer, constantly active in it
with thanksgiving, praying at the same time also concerning us,
that God would open for us a door for the Word, to speak the
mystery of Christ, because of which (mystery) also I have been
bound, in order that I may make it plain as it is necessary in
the nature of the case for me to speak. In wisdom be ordering
your behavior towards those on the outside, buying up for yourselves the strategic, opportune time. Your word, let it always
be with graciousness, with salt thoroughly seasoned, to the end
that you may know how it is necessary in the nature of the
case to answer everyone.*

All that relates to me, Tychicus will make known to you, the beloved brother and faithful minister and my fellow-bondslave in the Lord, whom I sent to you for this same purpose, in order that you may come to know the things concerning me and in order that he may encourage your hearts; with Onesimus the faithful and beloved brother, who is one of you. All things to you they will make known, the things here. There greets you Aristarchus, my fellow-prisoner, and Mark, the cousin of Barnabas, concerning whom you received commandments; if he comes to you, receive him; and Joshua, the one called Justus, who are of the circumcision. These are my only fellow-workers with respect to the kingdom of God who are of such a character as to have become a solace to me.

There greets you Epaphras, the one who is one of your number, a bondslave of Christ Jesus, always wrestling on your behalf in his prayers, to the effect that you may stand fast, spiritually mature ones, and those who have been brought to the place of full assurance in everything willed by God; for I bear witness to him that he has much toil on your behalf and on behalf of those in Laodicea, and those in Hierapolis. There greets you Luke, the physician, the beloved one, and Demas.

Greet the brethren in Laodicea, and Nymphas, and the assembly in her home. And when this letter is read in your presence, see to it that also it is read in the assembly of Laodicea, and the letter from Laodicea. see to it that you also read it. And say to Archippus; Look to the ministry which you received in the Lord, that you discharge it fully. The greeting by my hand, the hand of Paul. Be remembering my bonds. The grace be with you.

SCRIPTURE INDEX